CHINA
IN WORLD
POLITICS

for the normalization of relations: Soviet withdrawal from Afghanistan, Soviet pressure for Vietnamese withdrawal from Cambodia, and the reduction of Soviet military presence along its borders with China and in Vietnam.

To conclude the chapter, we will look at China's relations with the newly independent republics, which have also been in the process of removing their communist and Marxist institutions. Both China and the former parts of the Soviet empire have sought normalization and improvement of relations during the current era of transition, but many questions remain unanswered about the future of these relations, especially in matters of security and influence. Rather than suggest probable developments, we will consider a number of choices available to Beijing's leaders, with their relative risks and opportunities, especially in light of important changes taking place in the former parts of the Soviet empire in Central Asia.

Chinese-U.S. Relations

Throughout the Cold War years, U.S. policy in Asia had a greater impact on Beijing's policy choices than that of any other state. However, as we look at Chinese-U.S. relations in Chapter 5, we will see that the Soviet Union played an important role in these relations. In the latter stages of the Cold War, the Soviet Union became a greater security concern to the Chinese than the United States, especially with the withdrawal of U.S. forces from Vietnam and the buildup of Soviet military in the Far East, South Asia, and Southeast Asia during the Brezhnev era.

In discussing the different stages of Sino-U.S. relations, we will ask whether Beijing and Washington could have pursued different policies that might have avoided most of their Cold War confrontations. In any case, we will see how each side both initiated and responded to crisis situations, and that even though Richard Nixon and Henry Kissinger are usually given credit for the era of good feeling and peaceful coexistence in the 1970s, Mao Zedong also played a major role in the normalization of Sino-U.S. relations. With China's Open Door policies beginning in 1978, Chinese-U.S. relations became more complex as Japan, Hong Kong, Taiwan, South Korea, and a number of Western European countries also became involved in China's opening to the outside world.

We will also see how economic and trade relations have largely dominated Chinese-U.S. concerns, accompanied by both major conflicts of interest and efforts at accommodation. We will carefully consider human rights issues and the extent to which Sino-U.S. relations have been influenced by China's repression of student demonstrators.

A number of other factors, however, inside both China and the United States, have also affected political, economic, and security relations; these factors have created cross-boundary dependencies in which different constituencies have developed inside both countries for cooperation but also for the use of threats.

China and Its Neighbors in the Post–Cold War Era

Although the United States probably played a greater role than any Asian state in China's Open Door policy in the 1980s, there is now growing economic interdependence among China and its Asian neighbors in both investment and trade. What is lacking, with the decline of both Russian and U.S. military presence in Asia, is a stable balance-of-power system in the region. In Chapter 6, we will consider how these developments may have affected Beijing's policy choices (in terms of economics, politics, terrorism, and security) in dealing with an emerging regional system that is much more advanced in economic terms than in security cooperation. In fact, although economic and security relations are interdependent and trade and investment may lessen the danger of conflict in Asia, potential power rivalries may develop in what is currently a regional power vacuum. Because of the importance of Chinese-Japanese relations, we will deal with the topic separately in Chapter 7, but we will also note in Chapter 6 how Japan and China interact with their neighbors on specific issues.

All actors in Northeast Asia seem to have a common interest in defusing the long-lasting tensions and rivalry on the Korean peninsula: China, North Korea, South Korea, Japan, and Russia. Currently, Taiwan seems to be a loser as relations improve between China and South Korea, whereas the United States as well as other Western countries stand to gain by normalization of relations in the region.

As for Southeast Asia, China's policy choices involve both dangers and opportunities. In the early years of China's economic modernization policy, trade between China and the countries of the Association of Southeast Asian Nations (ASEAN) was quite limited compared with trade and investment involving South Korea, Japan, Taiwan, and Hong Kong. Security arrangements in the region were also almost nonexistent. The large Chinese population in all Southeast Asian countries provides both opportunities and risks in China's relations with these countries. The withdrawal of both U.S. and Russian influence in the region made ASEAN countries fearful of both Japanese and Chinese influence. At the same time, the ASEAN countries are seeking to improve relations among all states in the region, including both Japan and China, and China has reciprocated by expressing support for regional economic and security regimes.

South Asia poses a different set of issues for Beijing's decisionmakers. Long after the end of the Cold War, the United States, Russia, and China are seeking to limit regional rivalries, particularly between Pakistan and India, and traditional lines of alliance are shifting in the face of Pakistan's growing instability. Nevertheless, China could be a decisive factor in promoting order in the region—or in the further buildup of arms, including nuclear arms.

In addition to China's influence on the regional balance-of-power system, there is also the question of rivalry or cooperation between China and India. These are the world's two most populous states, and they are both going through a transition to modernization. In both countries, there has been a shift from state ownership and control of the economy to marketplace incentives, but India takes pride in its claim of being the world's largest democracy, with a combination of parliamentary government, federalism, and decentralization, in which considerable autonomy is given to the different regions. As in China, however, there have been severe human rights violations as well as social, economic, and political discontent. For both China and India, the greatest stakes involve internal stability and modernization, as well as the realization that little can be accomplished without reduced population growth rates. Sino-Indian relations seem to have improved, at least on the surface, but future policy choices involving the relations of these two Asian giants could be crucial to regional and global peace.

Current developments in the independent republics of Central Asia, on China's western boundary, are potentially destabilizing; as we will see, China's policy choices with regard to these new republics, which are largely Islamic, all suggest caution and perhaps a wait-and-see attitude. Historically, there have been close cultural and economic ties between the peoples of Central Asia and the province of Xinjiang, which is a very large but thinly populated region of western China. China's fears of instability, Islamic separatism, and terrorism all color its relations with its Central Asian neighbors.

Global Regimes

One of the most controversial issues in global politics is the future role of China in the emerging global regimes of the post–Cold War era. Regimes consist of the rules of behavior (or lack of rules) that seem to guide the actions of states as they become increasingly interdependent. In some types of transactions, such as international trade and finance, these rules have become systems of extensive cooperation and regularized behavior; whereas in other areas of interaction, such as regional conflicts, arms races, and arms trade, the current global system lacks effective rules for cooperation, although some states have called for more effective regimes in these areas.

In all of these emerging areas of interdependence and growing interaction, the need for global cooperation is increasingly apparent. However, China's leaders traditionally emphasized the principle of national sovereignty, and their interactions on economic, security, or environmental issues were more bilateral than multilateral. Yet, as we will see, there are signs that even

China may be moving gradually toward more cooperation in solving these global problems, especially if there is a general consensus within the United Nations on what rules of behavior should be adopted. With respect to the emerging global regimes, Beijing's leaders must choose between following their past policies (refusal to take a position, actual resistance, or hesitant cooperation) and taking a greater leadership role.

■ Alternative Scenarios for the Twenty-First Century

Today, China stands at the crossroads, uncertain about its own identity in a post–Cold War world, one in which Marxist ideology has largely been discredited. Changes are taking place inside China as its leaders move more rapidly and successfully toward a marketplace economy than has been the case with former communist states throughout the Eurasian land mass. With the exception of the 1989–1990 period, China's gross national product has increased at the rate of 9 percent a year since the 1978 reforms, much more rapidly than for the Western economies (including Japan, which has faced serious challenges since 1985).

In our final chapter, we will look at some of the reasons, despite recent economic success, that the Chinese people and their leaders have been unable to clarify their future role. There is a serious identity crisis inside China. The collapse of international communism wiped away many of Beijing's views of the outside world, and Tiananmen Square challenged the very foundations of order and the Chinese Communist Party's mandate to rule from above. No new ideology, not even nationalism, has filled the void in China's definition of itself domestically and internationally.

As we analyze China's current role in the international security system, we will see how Beijing's leaders remain the world's strongest supporters of the Westphalian system of power relations, which emphasizes sovereignty and noninterference in the affairs of other states. At the regional level, China until recently had been resistant to multilateral efforts to achieve collective arrangements such as those emerging in Europe. In considering China's future, we will summarize Beijing's risks and opportunities in continuing its current policies. We will also look at its choices in breaking new ground, both in its domestic policies and at the regional and global levels, and look at choices that may bring China into harmony with the emerging global regimes of the twenty-first century.

New Ideologies in the Twenty-First Century

You, O King, live beyond the confines of many seas, nevertheless, impelled by your humble desire to partake of the benefits of our civilization, you have dispatched a mission respectfully bearing your memorial. Your Envoy has crossed the seas and paid his respects at my Court on the anniversary of my birthday. . . . As to your entreaty to send one of your nationals to be accredited to my Celestial Court and to be in control of your country's trade with China, this request is contrary to all usage of my dynasty and cannot possibly be entertained. Swaying the wide world, I have but one aim in view, namely to maintain a perfect governance and to fulfill the duties of the state. . . . Our dynasty's majestic virtue has penetrated unto every country under heaven and the kings of all nations have offered their costly tribute by land and sea. . . . It behooves you, O King, to respect my sentiments and to display even greater devotion and loyalty in future, so that by perpetual submission to our Throne, you may secure peace and prosperity for your country hereafter.

—Excerpts from a memorial by
Emperor Ch'ien Lung to King George III of England

The Chinese World Order

The Chinese people call their nation the Middle Kingdom, the center of the natural order and the world order as they knew it for centuries. From prehistory until 1911, China's emperors ruled so long as they held the Mandate of Heaven, the natural force that dictated whether a dynasty had sufficient rectitude to provide moral guidance to the people. When the mandate was lost through immoral actions, corruption, or other behavior that offended the heavens, the natural forces would show their displeasure through disasters such as floods, earthquakes, or droughts. The Chinese people then would know that a change in dynasties was imminent. Chinese leaders did not rule on the basis of a social contract with the people or on the basis of a constitutional relationship with other political entities, as did leaders in Western Europe and the United States. Chinese rulers were the sons of heaven.

China was at the center of both heavenly forces and the earthly order. Surrounded for centuries by nations such as Korea and Vietnam, which sent emissaries periodically to bring presents to the Chinese emperor, the Chinese people believed that the tribute system confirmed the superiority of Chinese (Han) civilization. Relations between China and Korea or China and Vietnam were not analogous to relations between sovereign nations in an anarchic international system or even between a colonizing power and its colony; rather, the nations surrounding China were considered inferior because they were not Chinese. Only through adoption of Chinese civilization, which the neighboring elites would be exposed to during their voyages to pay tribute to the Chinese emperor, would the nations on China's borders be accepted as anything but barbarians.

Except for seven maritime voyages of exploration between 1405 and 1433, in which Chinese ships sailed as far as the Middle East and Africa, China did not seek information about the outside world. It neither fought external wars nor searched for external markets, and foreigners who came to China were welcome so long as they accepted the superiority of Chinese civilization. Those peoples such as the Mongols (1279–1367) or the Manchus (1644–1911) who dared to invade China and establish their own dynasties were quickly sinicized—that is, forced to accept the superiority of Chinese civilization. The Chinese nation could easily afford to practice what today would be called an isolationist foreign policy. All under heaven could be found within the Middle Kingdom.

The Western world did not understand the Chinese concept of the Middle Kingdom. The British, the Russians, and the rest of Europe and the United States discovered China and, beginning in the eighteenth century, demanded free access and free trade. China had tea, spices, silk, and porcelain, which the people in Europe and the United States wanted to buy, but the Chinese people had no particular desire to buy anything from abroad. And to Chinese emperors, the notion that emissaries from foreign monarchs should be treated as equals was even more absurd. Unless Westerners in China became sinicized, the Qing dynasty court believed they should not be in China. European demands for establishment of diplomatic relations and exchange of ambassadors were therefore repeatedly denied.

The Chinese did not understand the Western system of sovereign states jockeying for power within the international system. The West did not understand the Chinese system of a political system shaped by natural forces. The result was a battle between two civilizations, each equally convinced of its own superiority. Unfortunately for the Chinese people, by the nineteenth century Western nations had become more dynamic and more powerful than China. The result of the conflict was that China was no longer in accord with the Mandate of Heaven, nor was it a sovereign state in an international system dominated by Western powers. By the early twentieth century, the foreign powers in China had as much and perhaps more political, military, and economic power than did the remnants of the Qing dynasty.

The Unequal Treaties

The Chinese emperor Ch'ien Lung allowed a limited number of foreign merchants to establish a seasonal base near Guangzhou (formerly Canton) in the late eighteenth century, from which they were allowed to trade with thirteen authorized Chinese merchant groups (*hongs*). They quickly began to buy Chinese silks, porcelain, teas, and chinaware; the Chinese bought foreign furs, sandalwood, and ginseng. The balance of trade favored China. To redress this negative balance of trade, Great Britain began selling opium to the Chinese. By 1840 the balance of trade once again favored the West.

The Chinese emperor and his chief lieutenants, who were distressed by the negative effects of opium smoking on both the Chinese people and the Chinese economy, banned the cultivation, import, and smoking of opium. However, the emperor and his lieutenants were too weak to enforce their own regulations. In 1839, after a Chinese official blockaded foreign warehouses and forced merchants to turn over 20,000 opium chests for public burning, the British military launched a punitive military expedition. The Opium Wars ensued, which were handily won by superior British military forces.

As the price for peace, the Chinese emperor was forced to sign unequal treaties that gave the island of Hong Kong to the British and established five treaty ports. The treaty ports resembled European port cities with special zones for foreigners that contained warehouses, shops, restaurants, and homes, all of which were staffed by Chinese. Foreign nationals in the foreign enclaves (and eventually in all China) were exempt from Chinese law and subject only to the laws of their home country, a doctrine known in international law as *extraterritoriality* and usually accorded only to diplomatic representatives. The treaty ports were so advantageous that all the Western powers wanted one. Eventually, more than eighty treaty ports were established.

Even the United States, which never officially had its own treaty port, demanded all the rights and privileges in China that had accrued to the other Western powers and their citizens. Thus was established the international principle of most-favored-nation (MFN) status (the basis of the General Agreement on Tariffs and Trade [GATT]), which is defined as agreement by consenting states to grant each other equal access to their domestic markets. China and the United States struggled over the terms and conditions of MFN status. For many years, members of the U.S. Congress attempted to defeat reauthorization unless China improved its human rights record.

Free Trade

The Opium Wars, which were fought to establish control over the export of opium to China, were a victory for the Western advocates of free trade. The Western powers regarded this as just, because they believed that free trade was a right rather than a privilege. President John Quincy Adams, despite his abhorrence of opium, praised England for fighting a just war for the "Christian precept" of open trade. From the 1840s onward, when the first unequal treaties were signed, the foreign powers increasingly controlled parts of coastal China and Chinese foreign trade.

Free trade, in the Chinese context, was translated into increasing foreign control. Instead of being paid tribute, the Chinese emperors had become, in effect, the tributaries of foreign powers that had encroached on their own land. The last Qing dynasty emperors and empresses cooperated with the foreign powers to prolong their own rule, which could easily have been ended by foreign military forces, but the dynasty had lost the Mandate of Heaven.

Chinese Nationalism

The Chinese people chafed at the foreign presence in their country and began to develop a modern form of nationalism. Instead of viewing China's place in the world through the traditional context of the Middle Kingdom, a movement began in the late nineteenth century to develop a nation that had both wealth and power. With wealth and power, China would no longer be subject to the will of foreign nations.

Nascent nationalist sentiments were evinced throughout all strata of Chinese society, with the "recovery of sovereign rights" as the mantra of all groups. The Boxers, a secret society with some criminal connections, joined with the rural gentry and anti-Western officials to oppose foreign influence in China. The Boxer Uprising of 1900 was put down with the assistance of foreign troops, but not before approximately 250 foreigners had been killed. A more studied approach to the problem was adopted by the urban intelligentsia and merchant classes, who sent their sons to Japan to learn how an Asian nation had beaten the West at its own game. In Tokyo in 1905, Chinese reformers established a secret revolutionary league that was the antecedent to the Kuomintang (Nationalist) Party. Even the Qing government itself favored a reform initiative, but it was a case of too little too late, and in 1911 the Qing dynasty collapsed. The mandate had passed on to a new generation.

On May 4, 1919, came the defining moment in modern Chinese nationalism. Anti-Western and anti-Japanese demonstrations erupted in China to protest the terms of the treaty that ended World War I. The European powers, meeting in the Versailles Palace in France, had agreed that German enclaves in China would be handed over to the Japanese rather than returned to China. Inspired by the desire to force the victorious powers in World War I to redress the insults heaped on China and spearheaded by students and intellectuals, the May 4 movement spawned many political organizations dedicated to strengthening China and driving the foreigners out.

The Chinese Communist Party (CCP) was one political organization that had its roots in the May 4 movement. Founded in 1921 with some Soviet assistance, early Communist leaders actually worked together with the Kuomintang Party in the interests of developing a strong nationalist movement in China. The two parties had irreconcilable visions of a strong, nationalist China, however, and their united front lasted only through the mid-1920s. From the late 1930s through the late 1940s, the Communist Party's nationalism came to be more attractive to the Chinese people than that of the ruling Nationalist Party. Under the leadership of Mao Zedong, the Communist Party used the desire for a proud and independent Chinese nation to recruit supporters throughout the fight against Japan during World War II. The perception that the Communists, and not the ruling Kuomintang Party, were truly fighting the Japanese invaders was crucial to the Communist victory over the Nationalists in the Chinese civil war from 1945 through 1949. When Mao Zedong proclaimed the establishment of the People's Republic of China (PRC) on October 1, 1949, one of his foremost goals was the establishment of a Chinese nation-state that was independent of foreign influence.

The Cold War World System

The People's Republic was established in a world unlike any other in history. Two superpowers, both armed with sufficient nuclear weapons to destroy themselves and everybody else, dominated the international system. They did so not in the interests of creating a stable, bipolar balance-of-power system to prevent a world war that would be too costly to the superpowers; rather, the superpowers added ideology to the traditional power rivalry. Communism versus capitalism became an international security issue. For the first time in history, differences over economics defined the global regime.

The stakes were high—total annihilation—and so most nation-states in the world, big or small, felt compelled to join the bloc of one superpower or the other. Belonging to one of the two alliance systems provided a security umbrella, but at the price of limiting autonomy of action. Few nation-states could maintain strong diplomatic and trade relations with their counterparts in the opposing alliance system. The world became bifurcated, and each nation's scope of action was dictated from the center of the alliance system.

The bipolar balance of power was highly static between the United States and the Soviet Union, which prevented the Cold War from erupting into a real war, but transitions in the two alliance systems came about through competition on the fringes. Many countries in Africa and Asia bore the brunt of the Cold War as the two superpowers fought proxy wars in Vietnam, Angola, Korea, Mozambique, and many other countries around the world. The Cold War was costly not only to the two superpowers but also to the client states they courted and sometimes fought over.

The People's Republic of China

Mao Zedong and Zhou Enlai, the Chinese prime minister and foreign minister for most of the period from 1949 through 1976, sought to maintain China's autonomy while enhancing its security within the world system created by the Cold War. China's leaders always conceived of their nation as an independent and major actor in the international system, threatened at times by the United States, at other times by the Soviet Union, and sometimes by both superpowers. But China's leaders never considered themselves to be subordinate to either major power after World War II. Mao and Zhou's foreign policy goals were as follows: "China's leaders have regularly viewed international politics as a struggle for hegemony among superpowers, have maintained an abiding concern with their security and sovereignty against threats from abroad, have sought to preserve a high degree of independence and initiative in their international conduct, and have tended to identify their country with the developing nations of the Third World, rather than with either of the two superpowers."[1]

The "Five Principles of Peaceful Coexistence," which are cited by Beijing as its standard for international contact, are as follows:

1. Mutual respect for sovereignty and territorial integrity
2. Nonaggression
3. Noninterference in each other's internal affairs
4. Equality and mutual benefit
5. Peaceful coexistence

Mao and Zhou remembered the era of the unequal treaties all too well, so much so that autonomy and a fierce defense of Chinese sovereignty became the basic tenets of the foreign policy of the People's Republic of China.

Security

However much China's leaders may have desired autonomy, even a large regional power with nearly one-quarter of the world's population could not remain isolated from the bipolar system of the Cold War for long. Mao Zedong guided the People's Republic to "lean to one side," the Soviet side, from 1949 through 1960. Though still attempting to maintain an independent stance and ever prickly about issues relating to Chinese sovereignty, Mao believed that security imperatives and ideological similarities helped China's friendship with the Soviet Union. When Sino-Soviet relations broke down over controversies relating to sovereignty, security, and ideology, China tried to be truly autonomous throughout the 1960s. Border clashes with the Soviet Union convinced Mao and Zhou to lean to one side again, but this time toward the United States. Throughout the 1970s, China's relations with the United States were markedly better than its relations with the Soviet Union, and Washington promoted Sino-U.S. relations as a bargaining chip with Moscow. From 1949 through 1991, Beijing leaned at times toward Moscow and at other times toward Washington, but these special relations were based on tactical interests and never amounted to anything that might be perceived as permanent alliances.[2] Rather, Mao and Zhou sought, with some success, to enhance China's security by playing off the superpowers.

Autonomy

The constant element of Chinese foreign policy during the Cold War was the desire to participate in the bipolar international system only to the extent necessary to preserve and enhance China's autonomy. China would lean to one side and then to the other, and it would seek friends in the third world, but its continual security imperative was the jealous preservation of its sovereignty.

To a large extent, China succeeded. Nikita Khrushchev began to acknowledge China's demands for full sovereignty in the middle 1950s when he returned territory and economic concessions wrested from Mao by Stalin. Khrushchev became nervous, however, as China worked to develop its trump card in its battle for autonomy in the international system—a nuclear capability. A sovereign communist China was acceptable to Khrushchev, even though the ideological conflicts between the two communist nations were troublesome. A nuclear neighbor on the Soviet border was not acceptable, however, and a complete rupture of relations between China and the Soviet Union ensued.

By leaning to the other side, China also achieved U.S. acceptance of the sanctity of China's borders as defined by Beijing. In the Shanghai Communiqué, which was signed when President Richard Nixon visited China in 1972, the United States acknowledged that the island of Taiwan is a part of China and that unification of the island with the mainland is an internal Chinese affair. U.S. abdication of responsibility for the security of its Nationalist allies on Taiwan was deemed by the Communist Chinese as a victory. A reminder of the era of unequal treaties and foreign domination had been removed to the benefit of the People's Republic. Through a combination of obduracy and skillful diplomacy, China achieved international respect for the inviolability of its borders.

Friendship with the Third World

Although China was constrained by the bipolar international system of the Cold War era from true independence of action, its leaders believed it could acquire friends and serve as a model to third world nations still struggling to find their identity in the postcolonial world. Zhou Enlai therefore traveled to Bandung, Indonesia, in 1955 to join twenty-eight other nations in calling for a "nonaligned movement." In the era when China's relations with the Soviet Union were friendly if not warm and rapprochement with the United States was still in the future, promoting friendship with third world nations was often China's only way of reaching the outside world. In some states, such as Indonesia, Chinese friendship took the form of promoting communist rebels; in other states, such as Tanzania, Chinese friendship took the form of economic aid and technical advice. Some third world countries, such as India, came to be enemies, not friends. Yet from the late 1950s until 1972, China's attempt to define a role for itself in the international system beyond the bounds of Soviet or U.S. control was based on its relationship to the many nations that sought nonalignment in the Cold War.

Before the PRC's credentials were recognized by the United Nations in 1971, Beijing involved itself in international fora only when a Chinese security issue was on the agenda. In 1971, after the People's Republic finally assumed a seat at the UN Security Council, its position relative to the third world changed. Now the People's Republic was not only a supporter of third world aspirations, but also a powerful voice in the UN system, in which the nonaligned nations of the third world exerted their power most effectively. By virtue of sheer numbers, the third world nations could outvote the superpowers and their allies in the UN General Assembly. However, to make their voice heard in the UN Security Council, these nations had to turn to China.

The People's Republic of China had by default become a leader of the third world movement, and Chinese statements in the United Nations have always reflected a consciousness of this position. By its inclusion in the Security Council, however, China also became a power in the international system, and its votes in the United Nations reflect a caution that belies the People's Republic's old rhetoric identifying China with revolutionary forces in the third world.

An examination of China's changing role in the Cold War era from 1949 to 1991 reveals that the values pronounced in Beijing have often come in conflict with one other. As with every other actor in the international system, China's leaders have tried to balance changing perceptions of outside security threats with possible opportunities for increased power and influence, often with conflicting results. The demands of the Cold War system forced China to be creative in defense of its security and in seeking support from other nations. China's solution was to play the international system for all it was worth by siding with either superpower when necessary, courting the third world when isolated, and acting as a great power when it was in Beijing's interest to do so.

Origins of the New World Order

The end of the Cold War world order has offered China's leaders an entirely new set of foreign policy and security issues to grapple with. From 1985, when Mikhail Gorbachev became secretary-general of the Communist Party of the Soviet Union, to 1989, when the communist regimes in Eastern Europe fell, the leaders of the Chinese Communist Party became increasingly agitated. Gorbachev's attempts to restructure the Soviet Communist Party were considered by the Chinese to be hasty and ill-planned, a bad example to other communist regimes. When the Berlin Wall fell and Germany was rapidly unified, the Chinese leaders felt at once vindicated because their reservations about Gorbachev's program had been borne out; yet they were also nervous over what it meant for the remaining communist parties in the world. Many heated discussions took place in Beijing over how China should react officially, but ultimately moderation prevailed, and the People's Republic recognized the new regimes. Ideology was not a sufficiently strong factor to motivate China's leaders to isolate themselves from the changes in Europe.

The collapse of the Soviet Union was entirely different. Not only had the progenitor of all communist regimes on earth collapsed, discrediting the ideology that still defined the political myth of the People's Republic of China, but it also left in its wake a whole new international and regional security configuration. The international system was no longer bipolar. Instead, one superpower was predominant, with a number of regional powers such as the European Community and Japan becoming increasingly important. China, too, was transformed into a regional power with the potential to affect future security alignments in East Asia. As the world system is reconfigured in the post–Cold War era, a form of multipolarity may ensue.

How has China reacted? According to the *People's Daily,* "Three great trends are now evident in the world: (1) the emergence of the United States as the sole surviving superpower after the disintegration of the Soviet Union and the Gulf War; (2) the emergence of a multipolar world because of political, economic and technological changes; and (3) the resurgence of nationalism with accompanying ethnic, religious, and territorial disputes."[3] China, a nation-state with one-quarter of the world's population, an increasingly powerful military, and a rapidly growing economy, is likely to grow in power and influence as unipolarity is transformed into multipolarity. However, being surrounded by former republics of the Soviet Union, with all their ethnic and economic problems, and being emerged in several irredentist campaigns itself, China is likely to become involved in the resurgence of nationalist disputes, with the attendant external and internal security threats. Chinese involvement in military activities somewhere in central, eastern, or southern Asia is not improbable as tensions flare up on the borders with the former Soviet Union, on the Korean peninsula, and potentially with Taiwan. In the post–Cold War era, defending China's security interests in East Asia will entail selecting from an infinitely more complex series of options than was the case during the Cold War.

China's Goals in the New World Order

China will undoubtedly play an increasingly powerful role in defining East Asia's security configurations, whether as a peacemaker—a "police force" that uses a combination of diplomacy and threat to prevent conflict—or as an enforcer—a military power that achieves its goals through force. Statements from Beijing, particularly its "charm offensive" in South and Southeast Asia, continue to stress China's peaceful intentions and its desire to achieve a new world order that includes the following basic aspects:

1. All countries, big or small, strong or weak, rich or poor, are equal sovereign members of the international community entitled to participate on an equal footing in the consultations and settlement of world affairs, and such practices as the big bullying the small, the strong lording over the weak, and the rich oppressing the poor should be rejected.
2. Each and every country has the right to choose independently its own social, political, and economic systems and course of development in light of its specific conditions. No country should interfere in the internal affairs of other countries or seek to impose its own values, ideology, or mode of development on others.
3. In international relations, there must be mutual respect for sovereignty and territorial integrity. No country should invade or annex the territory of other countries under any pretext. International disputes should be settled in a fair and just manner through peaceful negotiations rather than the use or threat of force, let alone by means of war.
4. In order to attain common development and prosperity for all the countries in the world, the economic exchanges among countries should be carried out on the basis of equality and mutual benefit, a just international economic relationship should be established, and the assistance should be supplied without attaching any political conditions. With the world economy becoming more and more internationalized, the economies of various countries are increasingly interrelated. If the economies of the numerous third world countries remain underdeveloped for a long time, it will neither facilitate the economic development of the developed countries nor genuinely ensure peace and stability in the world.[4]

Peace and prosperity will ensue, according to official Chinese policy, if the people of the world work together and adhere to the UN Charter. Yet, as with any other nation-state in the world system, China's own foreign policy goals are limited and self-serving. The drive for security, economic and military power, and influence will be the focus of the next generation of Chinese leaders. How China accommodates its broad prescriptions for the international system with the foreign policy choices it will have to make in the early twenty-first century will determine China's status. It may also affect the stability of the international system, for although China may be only a regional power, it is a large and powerful nation in the center of a regional system that will become increasingly important in this century.

Policy Options in the Twenty-First Century

China's primary foreign policy goal for the twenty-first century is to cement political friendships and a stable international environment that will allow Beijing to develop its economy and its trade and to acquire advanced technology.[5] However, security issues may conflict with these economic goals. China's leaders will have to assess if and when security goals will necessarily supersede economic goals. Their decisions will have a profound effect on East Asia and the world.

Option 1: Nationalism Versus Communism

Communist ideology has been discredited throughout the world, except in official China. Although the Chinese Communist Party continues to aver that it is leading the Chinese nation toward socialism and then communism, in reality it seems to be leading the nation toward capitalism. As a result, a large portion of the Chinese people no longer are interested in making revolution; rather, they are interested in making money. Communism has been discredited abroad and has very little credibility in China. For the Chinese Communist Party to continue its leading role, it has had to seek the support of the people through an ideology other than communism. Nationalism has replaced communism as the validating principle of CCP rule. Since an appeal to the people's sense of national pride helped Mao Zedong win control over China in the first place, nationalism may be espoused as a doctrine without violating party principles.

However, whipping up nationalist sentiments can be dangerous and can even redound to the detriment of those who first raise the flag. Yugoslavia is one example. Perhaps more pertinent is the revival of nationalist sentiment in Russia, which is causing great fear among Russia's neighbors and drove Eastern European countries, former satellites of the Soviet Union, into joining the

North Atlantic Treaty Organization (NATO). If the Russian sense of encirclement increases as a result of NATO expansion, this might cause a future Russian government to react militarily.

The search by the leaders of the Chinese Communist Party to define a new political myth that justifies their continued rule is fraught with difficulties for China and its neighbors. Nationalism may be used positively by stressing the greatness of Chinese history and civilization and the Chinese Communist Party's efforts to continue that greatness. For a party that has already largely lost the support and even the interest of its people, however, the only sort of nationalism that is likely to serve as a factor to unify and motivate the Chinese people behind the banner of the CCP is the demagogic sort of nationalism. If the CCP chooses to assert itself in this manner, China's neighbors will feel increasingly threatened, and security in East Asia will be endangered.

Option 2: Nationalism Versus Irredentism

China has never allowed consideration of any option other than Taiwanese reunification with mainland China, with which the CCP has identified itself. Anything else would destroy the legitimacy of the party and its leaders. If Taiwanese leaders prod Taiwan to a more independent status, Chinese leaders might then be tempted to resort to the military option to effect Taiwanese reunification.

China also seeks control over groups of islands in the South China Sea, primarily because of the possibility of oil in the area. These islands are also claimed by Vietnam and the Philippines, and many believe that arguments over which nation rightfully owns the islands could easily flare up into open warfare. Alternative solutions, such as establishing joint control of the area, or dividing the islands among the contending powers, were dismissed until 2002 when China agreed to discuss these territorial issues. The South China Sea was long considered, and may still be, an international "hot spot" in the early twenty-first century.

How China handles each of its territorial claims will have a tremendous effect on its international credibility and on its position as a regional power in East Asia. If China resorts to heavy-handed political maneuvering or, even more alarming, to military actions, it will harm its own economy, its international standing, and its credibility as an adjudicator of peace on the UN Security Council. China may, however, engage in diplomatic maneuvering to effect expanded influence in Hong Kong, Taiwan, and the South China Sea without resorting to force or coercion. In the early years of the twenty-first century, China seems to be adopting both approaches. It is being heavy-handed in its approach to Hong Kong politics and in its reactions to the 2004 election in Taiwan, while wooing Southeast Asia, India, and the Central Asian republics. Only time will tell whether China will be able to maintain both approaches or whether, to fulfill its nationalistic credo, it will have to resort to force.

Option 3: Leninism Versus
Western Democracy and Civil Rights

Next to strong support for Chinese nationalism, perhaps the most strongly held value in the minds of China's leaders is the belief that the CCP is best able to promote not only the restoration of China as a great nation but also the people's well-being. Events in Eastern Europe and the Soviet Union, as well as the demonstrations at Tiananmen Square, have only strengthened the determination of CCP leaders to take whatever measures are necessary to maintain the party's Mandate of Heaven. All party factions agree, ironically, that the CCP is best able to maintain Confucian values such as order, stability, and effective rule from above.

- CCP leaders, whether conservatives, moderates, or reformers, believe that the well-being of the Chinese nation and its people requires economic growth and the social rights that communist societies traditionally define as human rights, including the following: modernization, higher living standards, the right to work, education, and the provision of life's essentials, such as food, health care, shelter, and clothing.
- Although moving away from totalitarian thought control and extreme forms of suppression, the CCP firmly believes in denying practices U.S. citizens consider to be their inalienable political and civil rights, as specified in the Constitution and the Bill of Rights. These practices include freedom of speech, freedom of assembly, freedom of religion, freedom of the press, an impartial judiciary, and freedom from arbitrary arrest and cruel and unusual punishment—what most U.S. citizens consider to be essential components of a representative democracy.

China's leaders have eliminated most of the totalitarian features of Leninism while retaining authoritarian controls. The question is whether China's leaders can maintain the support of the people, which is essential to continued rule by the CCP, through authoritarianism rather than some form of democratization. If the rest of the communist world serves as a model, party leaders may discover that the Chinese people will not accept the provision of social rights as a substitute for civil and political rights over the long term.

Option 4: Marxism Versus Capitalism

The rapid modernization and development of China's economy, with annual gross national product (GNP) growth rates averaging 9 percent or better, has been achieved through the adoption of a number of capitalist reforms, including creation of private markets, private agricultural households, rural cooperatives (largely independent of government or party control), and joint ventures with foreign corporations. China's leaders may prefer to call these developments "socialism with Chinese characteristics," but Westerners call them capitalism. At the same time, China's leaders strongly support the continuation of a public sector, which means that China in effect has a dual economy. The coexistence of both large public and private sectors creates many problems, but China's leaders support a dual economy because they hope to attain the best of both possible worlds (the good features of both socialism and capitalism without the bad features of either). Maintaining a large public sector is politically expedient for the CCP for a number of reasons:

- Public enterprises are a major source of party power and wealth. As the private sector grows, especially at the regional and local levels, the existence of a large public sector will give the CCP continued leverage because private enterprises cannot survive or prosper without access to basic commodities and services produced in the public sector.
- China, in the present and future, faces many serious economic bottlenecks, such as a lack of capital and finance, energy, transportation, and basic resources such as water, timber, and iron ore. Continued party control over key sectors such as most banking and other financial services, utilities, energy, transportation, basic industries, and water supplies gives the CCP and government leverage to deal with these bottlenecks.
- From the Chinese perspective, a dual economy, with many public enterprises and services, as well as extensive regulatory authority, can help avoid some of the severe problems and inequities found in highly individualistic and capitalist societies such as the United States.

Yet despite the many economic successes since the 1980s, China's leaders may not be able to control a dual economy over the long term. One of China's leading dissidents predicts that the Communist Party will fail:

> What will emerge in China is a mixture of these many forces, but it will not be the kind of mixture this regime wants. It will not mix economic freedom with political unfreedom. Communism and capitalism are so completely different that no one will be fooled for long that they can be joined. In the end there will be a Chinese path, but it will be a different path to freedom, a different path to democracy. The Chinese people do not speak in Western phrases and political philosophies, but they know what kind of political and economic system best serves their own welfare.[6]

Option 5: Rural Versus Urban Interests

The Chinese communist revolution was different from all other communist revolutions throughout the world because it was in large part a peasant revolution. In the 1990s, over 800 million Chinese (over two-thirds of the population) lived in rural areas. China's decisionmakers must pay careful attention to the well-being and further development of rural China if they are to lead their country's emergence as a successful and powerful nation in the twenty-first century:

- If the party is to maintain its Mandate of Heaven, it must take measures to maintain the support of China's rural masses, who continue to provide most of China's party cadres and soldiers, and most of the human resources for its rapidly developing economy (both in rural China and in urban centers through the migration of over 100 million peasants to China's burgeoning cities).
- Even with migration to the cities (which is causing increasing urban unemployment and other problems, including crime), millions of working-age men and women are either unemployed or underemployed in rural areas, creating enormous hardships and human suffering.
- China's leaders must make greater efforts to overcome severe inequities both between rural and urban areas and between China's more prosperous coastal areas (which contain much of the best farmland) and its interior provinces. These inequities involve educational and employment opportunities (especially for women), level of health care, quality of consumer products (which are in increasing demand throughout China), entertainment, and basic human needs such as an adequate diet. These inequities are also responsible for growing disparities in rural and urban lifestyles.

To overcome these differences, especially in the creation of new services and the availability of consumer goods, China's leaders will have to provide more incentives for overseas Chinese to invest in rural China. Because of their ability to adjust to conditions inside China, rural areas included, overseas Chinese are better able than Westerners and other foreigners to move beyond China's special economic zones in the coastal provinces to the vast hinterlands, the development of which will determine the future of China in the twenty-first century. How Beijing treats Hong Kong and Taiwanese Chinese could greatly affect the future contributions of over 55 million overseas Chinese, who continue to provide a majority of China's overseas investment, especially in rural areas. How Beijing manages China's peasantry will have a profound effect on the longevity of the CCP.

Option 6: Alignment Versus
Nonalignment and Splendid Isolation

Some of China's most difficult policy choices in the post–Cold War era will involve efforts by China's leaders to avoid external interference in China's internal affairs. At the same time, they will try to take advantage of changing global political-security and economic structures in order not only to benefit China at home but also to increase its influence abroad. China's leaders have, in fact if not in theory, followed the axioms of structural realism, the predominant theory explaining international relations in the post–Cold War era.[7] Whereas traditional realists view the intentions of states with constant suspicion, structural realists (sometimes referred to as neorealists) make no prior judgments of the intentions of other states. Instead, they believe nations constantly reassess their intentions and capabilities in a geopolitical system in which intentions and capabilities are continually changing. Each state, after assessing how these changes can affect its own vital interests, then determines which policy options can minimize dangers and maximize opportunities. This occurs through alignment, nonalignment, or isolation. Some of the following considerations may help to clarify China's future alignments in the twenty-first century:

- Major external threats to China in the near future seem to have diminished, and China's continuing internal weaknesses and primary emphasis on economic growth and development largely preclude any external involvements that divert major Chinese resources from domestic problems.
- At the global level, Beijing may wish to be consulted as an emerging world power; however, China's leaders expect other, more wealthy and powerful states to bear most of the burdens of dealing with international political-security, racial-ethnic, economic, and environmental problems. Logically, if China's GNP continues to grow at 9 percent or more a year, Beijing may be willing to assume more global responsibilities in the twenty-first century.
- China will seek outside help from many sources but will try to avoid dependence on any one country, especially Japan or the United States. European and overseas Chinese investors, as well as investors from other Asian countries such as Korea, help to give China greater leverage in its relationships with the outside world.
- China's Open Door policy continues to be ideologically and politically neutral, without trade or investor preference for either capitalist or former communist countries. Global economic regimes (the World Bank and the International Monetary Fund), although capitalist in nature, are also viewed as major sources of assistance.

- Global security regimes, such as the Nuclear Nonproliferation Treaty and the Missile Technology Control Regime, are viewed pragmatically, as are Chinese arms sales. Beijing will continue to assess these security regimes and the arms sales of other countries, as well as its own, according to China's perceived interests, not according to the wishes of countries such as the United States or the wishes of the majority of members in the United Nations.

Faced with external threats and limited means of dealing with external dangers throughout the twentieth century, China's leaders have at times sought alignment with one power or groups of powers and at other times have sought to avoid entangling alliances. Ideological affinities have been secondary to perceived national interests, as demonstrated by China's behavior in the early Cold War years, when it first aligned with the Soviet Union in opposing the United States, later followed a policy of isolation in its relations with both the East and the West, then aligned with the United States against the Soviets, and finally sought friendly but nondependent relations in the 1990s with all major powers. In the post–Cold War era, with its changing geopolitical structures, however, China's security imperative will be to work with other nations to prevent any state or group of states from dominating the international system militarily or economically, especially in Asia. China will have to learn how to become a major power broker within a multipolar international system and a fragmented power system in Asia.

Suggested Readings

Barnett, A. Doak. *China and the Major Powers in East Asia*. Washington, D.C.: Brookings Institution, 1977.

Choudhury, Golam W. *China in World Affairs: The Foreign Policy of the PRC Since 1970*. Boulder, Colo.: Westview, 1979.

Garver, John W. *Foreign Relations of the People's Republic of China*. Englewood Cliffs, N.J.: Prentice Hall, 1993.

Harding, Harry. *China's Foreign Relations in the 1980s*. New Haven, Conn.: Yale University Press, 1984.

Huntington, Samuel P. *The Clash of Civilizations and the Remaking of World Order*. New York: Touchstone Books, 1997.

Kegley, Charles W., Jr., and Gregory Raymond. *A Multipolar Peace? Great-Power Politics in the Twenty-First Century*. New York: St. Martin's Press, 1994.

Kim, Samuel S., ed. *China and the World: Chinese Foreign Policy Faces the New Millennium*. Boulder, Colo.: Westview, 1998.

———. *China, the United Nations, and World Order*. Princeton, N.J.: Princeton University Press, 1979.

Lampton, David, ed. *The Making of Chinese Foreign and Security Policy in the Era of Reform, 1978–2000*. Stanford: Stanford University Press, 2001.

Nelsen, Harvey W. *Power and Insecurity: Beijing, Moscow, and Washington, 1949–1988*. Boulder, Colo.: Lynne Rienner, 1989.

Ogden, Suzanne, ed. *China.* 5th ed. Guildford, Conn.: Dushkin, 1993.

Shih, Chih-yu. *China's Just World: The Morality of Chinese Foreign Policy.* Boulder, Colo.: Lynne Rienner, 1992.

Zhao, Suisheng, and Jonathan Pollack. *Chinese Foreign Policy: Pragmatism and Strategic Behavior.* Armonk, N.Y.: M. E. Sharpe, 2003.

▓ **Notes**

1. Harry Harding, "China's Changing Roles in the Contemporary World," in Harry Harding, ed., *China's Foreign Relations in the 1980s* (New Haven, Conn.: Yale University Press, 1984), p. 214.

2. For an analysis of the emerging multipolar system in the 1990s as well as a detailed comparison of the current system with earlier geopolitical power structures, see Charles W. Kegley Jr. and Gregory Raymond, *A Multipolar Peace? Great-Power Politics in the Twenty-First Century* (New York: St. Martin's Press, 1994).

3. Quoted in Wayne Bert, "Chinese Policies and U.S. Interests in Southeast Asia," *Asian Survey* 23, no. 3 (March 1993): 319.

4. People's Republic of China Mission to the United Nations, "China's Position on Certain International Issues," press release, January 1992, pp. 14–15.

5. Bert, "Chinese Policies."

6. Liu Binyan, "Civilization Grafting: No Culture Is an Island," *Foreign Affairs* 72, no. 4 (September–October 1993): 21.

7. The major study of structural realism is Kenneth N. Waltz, *Theory of International Relations* (Reading, Mass.: Addison-Wesley, 1979). Also see Waltz's chapter "Realist Thought and Neorealist Theory in the Evolution of International Relations," in Robert L. Rothstein, ed., *The Evolution of International Relations* (Columbia: University of South Carolina Press, 1991), pp. 21–38.

Chinese Politics and Ideology

What does China need most today? The fruits of our 24-year-old program of "reform and opening" are impressive, but we still face numerous problems, many of them extremely challenging. Among these are an inadequate awareness of the rule of law, political corruption that grows worse by the day, [a] mounting pile of bad loans, a widening gap between rich and poor, rural poverty, and worsening environmental degradation. But the biggest and most fundamental problem we face is reform of the political system to build the democracy that is the dream of people from all walks of life throughout the land. In short, most of the problems China faces are domestic problems.

—Ma Licheng, a writer for China Youth
Daily and editorial writer for the People's Daily,
official organ of the Chinese Communist Party[1]

China's Traditional Foreign Relations

One can better understand China's external relations, even today, by turning back the pages of history to ancient times. For thousands of years, the Middle Kingdom has been one of the world's richest, most developed, and powerful civilizations. Supreme self-confidence and a lack of understanding of the world beyond its outer boundaries, however, poorly prepared its rulers for the colonial and imperial outreach of Western European powers, beginning with the Dutch and the Portuguese in the sixteenth century and later including the British, French, Germans, and Russians.

During periods of strong rule from Xian (China's ancient capital in the interior) and later in Beijing, China's dynasties extended their influence outward to Tibet and Central Asia to the west and the regions known today as Indochina to the southeast. During weaker periods, however, when rival regional warlords struggled with each other and with China's national dynasties, power contracted. European powers were able to take advantage of internal rivalries and weaknesses to establish colonies in China's coastal regions, such as Macao (a Portuguese colony) and Hong Kong (British), and on the Shandong peninsula in eastern China (German). In the late nineteenth century, the Japanese also gained control of traditional Chinese territory, such as the island of Taiwan in the East China Sea, as well as a number of other smaller islands in the region. In the north and northeast, China's dynasties also suffered humiliation and conquest at the hands of the Russian czars as they extended their area of control across Siberia to the Pacific Ocean in the nineteenth century, exercising control over territories formerly under the influence of the Middle Kingdom.

Unlike the European militarists who came in boats from far across the sea, China's ancient rulers extended their influence to the outer periphery of the Middle Kingdom through cultural influence and deference. During strong dynastic periods, distant rulers would send envoys to Xian and Beijing with gifts and homage, in the manner in which lords paid fealty to overlords in feudalistic societies. In Southeast Asia, Chinese influence in ancient times, as in the modern era, was based on the migration of overseas Chinese, who became the backbone of business, finance, and trade in many parts of Southeast Asia.

Twentieth-century Chinese, remembering the glories of ancient Chinese civilization in which Chinese culture, including its written language, spread throughout much of Asia, felt deeply humiliated at the hands of the Western imperialists and the Japanese invaders. These outsiders showed little respect for Chinese culture and sought to impose political, military, and economic control over China's coastal regions. Modern Chinese nationalism, which has a strong appeal to the mass ethnic-racial stock known as the Han people (over 93 percent of the population in modern China), gained its strength as a protest movement against the foreign "devils." In southern China, provinces such as Guangdong and Fujian rose up against the British in the Opium Wars of the 1840s, only to be humiliated by further British penetration of the region. The British took control of Hong Kong during this period and forced Beijing to sign a humiliating treaty at the turn of the twentieth century that gave Britain a ninety-nine-year lease over some mainland territory adjacent to Hong Kong (known as the New Territories).

Support for China's nationalist revolution of 1911, which did away with dynastic rule, came from the Chinese masses, who wished to create a strong modern China as a means of liberating the Middle Kingdom from foreign domination and humiliation. Sun Yat-sen, in the same year, was recognized as the founder of modern China when he returned from overseas to help establish a new Chinese republic. Sun pushed for three goals simultaneously, the *Three Principles of the People,* although he did not live to see them accomplished. First, he wished to instill a feeling of nationalist pride to unify the Chinese nation and free it from foreign control. Second, he sought to establish modern democratic institutions, which he believed were essential to mobilize the people to bring about his other goals. Third, he sought to bring about the modernization of China through education, technology, and improvement in social well-being. During his last days, Sun Yat-sen worked closely with other nationalistic leaders in China, who shared Sun's aspirations for national unity and modernization, although differing with him on the political strategy (type of political mobilization) to restore China to its rightful role as a great Asian nation.

The Mandate of Heaven and the Chinese Communist Party

Early Party Days and the Long March

The Chinese Communist Party (CCP) was founded in 1921, four years after the Bolshevik Revolution in Russia. On instructions from Moscow, China's fledgling Communist Party worked with the Kuomintang (KMT), led by Chiang Kai-shek, who had been trained as a revolutionary in Russia. In 1927, however, Chiang turned on his Communist partners, wiping out their urban bases and forcing the remnants of the CCP to flee to the interior countryside. Mao Zedong, who had joined the CCP in 1923, and other party stalwarts formed the first Chinese Soviet Republic in a region protected by surrounding mountains in southern China in 1931. When Chiang's forces threatened to overrun their mountain retreat, Mao and a small band of dedicated Communists retreated to Yenan in northwestern China. This difficult journey, covering thousands of miles through China's interior in 1934, became known as the *Long March,* one of the central myths of Chinese communism, showing how the Communists, supported by the people, could overcome all adversity. It was during the Long March that Mao Zedong finally assumed leadership of the CCP after defeating the more urban-oriented members of the Communist Party. Mao's strategies and tactics were unique, different in essential ways from the system of Marxism-Leninism practiced by the Bolsheviks in the Soviet Union. His unique system of politics, based on the support of the peasantry, was one of the great twentieth-century contributions to revolutionary theory and practice and contributed to the eventual triumph of the CCP over both the Kuomintang and the Japanese invaders.

The Mass Line and Rural Revolution

Mao abandoned standard Marxist orthodoxy to favor a rural, peasant revolution out of necessity. The CCP had little choice, because most of the Communists in China's cities had been wiped out by the Kuomintang. Unlike the traditional warlords, who robbed the peasants and used them in their rival struggles for power, Mao and his followers worked with the peasants and helped them with their harvests and in their struggles to gain control of the land from ruling landlords. Mao referred to this relationship between the party cadres and the peasants as the *mass line,* in which party cadres learned from the peasants, refined the peasants' views based on party doctrine, and developed policies that reflected the people's will refracted through CCP ideology. For China's peasants, being listened to by their leaders was an unprecedented experience.

Mao and his initially small band of followers in Yenan gained strength by recruiting peasants into the CCP and the People's Liberation Army (PLA). Mao also gained strength by appealing to Chinese nationalism. Many believed that the Communist military was far more dedicated to fighting the Japanese than were the Kuomintang forces. To show their patriotism, young urban intellectuals began to journey to Yenan to join the movement.

After the defeat of the Japanese, Mao and Chiang fought for control of China, and Mao's combined appeal to the peasantry and to Chinese patriotism won the day. The Nationalists, who were holed up in the cities with little support in the countryside, were no match for Mao's rural-based revolutionary forces. Militarily, the triumphant People's Liberation Army had little in the way of modern military equipment, except for the U.S. equipment it appropriated from Nationalist forces. It triumphed instead through the support of the masses and through sheer determination.

With its final triumph on the mainland in 1949 and the retreat of the Kuomintang to the island of Taiwan in the East China Sea, Mao's Communists gained a new Mandate of Heaven from the people. The Chinese people celebrated the establishment of the People's Republic of China (PRC) on October 1, 1949, as Mao's portrait was hung in triumph from the outer wall of the Forbidden City, the former home of China's emperors and empresses. China's modern unification, which began with the 1911 revolution that ended the Qing dynasty, had now come full circle. A new regime, a people's regime, had seized the Mandate of Heaven.

The Korean War

The new government of China did not have to wait long to receive its first major test. On June 25, 1950, North Korean troops swept into South Korea. U.S. forces, under a UN umbrella, soon landed on the Korean peninsula and started marching northward. Mao Zedong and the other Communist leaders grew increasingly uneasy as General Douglas MacArthur, who led the U.S. effort, spoke of marching to the Yalu River. Mao, we now know, agonized over how to respond. Ultimately, however, he felt compelled to protect his nascent regime from possible invasion by committing Chinese "volunteers" to fight with the North Koreans. For the next three years, the Chinese sustained large losses, both from battle and from frostbite, but they did succeed in stalemating the Korean conflict. In the 1953 armistice, the UN forces agreed to stay below the thirty-eighth parallel. Mao's northeastern flank was now safe.

Even though the Korean War severely strained China's weak economy, the patriotic support of China's people (through the Resist America campaign) helped the party to consolidate its power and extend its control throughout Chinese society. Largely through its own efforts—the United States led an international commercial embargo, and the Soviet Union was miserly in its aid—the party mobilized the masses to build a new infrastructure and industrial base. What modern industry, transportation networks, communications systems, and energy utilization had existed in China before 1949 had been concentrated in the coastal areas and was destroyed during the anti-Japanese war and the civil war.

Mass mobilization was achieved in a number of ways, most importantly through land reform. The old landlord system was destroyed to allow the peasants to work under party supervision in rural collectives and workers' brigades. In addition to working the land, peasants spent slack time building roads, expanding irrigation systems, working in small-scale factories, and other infrastructure tasks. Living standards were sacrificed to provide capital for large-scale industrialization in the Soviet style of quick modernization. In return for the people's—men's and women's—sacrifices, the party promised all Chinese vastly improved medical care, sufficient food, and improved educational opportunities. These egalitarian benefits, provided by the production units in the countryside or the work units in the urban areas, became known as the *iron rice bowl*. Like in the early days of Soviet communism, the people were told that their sacrifices would create a better tomorrow for their children. Sacrifices in an era of state socialism would lead, the Chinese leaders said, to better living standards in a future era of communism.

Let One Hundred Flowers Bloom

By 1957, Mao, who was always impatient, was dissatisfied with the pace of the party's efforts to achieve socialism. Temporarily abandoning the Leninist principle of silencing all overt criticism of the party, Mao called on the people, especially the Chinese intellectuals, to speak out about what needed to be done to improve conditions in China. Many Chinese responded to Mao's call to "let one hundred flowers bloom" by voicing criticism against existing party policies and rule. After a year of officially sanctioned criticism, Mao reversed himself and announced that there were weeds in his flower garden that needed to be pruned with a shovel. Those intellectuals who had spoken out were punished and received a black mark on their records that would come to haunt them during the Cultural Revolution.

Mao achieved two goals through the Hundred Flowers campaign. First, he exposed those who were not totally supportive of the Communist regime. Second, he was able to manipulate the people's criticisms to attack the party members who favored a rational, planned march toward socialism and communism.

Fearing that he was losing ground to party members who favored development in a Soviet style, Mao sought to undermine their authority. He succeeded, but at a terrible cost. No longer would the intellectuals voice their doubts about Communist policies, and their quiescence hindered the free interchange of ideas necessary for advanced economic development and industrialization.

The Great Leap Forward

After the collapse of the Hundred Flowers campaign, Mao sought to restore momentum to China's revolution by mobilizing the masses in new forms of social and economic efforts that would be unique to China. In 1958, collectivized farming was abandoned in favor of the creation of huge, county-size communes in which family life gave way to total sharing of resources, services, and even home chores such as cooking. To promote industrialization in the countryside, backyard steel furnaces were built all over the country, and dams and irrigation networks were built by hand. But the complete reorganization of the countryside did not suddenly produce a communist society, as Mao predicted it would. Rather, the people, who remained attached to fundamental values such as the nurturing of the traditional family, refused to accept the experiments in community living. Backyard steel was of such poor quality that the farm utensils melted down to make it would have been worth more. The irrigation networks could not withstand China's frequently adverse climatic conditions. The real results of the Great Leap Forward were economic dislocations and a drastic decline in agricultural productivity from 1958 to 1961. Widespread famine ensued. The Communist government now acknowledges 16 million deaths from malnutrition; other estimates range from 20 to 50 million deaths.[2]

The other members of the international socialist fraternity were appalled by the Great Leap Forward. The Soviet Union, in particular, resented Mao's claims that he had found the way to skip the socialist stage and immediately move into pure communism. If the first socialist country still had not advanced to Marx's second stage, how could Mao claim to have done so in an impoverished, rural society? Many CCP regulars were as appalled as the Soviets, and Mao was forced to abandon the communes in 1961 and revert to Soviet-style economic planning. The peasants were organized into workers' brigades within agricultural collectives, which were controlled by party cadres. Normal family life based on individual households was restored.

The Cultural Revolution

After several years of ascendancy of those in the CCP whom Mao perceived to be opposed to his romantic notions of revolution, Mao came to believe that he was being treated with respect but that nobody was listening to him. The

"Great Helmsman" became increasingly fretful that pragmatists—not idealists—pervaded the party and the state bureaucracy. Unlike Joseph Stalin, who sought to consolidate his power by using the secret police to purge his perceived enemies, Mao adopted an original approach. He called on Chinese youth to join together in groups, the Red Guard, to struggle against party cadres, government officials, enterprise managers, educators, and anyone else who may have had a blot on their revolutionary dossier.

China's youth obeyed Mao's commands with blind devotion as they traveled around the country exposing and punishing Mao's enemies. Most of China's leaders, government officials, educators, and intellectuals underwent "reeducation" through cleaning latrines and pigsties in remote rural areas. They were replaced by cadres who had the requisite political ardor but mostly no other credentials, including higher education because the schools were closed. Because of international disapproval of these internal developments, China became increasingly isolated from the international community, with many countries withdrawing their ambassadors.

It did not take long before various Red Guard factions were fighting each other (with guns) for the honor of being the purest defender of Mao's beliefs. When the People's Liberation Army splintered along similar lines, China nearly disintegrated into complete chaos. Mao then decided that some sort of order had to be restored. He called in loyal units of the PLA to prevent complete disintegration of the public order. Many of the Red Guard were then shipped off to the countryside, where they would not be able to cause any more problems, to "learn from the peasants."

The active phase of the Cultural Revolution lasted from 1966 through 1969, but it continued in milder form until Mao's death in 1976. The Cultural Revolution changed the course of Chinese history by dismantling the existing political, social, and economic structures in China and replacing them with others that barely functioned. It was a disaster for nearly all elements of Chinese society, setting back modernization and production, disrupting education and science, and further isolating China from the outside world. Perhaps its most long-lasting effect, however, has been an increasingly pervasive cynicism among the Chinese people about the credibility of the party's leadership. Knowing that the direction of any political campaign can be reversed without warning, many Chinese now turn a deaf ear to party exhortations.

The Rise of Market Socialism

Mao Zedong, in spite of the mistakes he made in his later years, will always be remembered as the leader who created a modern, relatively classless Chinese nation that was free of imperialist interference. If he had retired before the Great Leap Forward, he would undoubtedly be remembered as one of the greatest Chinese leaders of all times. As it was, at the time of his death in 1976

China was still chaotic. The chaos continued as supporters of the Cultural Revolution struggled for power against party members who favored rational, planned economic development over revolutionary zeal. The *Gang of Four*—Mao's widow and three other supporters of the Cultural Revolution—struggled against Deng Xiaoping and his supporters for control of the nation. By 1978 Deng had won, and he began to pursue the Four Modernizations.

To modernize China, Deng introduced market incentives to the peasants and ultimately to the urban economy. To gain the support of the peasantry, Deng authorized the creation of household rural production units in which farmers leased the land they tilled. Base levels of grain production were established, and each family farm was required to sell a certain amount of grain to the government at a set price. Beyond that, farmers could produce what they wished and sell to whom they wished. At the same time, Deng encouraged the establishment of private and collective rural industries. He also established special economic zones, where joint ventures with foreign companies were allowed. More than 100 million peasants eventually migrated to work in China's burgeoning coastal industries.

Under Deng, China embarked on a new course that may ultimately be more revolutionary than anything Mao could ever have imagined. Deng stressed marketplace incentives over Mao's reliance on political consciousness. Whereas Mao stressed self-reliance and separation from the international system, Deng opened China to the outside world. He believed that modernization of the nation's economy was the most important goal for the regime. If the people's living standards rose, Deng believed the party would win back its credibility both internally and externally. Indeed, the Chinese people's living standards have risen, more dramatically than anyone could have imagined in 1979. What Deng also could not imagine at the beginning of his rule was that increased prosperity would slowly but surely erode the power and control of the party over its people.

Deng's successors have continued Deng's policy of maintaining party rule through the dual appeals of economic development and nationalism. While they have succeeded in these areas, at the same time they are ruling over a less coherent and potentially fractious China where economic inequities are increasing, central control has declined, and disaffection may easily develop.

Nationalism, Irredentism, and Chinese Minorities

Restoration of the Middle Kingdom?

While Deng Xiaoping made economic development the cornerstone of his new China, the other pillar of popular appeal through which the party sought to renew its Mandate of Heaven was fulfillment of Chinese nationalism. All modern Chinese leaders have emphasized the restoration of the Middle Kingdom, which in ancient times included most of continental East and Southeast Asia. Even in the 1930s, Mao had visions of restoring China's ancient grandeur. With the end of the Cold War, the decline of the superpowers, and an emerging power vacuum in Asia, China's leaders, strongly supported by the majority Han population, have proclaimed an interest in restoring ancient boundaries that had been lost to foreign aggressors in the nineteenth and twentieth centuries.

China's leaders disagree with Westerners as to what constitutes internal restoration and consolidation versus external aspirations. Because the phenomenon of irredentism can go beyond national restoration to jingoistic expansion abroad, there is a real possibility that Chinese nationalist aspirations could threaten some of China's Asian neighbors in the twenty-first century. Legitimate nationalist goals are in the eyes of the beholder. Western nations, after practicing their own imperialism for many centuries, now question the legitimacy of Beijing's military occupation of Tibet. Chinese on both sides of the Taiwan Straits, however, agree that Tibet is an integral part of China. They also agree that parts of Indochina, the South China Sea islands, both Inner and Outer Mongolia, parts of what is now Russian Siberia, the foreign enclaves of Hong Kong and Macao, and the Japanese-controlled Ryukyu Islands were all integral parts of the Middle Kingdom and that parts of these areas should be restored to Chinese suzerainty. With the decline of party legitimacy, the CCP seems to be relying more heavily on nationalist sentiments to help legitimate its right to lead the Chinese people. If this nationalism is combined with irredentism, the results could be dangerous to China's neighbors.

China's Minorities

China's minorities, which form less than 10 percent of the population, are either dispersed along China's periphery or located in small pockets scattered throughout China. To lessen even the minimal control China's minorities have over their governance, Beijing is encouraging a rapid migration of the Han people to areas such as Tibet, Xinjiang, and Inner Mongolia.

In Tibet, Chinese control is controversial primarily because of international awareness of the conflict between Tibetans and Han Chinese. After the People's Liberation Army rolled into Lhasa, the Tibetan capital, in 1950, the native population became increasingly unhappy with their Chinese overlords. After conditions became worse, the Tibetan spiritual leader, the Dalai Lama, fled to India with over 100,000 supporters in 1959. From there he has devoted himself to publicizing his people's cause throughout the world, for which he was eventually awarded the Nobel Peace Prize, much to the chagrin of the leaders in Beijing.

Tibetans maintain that their nation should be independent from China, or at least autonomous in domestic affairs if not foreign affairs. They accuse Beijing of using force to destroy their sense of national identity and their particular form of Buddhism. Recent drives to encourage Han migration are seen as an effort to make Tibetans strangers in their own land, and Tibetans in exile have denounced China's economic development plans for Tibet as a "smoke screen" for mass Han settlement.

The Chinese maintain that Tibet was historically a part of China and that Communist rule has resulted in increased living standards, better health care, and easier access to education. Beijing maintains that the Tibet issue is not an ethnic issue, a religious issue, or a human rights issue, but rather an issue manufactured by a handful of former Tibetan gentry and religious leaders who want to reinstitute serfdom and religious oppression.[3]

A similar process is taking place in Inner Mongolia, where Han migrants now outnumber native Mongolians by a five-to-one ratio. With the emergence of Outer Mongolia, formerly a Soviet client state, as a nonsocialist state with a resurgent Buddhist faith, Beijing is increasingly nervous. Beijing is concerned that the regime in Ulan Bator (a city in Outer Mongolia) has become a base for supporting dissidents and separatists in Inner Mongolia. Beijing is reportedly justifying to itself the right to control all of Mongolia.[4] If it attempts to justify extending Chinese influence or control to Outer Mongolia, open conflict is possible.

Beijing's leaders believe that China's protesters, whether Uyghurs in Xinjiang, Tibetans, or others who challenge Communist authority, should all be lumped together, with little distinction between civil rights movements, separatists, or terrorists. As in Tibet, China's leaders have cracked down on dissenters in Xinjiang.

After the September 11, 2001, terrorist attacks on the World Trade Center and Pentagon, China joined the United States and other countries in the war on terrorism and began equating Uyghur separatists in Xinjiang with terrorist groups in Central Asia. In fact, China is taking advantage of the global efforts against international terrorism to crack down even harder on dissenting groups in western China. Beijing has also stationed troops along the border between Xinjiang and Afghanistan to cut off any outside support for separatist groups there.

As in Tibet and other western regions, Beijing has encouraged increasing numbers of China's Han majority to take up jobs in Xinjiang. While China claims that it is supporting education and other rights for the local population, in fact the Hans are becoming the new majority in urban areas. They hold most of the key jobs, including government and business positions.

China's primary goal in the minority regions is to maintain exclusive political control. The creation of new, formerly Soviet nations on its borders, many of which are populated by ethnic groups similar to China's minorities and with restive Muslim populations, is tremendously unsettling to Beijing. China is likely to combine a carrot-and-stick approach. Minority areas will not be allowed to break away from the Middle Kingdom or exercise any real political power, but they will be allowed limited social and cultural latitude, such as exclusion from China's one-child policy. In interior areas, this approach is likely to be successful. Western Chinese regions include most of China's basic resources, and in the twenty-first century they will become China's new frontier, with improved transportation, communications, and economic development. Though efforts are being made to preserve local culture and minority rights, local religious values and languages will face problems similar to those facing Indian populations in the United States. Revolt and separation will become less likely, as China works with Russia and countries in Central Asia to suppress separatist and terrorist activities throughout the region.

Solutions to Irredentism: Hong Kong and Taiwan

Restoration of the Middle Kingdom is also at the heart of China's policy toward Hong Kong and Taiwan. The question of the unification of Hong Kong and Taiwan with China is a political issue, not an ethnic one. Virtually all of the 6 million residents of Hong Kong and the 20 million residents of Taiwan are Han Chinese.[5] Many still have close cultural and family ties to people in neighboring provinces on the mainland. When Hong Kong became a part of the People's Republic of China in 1997, analysts predicted that the way that Beijing handled the transition would determine if, how, and when Taiwan would follow Hong Kong back into the fold.

With Hong Kong a special autonomous region of China, the colonial era in Chinese (and British) history finally came to an end. The people of Hong Kong and their supporters hoped that the transition would proceed smoothly, following Deng's stated policy of "one country, two systems." China was set to assume control over Hong Kong's foreign and defense policy, but economic, political, and social conditions in Hong Kong would supposedly remain unchanged for fifty years.

After June 1989, however, China, the United Kingdom, and the various parties within Hong Kong began reassessing prospects for the future. After 150 years of British rule without provisions for self-rule, the new British governor of the colony proposed reforms

> "The socialist system and policies shall not be practised in the Hong Kong Special Administrative Region, and the previous capitalist system and way of life shall remain unchanged for 50 years" (Hong Kong Basic Law, Article V).

to enhance democracy in Hong Kong. His efforts were denounced with unbelievable fury by Beijing, which also threatened to set up a shadow government. Observers believe that "Beijing could not allow this because it did not want to encourage demands for free elections in other parts of China, since that might one day lead to the demise of the Communist Party and to the loss of the current leaders' own personal power."[6] By insisting that Hong Kong is an issue of national pride, not democracy and human rights, Beijing has deftly appealed to Chinese nationalism and garnered support even from those who protested at Tiananmen Square.[7]

Disagreements over the future of Hong Kong could have wide-ranging political and economic consequences, both for Hong Kong and for China. In the 1990s, 55 percent of all external investment in China came from Hong Kong. The economies of Hong Kong and Guangdong province are becoming increasingly integrated, with over three-fourths of labor-intensive production in Hong Kong already transferred to enterprises within China that are controlled by Hong Kong businesses. In turn, Hong Kong has become a trade transfer point and financial service center for all of southern China. With over $13 billion ventured, China is now the largest investor in Hong Kong. Any political disputes over the future of Hong Kong could therefore disrupt both the Hong Kong and the Chinese economies.

Should the stability and well-being of Hong Kong be threatened, China's future relations with the United States and with Taiwan could also become highly problematic. The United States has over $7 billion invested in Hong Kong. Any political or economic disruptions of the Hong Kong economy would not only affect U.S. investments but also involve the U.S. government, particularly Congress, in efforts to sanction China. Perhaps more important, political and economic disorder in Hong Kong would have a negative effect on the possibility of Taiwanese unification with the mainland. Abridgment of the "one country, two systems" policy would send the wrong signal to Taipei and reverse the remarkable progress toward economic integration between Taiwan and China that has occurred since the early 1990s.

China's worst fears about the role of the people in Hong Kong politics, which were outlined in the Basic Law agreement between the United Kingdom and the People's Republic of China, came to pass in the early years of the twenty-first century. In 2003, Beijing sought to impose a security

"Do you think Hong Kong was democratic under British rule? Did the British raise concerns about that? Did the Americans raise concerns? No. Why don't you take a look at this double standard?" (Chinese foreign minister Li Zhaoxing, quoted in Keith Bradsher, "China Bristles at Criticism of Hong Kong Restrictions," *New York Times,* April 28, 2004, p. A10).

law on Hong Kong, sparking such surprisingly large and vehement protests that the law was withdrawn. Similarly, in 2004, demonstrators protested Beijing's interpretation of clauses in the Basic Law regarding approval of changes in electoral procedure. According to one analyst, a political expert at the People's University in Beijing, "The problem for China is not legal. It is not whether Hong society is capable of handling democracy. The problem is that if Hong Kong holds direct elections now, it will probably elect people who are not loyal to Beijing. Frankly speaking, that is something Chinese leaders are not ready to accept."[8] How China handles nascent demands in Hong Kong for a greater role for the people in politics will have a tremendous effect not only on the special administrative zone's internal political, social, and economic well-being, but also on the international perception of China. Taiwan, in particular, is watching.

The Future of Taiwan

Dramatic changes have taken place in Taiwan since the Kuomintang retreated to the island in 1949. In 2003, with 23 million people, Taiwan was the second most densely populated region in the world. In 1949, per capita income was $150 and external trade was $300 million. In 2003, per capita income was over $13,000 and annual trade exceeded $230 billion. In 1949, Taiwan was under the dictatorship of the mainland Kuomintang regime. In 2003, Taiwan held direct elections at nearly every level.

From the perspective of China's leaders, however, it is just a matter of time until Taiwan is reunited with the mainland. From the perspective of the Chinese who came to Taiwan with Chiang Kai-shek in 1949, Taiwan will eventually be reunited with the mainland but, they hope, not until a non-Communist regime rules in Beijing. From the perspective of a growing number of native Taiwanese,

"The basic position of the Chinese Government regarding the settlement of the Taiwan question is 'peaceful reunification; one country, two systems.' To put it briefly, it is to realize the reunification of the country by peaceful means, and inside the reunified country, two different social systems—socialism and capitalism—are allowed to co-exist. Socialist system will be practised in the main part of China and the capitalist system will be practised in Taiwan, Hong Kong and Macao areas. The two different social systems will co-exist peacefully for a long time without one swallowing up the other" (PRC Ministry of Foreign Affairs, http://www.fmprc.gov.cn/eng/ljzg/3568/t17796.htm, accessed April 23, 2004).

who represent 85 percent of the island's population, Taiwan should become a democratic and independent nation with representation in the United Nations. These Taiwanese gained more visibility as the ruling Kuomintang allowed greater freedom of expression in the 1990s, and particularly since the KMT lost power to the rival Democratic Progressive Party in the 2000 election.

The Case for Reunification

Since 1987, when the Kuomintang leadership allowed Taiwanese citizens to move back and forth freely to the mainland and to trade with the mainland, interactions have grown with amazing speed. By 1990, Taiwanese business leaders were investing U.S.$1 billion annually in mainland enterprises. By 1993, these investments had grown to U.S.$2.5 billion annually. By the early years of the twenty-first century, the figures were even more compelling. Total value of cross-strait trade in 2000 was U.S.$37.39 billion, and total Taiwan investment in China was U.S.$3.86 billion. Trade between China and Taiwan in the first 11 months of 2003 rose 23.2 percent from the previous year to U.S.$41.69 billion, which represented 17.1 percent of Taiwan's foreign trade. From January to November 2003, Taiwan registered a trade surplus with China of U.S.$22.13 billion, up 13 percent from a year earlier. Exports in the eleven-month period rose 19.5 percent to U.S.$31.91 billion, while imports increased 37.3 percent to U.S.$9.78 billion. The U.S.$31.91 billion worth of shipments to China accounted for 24.5 percent of Taiwan's total exports in the eleven months, compared with 22.4 percent a year earlier. In November 2003 alone, the island's China-bound shipments rose 25.5 percent from the previous year to U.S.$3.53 billion, while imports from China surged 54.7 percent from the previous year to U.S.$1.16 billion.[9] Economic, if not political, integration is moving ahead with amazing speed.

Personal ties are also pulling Taiwan's people closer to the mainland. Relatives and families, long separated by the Cold War, are being reunited. In 1993, over 1 million Taiwanese visited the mainland. In 2000, 3,660,600 Taiwan residents visited China and 154,770 Chinese residents visited Taiwan. Over 300,000 Taiwanese now live in the Shanghai area alone.

Startling developments are also taking place at the governmental level. In 1993, for the first time in over four decades, official meetings between Chinese and Taiwanese government officials took place. Although there were no major breakthroughs, four limited agreements were reached: cross-delivery of registered letters; verification of official documents by the two sides; a statement setting forth topics to be addressed at future dates; and a schedule for future meetings between representatives, to be held several times each year. Beijing has been pushing hard for even more interactions, including official trade and movement of people directly across the Taiwan Straits rather than through Hong Kong. Fearing that acceding to these demands could lead to further integration with the mainland on China's terms, Taipei has been holding back. Yet given its lack of official international status and the integration that has occurred thus far, accelerated integration with the mainland may be the only obvious route for Taiwan. Official direct negotiations were broken off in 1998 due to Taiwan's refusal to accept Beijing's precondition of accepting the "one China, two systems" principle; however, informal cooperation is actually increasing.

Other forces are also at work. Major actors in Asia, including the United States, Japan, and Russia, prefer the present arrangements to either a unilateral declaration of Taiwanese independence or forced integration into Beijing. Growing global concerns about dangers on the Korean peninsula and terrorism are also working to keep relations between Beijing and Taiwan at a lower level of confrontation. Over the long term, if the mainland becomes more democratic and the two entities grow closer together through economic and cultural ties, a political solution is likely. Indeed, barring any unforeseen changes in Asian power configurations, many analysts do not believe that time is on the side of Taiwan's emergence as a formal independent state that is extended diplomatic recognition in the international community.

The Case for Independence

Nevertheless, a number of factors beyond China's control may be moving Taiwan toward separation and independence from the mainland. With the end of the Cold War, the West no longer needed China as a counterweight to the Soviet Union. This led France and the United States to break previous pledges to China by selling military equipment to Taiwan. As defense contracts shrink in Western countries, Taiwan has become one of the major markets for Western defense industries. Although Beijing denounces military sales to Taiwan with vigor, counteractions against Western trade and investment in China would hurt the Chinese economy without necessarily stopping the sales. Nevertheless, given China's rise as a major political and economic force in the international area and its implacable opposition to any conference of legitimacy on Taiwan (for example, Taiwan was allowed to join the World Trade Organization in 2002 but China blocked its entry into the World Health Organization even during the severe acute respiratory syndrome [SARS] crisis), most nations are not willing to incur the wrath of Beijing by favoring Taiwan's positions.

Political and social factors also favor continued Taiwanese separation from the mainland. With the passage of time, the Kuomintang leaders from the mainland are being succeeded by native Taiwanese and by children of mainland families who were born and raised in Taiwan. Both groups have much less attachment to the mainland and to reunification than do their elders. The notion of two Chinas is an attractive option to these groups. In January 1993, Tai-

In his inaugural speech on May 20, 2000, President Chen established a "Five No's" policy on cross-strait relations. He pledged that unless the Chinese Communists used military force against Taiwan, he would not: (1) declare Taiwan independent; (2) change the name of the nation; (3) push for the inclusion of former president Lee Teng-hui's "special state-to-state relationship" in the constitution; (4) hold a referendum to change the status quo on the question of independence or unification; nor (5) move to abolish either the Guidelines for National Unification or the National Unification Council (Republic of China [Taiwan], Government Information Office, http://www.gio.gov.tw/, viewed April 13, 2004).

wanese president Lee Teng-hui stated, "We should make good use of our overseas development fund and all other possible resources to promote more pragmatic participation in world organizations. . . . This will expedite our ultimate goal of returning to the United Nations."[10]

By the late 1990s, the Taiwan issue had become increasingly complex. Threatened by the tone of the 1996 presidential campaign in Taiwan, China built up its military presence across the straits, which led to an anti-Chinese backlash. First, popular sentiment in Taiwan took a dim view of China's actions, leading to an upsurge in support for the Taiwanese wing of the KMT Party and for continued autonomy if not independence. Second, U.S. president Bill Clinton responded by sending a symbolic U.S. military presence into the Taiwan Straits. Beijing got the message, the crisis was defused, and cross-strait relations were stabilized. With the 2000 presidential election, however, Beijing was thrown a nasty curve. Two KMT candidates split the vote, and for the first time since 1949 a non-KMT president was elected in Taiwan. Chen Shui-bian, the head of the Democratic Progressive Party, was suspected by China of tacitly supporting Taiwanese independence. The 2004 presidential election in Taiwan, which was almost too close to call and involved the shooting of Chen Shui-bian and the Taiwanese vice president, was equally unsettling. China verbally admonished Taiwan to adhere to the one-China policy, and it sternly warned that political chaos would not be tolerated, but in reality China observed rather than sought to influence the 2004 election.

All parties involved in the future of Taiwan hope for the best possible outcome: eventual loose integration into the mainland based on increasing political, economic, and social ties and based on democratic principles. Certainly China, with its economic concerns, as well as its desire to be a respected international player and a good neighbor in Asia, would prefer not to resolve the Taiwan issue by force. Both Taiwan and China have a great deal to lose if integration is not the final outcome; however, given the Chinese leadership's increasing use of nationalism to justify its continuation in power and the role that the reunification of Taiwan has come to play in that nationalism, combined with Taiwan's increasingly diverse political atmosphere, the possibility for alternative, more belligerent outcomes cannot be dismissed.

Human Rights and Political Freedoms

You know the biggest surprise after 14 years (in prison) was not the new buildings, shops and highways, but the people. They are more open than before, they know more and they care about democracy, about their rights. What I have learned so far is that this economic system needs a modern political system to operate it. If China's government refuses to bring about these changes soon and fast, there is a good chance the people will push for it, that there will be unrest and turmoil, like in 1978 and 1989. And nobody wants to see that happen.[11]

These were some of the comments of Wei Jingsheng, China's most famous dissident, following his release from prison in September 1993 after serving over fourteen years for his activities during the democracy movement of 1979. Known as the father of Chinese democracy, Wei is convinced that the Chinese people want freedom and democracy and says that he does "not believe that they only want more money." Deng's reforms have brought new activism among the people. Even before Wei's *dazibao* (large character poster), millions of China's youth became politically active during the Cultural Revolution. Having tasted power when Mao turned to them in the 1960s and 1970s, they challenged existing authorities again in the 1980s after learning that the party is not infallible and that China's youth can play a role in eliminating corruption and promoting the well-being of the people.

But it was not just the students who challenged the existing order at Tiananmen Square. College students and their instructors make up less than half of 1 percent of the population, and the million or more people who supported the students at Beijing in the spring of 1989 came from all walks of life and included blue-collar workers, government officials, intellectuals, service personnel, media people, and even some party cadres. Tiananmen Square must also be viewed as a continuation of earlier frustrations. For example, Deng Xiaoping removed his protégé, Party Secretary Hu Yaobang, for his failure to put down student demonstrations in 1987 and 1988.[12]

Why Tiananmen Square?

Hu Yaobang had become a popular symbol of reform and freedom, and his death on April 15, 1989, served as an excuse for students to gather and express their views. There was also the precedent of demonstrations and memorials in 1976 in honor of Premier Zhou Enlai, who was popular with the people. Zhou was recognized for his moderate views and his help in bringing an end to the Cultural Revolution. The demonstrations in the spring of 1989 also came while Secretary-General Mikhail Gorbachev was visiting Beijing, a major step in normalizing Sino-Soviet relations after many years of turmoil between the two communist giants. Gorbachev agreed to visit a student delegation at Tiananmen Square, and the students viewed him as a leader of economic and political reform.

At first, Party Secretary Zhao Ziyang, Deng's new heir apparent, advocated leniency with the students. The demonstration started out largely as a protest against government and party corruption, and there was considerable sympathy for the demonstrations by a broad sector of the population who felt left out of the new prosperity. Student demands for political democracy came only during the latter stages of the demonstrations, and no one, including the students themselves, seemed to have any idea what democracy would mean for China.

By the end of May, the demonstrations were diminishing, but the party leaders, divided between reformists and conservatives, were undecided as to how the demonstrations should be brought to an end and whether the students should be punished. At this point, Deng Xiaoping and the older hard-line leaders took charge, fearing that to leave the demonstrators unpunished would be a sign of party weakness and would threaten its future authority. No doubt the Old Guard was looking over its shoulders at the tumultuous events taking place simultaneously in Eastern Europe, which Deng and his cohorts blamed on weakness and basic errors in Moscow. Beijing's hard-liners were convinced that unless opposition to party rule in China were ruthlessly crushed, challenges to party authority similar to those in Eastern Europe and the Soviet Union might very well succeed in China. As for the demonstrators and their supporters, they may have had illusions resulting from economic and social reforms over the previous ten years that the party could be persuaded to accept political reforms as well. If so, they were wrong. The leaders in Beijing never intended that economic reforms should also lead to the demise of party authority.

Believing that party authority was being questioned, Deng and the Beijing leadership felt that they had no choice but to suppress the students with military force. The party leadership was also increasingly alarmed that the student demonstrators were receiving growing support from blue-collar workers, the middle class, intellectuals, and important elements within the mass media, which up to then had always been under the tight control of the Ministry of Culture. Even the military units around Beijing seemed divided as to whether they should use force to quell the student demonstrators.

The Consequences of Tiananmen

Much of the favorable opinion of China that had been built up over the previous decade came to an end with the military crackdown on China's young people on the night of June 4, 1989. In fact, the outside world had a much better view of events in Beijing than most of China's vast population (mostly rural), which never saw all the Tiananmen events shown on Western television screens. There were also demonstrations in other cities such as Shanghai, but these were quickly crushed once the decision was made to quell the demonstrations in Beijing. Prior to June 4, China's own media services had shown some sympathy for the students, but afterward media personnel who had shown such sympathy were quickly removed, and the print and electronic media returned to the official party line. Any opposition to party authority and control of the media was suppressed, and dissenters who were not arrested went into hiding.[13]

Although the physical power of the party, with the crucial help of the military, was preserved, its legitimacy, which had suffered severely from early steps such as the Great Leap Forward and the Cultural Revolution, was further undermined. In addition, as in the former Soviet Union (in both December 1991 and October 1993), the military became the key to stability and political order, a major deviation from communist doctrine. In the 1990s, a major result of developments inside China has been the increased role of the military in deciding China's future, including the future of the party itself.

Since Tiananmen, Beijing has continued to push for more economic growth, mainly through further market incentives, foreign investment, and foreign trade. But annual economic growth, as we shall see in Chapter 3, is producing social and economic contradictions. These include inequities in wealth in both rural and urban areas; quandaries facing Beijing as de facto political participation grows at the local level; and mass consumerism and growth in Western cultural values accompanied by greed and party corruption.

All of the contradictions leading up to the 1989 student demonstrations remain in some form in today's China. As long as the dual economy exists (which we will discuss in Chapter 3), there is the temptation for party members to take advantage of dual pricing to use their position to obtain cheap public goods and sell them at high prices on the private market. Public criticism of the personal lives of high-level party officials is ruthlessly suppressed in order to try to protect the legitimacy of the party rulers. Party members themselves are now being encouraged to go into private business and make money, a practice known as "plunging into the sea." Since Tiananmen, moneymaking seems to be the dominant ideological value in China. Some party and government officials are moonlighting to make a profit, with only a small proportion of their time dedicated to the performance of their public duties. This can occur in contemporary China because there is no effective system of accountability for party and government officials, especially when the mass media is controlled by the party and any investigation of party behavior is squashed. One of the results of Tiananmen was an even greater determination of party leaders to crush any thoughts of popular or free elections, oppose an independent judiciary and investigative corps, or permit media free of party control.

China's Youth After Tiananmen

In the past, China's youth served as Mao's instrument for cleansing the party and bureaucracy of corruption and also as a means of renewing revolutionary fervor. Since Tiananmen, China's youth remain silent. Although they discuss their concerns privately, the price of public expression is the threat of punishment, including the loss of educational privileges or even jail. There is, however, a basic contradiction in the silencing of youth. Both the Cultural Revolution, spearheaded by millions of active youth in the Red Guard (in the 1960s and 1970s), and the student demonstrators (in the 1980s) culminating in the Tiananmen events, have taught China's young people that they indeed are the wave of the future; they have learned that, sooner or later, they will be a major force in restoring Chinese idealism, as well as in achieving social and political reform. Today in China, most of the youth and intellectuals have little faith in the ability of the party to solve China's problems in the twenty-first century. Most students and intellectuals would agree, however, that breakdown of order in China, which appeared imminent in 1989, could cause great suffering, such as has occurred in other former communist lands. Those in China who question authoritarian party rule today seem more concerned with achieving economic prosperity and social well-being than with obtaining freedom of expression or political participation. Because open dissent is not allowed in China, one Western observer believes "a regime of suppression has difficulty detecting the sincerity and strength of individual loyalty. Considering its tight control of society, the PRC's claim of widespread loyalty from the people is certainly questionable."[14]

Prisoners of Conscience

Long prison terms, reports of torture by student prisoners released from jail, and further arrests for speaking out against the government or party are a continuing reminder that lack of freedom of expression has been a Chinese legacy. Better-known demonstrators, at the urging of Western human rights groups, have occasionally been released as a sign that the government wishes to improve its international human rights image. But lesser-known dissidents continue to languish in jail, refusing to renounce their dissenting beliefs.[15] There are signs that the rage of dissidents is diminishing with the passage of time. A Western observer who closely follows human rights issues in China notes, "These days, especially outside Beijing, many Chinese seem to have forgotten—not the attack itself, but at least the fury they once felt." But he then points out:

The great majority of Chinese intellectuals still seem to expect that the set-back is temporary and that the official verdict on June 4 will be reversed. Alienation is as widespread as ever, few people believe in Marxism, and many Chinese and foreigners alike regard Communist rule as a crumbling dynasty. But outside the capital, the reason for discontent has more to do with corruption and rising prices than with killing students.[16]

The Party in the Twenty-First Century

In the twenty-first century, China is a mass of contradictions. The Communist Party still fears an open discussion of the past and of the future; yet controlled conversation on a whole variety of issues is allowed, often as a safety valve. Thus, although the government controls the Internet and censors it, chat groups address issues that would have been forbidden not that long ago. Controlled local elections are allowed in many areas. The media is allowed varying degrees of lassitude, depending on the way the Beijing winds are blowing. Private entrepreneurs have been invited to become members of the Communist Party, and many believe that China is headed toward market capitalism rather than market socialism. But the party remains in control and ruthlessly clamps down on any form of expression that might threaten its legitimacy.

The party allowed direct village elections in 1988. Today, village elections occur in some 700,000 villages across China, reaching 75 percent of the nation's 1.3 billion people. To convince the outside world of the legitimacy of its electoral process, China's Ministry of Civil Affairs granted the Carter Center, founded by former U.S. president Jimmy Carter, permission to observe village election proce-

"First of all, we should develop democracy to safeguard people's democratic rights and to respect and protect their human rights. Secondly, we should improve on the legal system through better legislation, better administration according to law, and greater judicial reform. Thirdly, we should run the country according to law, making our socialist democracy more institutionalized, standardized and proceduralized, and in this way we can make sure that it will not change because of changes in the leadership and changes in the views and focus of attention of leaders. Fourth, we must strengthen supervision, and we should make sure that the government is placed under the supervision of the people. We have to develop democracy and strengthen supervision" (*Washington Post* interview with Premier Wen Jiabao, November 23, 2003, http://english .peopledaily.com.cn/2003 11/23/ eng20031123_128838.shtml).

dures and to provide assistance in gathering election data, educating voters, training election officials, and hosting Chinese officials to observe U.S. elections. The Carter Center also began observations of township elections—elections above the village level—in conjunction with the National People's Congress in 1999.[17] While some dismiss these elections as controlled by the party, which vets all the candidates, they are nevertheless useful in forcing candidates to be more responsive to the people's needs, be less inclined to corruption, and once in office, be more likely to accomplish popular projects.

An apt illustration of today's contradictions is the recent government effort to encourage foreign investment in its media outlets. Officially, news outlets will be off limits; however, even Chinese officials acknowledge that over the long term the party will not be able to exercise total control over media outlets with foreign interests.[18] At the same time that the government is encouraging privatization of and foreign direct investment in the media, it has mounted a ferocious campaign against at least one journal known for the quality of its investigative reporting, not all of which is flattering to the Communist Party. According to an editor from *Southern Metropolitan Daily,* an investigative journal in Guangdong province, "All Chinese media have three functions: mouthpiece for the government and party, to support themselves by making money and, thirdly, to give journalists a means to influence society. . . . The three goals are irreconcilable, and if you go too far in any one direction, the result is trouble. We are all learning there is a bottom line somewhere, and although nobody wants to be punished, no one knows where it lies exactly."[19] In all likelihood, the party itself does not know exactly where the bottom line lies.

The Chinese premier advocates development of the legal system—certainly a change from the Maoist era, when the party was the law and there was no other legal system; yet the judiciary is subject to party control and defense lawyers often have a hard time making their case. Contract and business law are being developed, yet the laws can be flouted with impunity if the interests of connected officials are involved. In all these areas—elections, the media, the law—the systems, structures, and regulating systems are not above suspicion. Yet clearly, as Premier Wen indicates, the party leadership understands that over time it must develop more rigorous and independent standards to truly succeed in the international arena as well as maintain the people's loyalty. The question is whether the party will be able to loosen its grip and maintain its power.

Beijing's leaders hoped that China and the world would be able to forget Tiananmen by bringing the Summer Olympics to Beijing in 2000. Although Beijing's leaders went to great lengths to persuade the Olympic Committee to select Beijing, including releasing of dissidents such as Wei Jingsheng just before the committee was to vote in September 1993, their efforts were to no avail; the committee narrowly voted for Sydney, Australia, over Beijing on the final vote. World opinion on the issue was divided, with some Western observers believing that the choice of Beijing would have drawn China into the mainstream of the international community and brought pressure in the years leading up to the 2000 Summer Olympics for the country to improve its human rights image. By 2001, China had been vindicated. Beijing was chosen as the site for the 2008 Summer Olympics. Chinese leaders and the Chinese people view the Olympics as a validation of their acceptance into the international community as an equal partner. Beijing is being physically transformed for the games. China's image abroad, the CCP hopes, will also be transformed by its Olympic glory.

The Problem of Decentralization: Empire, Federation, or Anarchy?

> What remains in question today is how communist rule will end in China. Among the many scenarios suggested by China experts . . . [is that] the regime on the Chinese mainland may well disintegrate under the stress of increasing regionalism.[20]

One of the continuing trends has been the movement of power away from the center to the regional and local levels. These trends, which may greatly affect China and its global role in the twenty-first century, can be observed through a number of changes taking place at the local level, especially in rural China. Some Western observers who have recently lived in a number of China's rural villages think that the CCP's ability to influence local farmers has declined because of the easing of social regimentation and the introduction of market reforms.[21] In prosperous areas the farmers seem interested only in cadres who have the skills to help the peasants make a profit, including the ability to run factories and market products. Although Deng's household responsibility system increased agricultural production, it also reduced the ability of the party to control the land and its farmers. Now the party competes with other groups for influence, and sometimes party cadres are viewed as an impediment rather than a benefactor in promoting the people's needs. Who are some of these competing groups?

The Breakdown of Order and the Emergence of Local Organized Crime

With the relaxation of totalitarian central control, crime bosses have emerged, especially in southern China's rich coastal regions. Many of the social problems in contemporary Western societies, assumed to be absent during Mao's iron rule, are emerging since Deng's reforms. Criminal elements "promote prostitution and gambling, trafficking in narcotics, rural women and children, and slip hired outlaws across the border to rob Hong Kong banks."[22]

Local Religious Revival

In the past, Western religions influenced only a small percentage of the Chinese population, but unless local congregations have governmental approval to practice their religion, they must go underground and gather at night to worship. Government concern about growing numbers of Christians has led to a crackdown on Protestant and Catholic groups that are not officially registered, and there has been increased religious oppression against Muslims and Tibetan Buddhists, including beatings, forced relocations, surveillance, arrests, and property confiscation.[23] The furious government campaign against the Falun Gong, a group that combines quasi-religious elements with exercise, demonstrates the leadership's continued sensitivity to any group it does not control. According to the Law Yearbook of China, arrests for disturbing the social order (which include membership in unapproved religious groups) totaled 12,826 in 2002, down from previous years.[24]

The Reemergence of Family Clans

One consequence of declining local party control has been the takeover of power in some local regions by clans, based on warlord-type rivalries. Local leaders, supported by extended family connections, may assume actual power at the village level, control local government, and allocate privileges. Rivalries between clans can lead to violence. In fall 2004, violence erupted between Han and Hui (Muslim) villages in Henan province. Martial law was imposed, and as many as 150 people may have died.[25]

Economic Decentralization

The significance of China's economic reforms will be discussed in detail in Chapter 3. But it is important to note here that much of China's economic miracle has been due in large part to economic decentralization, especially in rural areas, where over 100 million peasants now work in local service industries and factories that are locally controlled.

The redistribution of power has been magnified by the continuing losses of state enterprises, one of the major sources of power of the CCP and central government in Beijing. Although the party continues to proclaim the values of socialism with Chinese characteristics, state enterprises are hamstrung by a growing national debt, much of which results from the inefficiencies of the public sector. At the same time, decentralization of power is growing because of the ability of rich coastal provinces to increase their taxation of local enterprises, both domestic and foreign owned. Beijing's choice seems to be either to allow regional and local taxation and investment to increase, which risks an increase in inflation and loss of central power, or to risk instability and political challenge by trying to restrict the actions of local authority. The latter choice is becoming increasingly difficult because these authorities no longer depend on Beijing for finance, which can be obtained directly from foreign investors or through the reinvestment of local profits.

The problem of decentralization is compounded by uneven economic growth, with growing discontent in poorer interior provinces, while the southern and eastern coastal provinces get rich. It is important to note here how decentralization is redistributing both economic and political authority, while economically integrating the rich coastal provinces with other Asian economies such as Taiwan, Hong Kong, South Korea, Japan, Indonesia, and Singapore, through trade and investment. Not only are their economies becoming more interdependent, but cultural lifestyles are also converging based on mass consumerism. Life is more relaxed in Guangdong province (next to Hong Kong) and Fujian province (across from Taiwan). In many respects, coastal cities such as Shenzhen and Xiamen seem to have more in common with Hong Kong and Taipei than with Beijing, 1,000 miles to the north, where living standards are much lower and people's lives seem more controlled by public authority.[26]

Rights of Women and Children

Continued privatization, both before and after Tiananmen, has increasingly affected the human rights and social well-being of women and children. Although Mao's socialist revolution emphasized gender equality, women are now more likely to be laid off first and hired last. In 2003, "47 percent of laid-off workers were women, a percentage significantly higher that their representation in the labor force . . . [and] women were paid only 70.1 percent of what men received for the same work. . . . Moreover, a 1998 Asian Development Bank report estimated that 25 percent of all women were semiliterate or illiterate, compared with 10 percent of men. Official government statistics claimed that the illiteracy rate among women ages 15–40 was only 4.2 percent."[27] Similarly, the use of child labor in China's new factories is seemingly increasing, although statistics are difficult to obtain.

Military Decentralization?

One of Mao's greatest accomplishments was the unification of military power throughout the Middle Kingdom, which even made it possible to extend the party's control quickly to far-western regions such as Tibet and Xinjiang soon after he came to power in 1949. Although the military has always backed the central party leadership, which was crucial to the party's retention of power at the time of the Tiananmen demonstrations, recent developments inside the military raise important questions about the future role of China's military forces, which now number approximately 3.2 million, perhaps the largest military force in the world, depending on developments inside Russia.

As a result of the army's decisive role at Tiananmen Square, there was a reemphasis on ideology and party discipline; however, the government now emphasizes the professionalism of the military as well. But there is another Chinese military that is largely unknown to the outside world. After the Cultural Revolution, the authorities in Beijing cut back on funding of the military as the government's resources shifted to building China's infrastructure and revitalizing the economy. Interestingly, military units were told to create their own economic enterprises and convert many of their military factories to civilian production. China's military has always been largely self-reliant, producing much of its own food supply. Through encouragement from Beijing, 65 percent of production from military-owned factories now goes to civilian goods. Many of these products, such as motorcycles, refrigerators, and color televisions, are in great demand. Factories still producing military products sell their goods on the world market. Sometimes high-level government and party officials are involved in these transactions, which is a major source of independent income for the military establishment as well as for high-level party officials and many of their children, who are involved in overseas sales. One of the more interesting examples of these capitalist-type military sales operations is the establishment of import companies inside the United States, controlled by China's military. In the 1990s, they sold over $1 billion of light weapons to the private arms market in the United States, including highly sought after AK-47 automatic weapons.

The sale of both civilian and military products has not only made the military partially independent of central funding, but has also helped make a major proportion of the armed forces avowed capitalists who are strongly dedicated to China's market reforms and strongly supportive of a market economy. Dependence on Beijing has been further diluted by growing ties between local military units and local officials. These relationships have been mutually beneficial. Local military units have provided work brigades to perform essential functions such as bridge and road repair, maintenance of irrigation ditches, and other needed services that local authorities do not have the money to pay for. Local authorities, in turn, provide the military education, housing, and other essential needs.

Local military units produce over 50 percent of their own food, such as meat, vegetables, and eggs, and they also provide much of their own chickens, grain, and fruit. Military food production and factory units have become an important part of the local economy, working with private and cooperative farms, factories, and retail services at the local level. In effect, China now has two military forces: the professionalized forces, which are being rearmed with modern equipment, especially naval and air units; and the local economic production units, which are to a considerable extent self-reliant and tied in to local community services and market operations, as both consumers and providers.

In order to further improve relations between the military and the civilian population, the CCP has increased the role of paramilitary units, independent of the army. These units now have prime responsibility for putting down future demonstrations, disturbances, or challenges to authority, whether in Beijing or at the regional or local level. The future role of the military may become more problematic, however, as local authorities and economic units take more initiative, based on their own resources and bargaining power, in speeding up economic development as well as bargaining overseas for more trade and investment. Significantly, local military-controlled businesses are heavily involved in setting up their own sales and investment arrangements, often in cooperation with parallel private and local public enterprises.

Implications of Decentralization

Historically, large empires have been held together by highly authoritarian regimes, such as in ancient Rome or the Russian empire. When the central authorities of Western colonial empires such as Great Britain turned to democracy at home in the twentieth century, overseas colonies demanded the same rights, and today traditional Western imperialism is largely relegated to history books. As for the unification of large territories into single governmental units, the preferred way of achieving the advantages of large markets and economies of scale has been through the creation of democratic federal systems, with the people directly electing and controlling governing bodies at the local, regional, and national levels. The United States led the way in 1789, followed by Canada in 1867 and Australia in 1900. Other large former colonies of Western countries, such as Brazil, Mexico, and India, which are now formally democracies, have all adopted federal systems with varying degrees of democratically controlled national, regional, and local units of government.

But what about China? Federalism, with a real division of power between different levels of government—based on experience going back to Rome, Sparta, and Athens—seems to be incompatible with highly authoritarian forms of government. Under authoritarian systems, power is either highly controlled from the center or else the system breaks up into parts, as in the case of the Roman empire or what was formerly the Soviet Union. Whether Russia, with its difficulties, will be able to hold together or to join together in a federal system with other parts of the former Soviet Union is highly problematic. As for the Middle Kingdom, outsiders may hope there will be a peaceful evolution to a more democratic society, which might in time lead to effective popular control at the local, regional, and national levels. But inside China, the problem of decentralization, which is becoming an increasing reality as economic power devolves from the center, seems to pose one of the greatest Chinese enigmas of the twenty-first century.

No one seriously wishes to see the breakup of China into rival regions, which would probably undermine the remarkable economic development and stability that has enabled China to become more economically and politically integrated into the global system, something that benefits both China and the world community. Western social scientists like neat explanations of social, economic, and political power structures, but perhaps future relationships inside China may confound the outside critics. Could it be that party and central control will continue in varying degrees far into the twenty-first century, with an informal type of bargaining system allowing considerable devolution of power in response to local needs? In reality, the process may have already begun, as well as the pluralization of Chinese society at different levels. Few, either inside or outside China, seem to feel that there is any advantage in pointing out the loss of party power and central authority.

▓ The Problem of Succession and China's Political Future

One of the major weaknesses of communist political systems, including the People's Republic of China, is the lack of any orderly process for selection of new leaders. In China, following Mao's death, a number of heirs apparent failed to consolidate their power, and it was nearly two years before Deng Xiaoping, who was not one of Mao's favorites, was able to establish his power base and institute major economic reforms. In the 1980s, two of Deng's proposed successors, Hu Yaobang and Zhao Ziyang, were both removed from power, and his next heir apparent, Jiang Zemin, was at first viewed as an interim figure in spite of his appointment as party general secretary, president of China (following the National People's Congress in March 1993), and head of the Military Advisory Commission (a structure set up to give the senior brass an honorable place to retire). Jiang held on to power for a decade, however, during which time China continued its astonishing economic growth and its rise in the international community.

Deng's Strategy for Ensuring the Future of the Party and the Nation

In his last political campaign to revitalize and ensure continued market reform after he was gone, Deng Xiaoping toured Guangdong province in southern China in January 1992, where he visited the special economic zones in Shenzhen and Zhuhai. He noted the tremendous economic development and prosperity that had occurred since his previous visit in 1984. With an eye to the mass media, he announced to the world that he had now seen the future, and that it worked. Deng's purpose was to mobilize mass support for further market reforms, which he said would ensure China's place in history and provide for the well-being of the people, as well as the legitimization of the CCP.

Deng was convinced that further and even faster development, based on market reforms, was the key to the future. This could best be accomplished by combining economic reform with the four cardinal principles that he said were essential to the achievement of socialism with Chinese characteristics: party leadership, socialism, proletarian dictatorship, and Marxism-Leninism-socialism. The conservative wing of the party, which still controlled the mass media, saw that Deng was trying to mobilize overwhelming support for the speeding up of market reforms, so that after he was gone no one would be able to reverse the process.[28]

Evidence of party conservative control of the media and Deng's difficulties in publicizing his campaigns was confirmed by the immediate refusal of the Chinese mass media to publicize Deng's last campaign in southern China. Although the Hong Kong press told the world about Deng's last hurrah, giving immediate coverage to his campaign across the border from Hong Kong in Shenzhen, it was over two months before anything appeared in the conservative-controlled Chinese mass media, including any story in the *People's Daily,* the leading party-controlled daily, published in Beijing. The Leninist antireformers in the party had good reason to be concerned. Once the news of Deng's last campaign to reaffirm and gain support for market reforms did reach the public, there was a ground swell for Deng's policies, and the reformists within the party rallied to Deng's efforts to weed out the conservatives and put reformers in key positions of leadership at the 1992 Fourteenth Party Congress and the 1993 National People's Congress. Building on his momentum of support from his campaign in the south, even though he was eighty-eight and unable to attend events, Deng worked behind the scenes through his cohorts to remove his opponents and place his supporters in key positions in the party and government.

Eliminating the Old Guard

In China, because there is no democratic process for the selection and removal of leaders, political selection takes place through intraparty struggles behind the scenes. The process involves key leaders seeking to place their own cliques in power positions while countering the maneuvers of rival leaders and their followers. In order to reduce the temptations of the military to become actively involved in the succession process, Deng arranged a major overhaul of the leadership, removing or transferring key officers who had become politically involved in putting down the Tiananmen student demonstrations on June 4, 1989. Those who advocated ideological fervor and communist indoctrination were replaced by those who strongly supported a professionalized army. In order to stem criticism of party nepotism and accusations of corruption, Deng Xiaoping deliberately removed the children of prominent party members (known as *tazi*) from key positions in the party, government, and business community. None of his own five children were allowed to hold important positions, although some of them had gained prominence since his rise to power in 1978.

Deng, in his last hurrah, also sought to strengthen the position of the economic reformists in the Party Central Committee, the ruling Politburo, and the seven-member Party Standing Committee of the Politburo. As a result of changes made at the Fourteenth Party Congress, the Old Guard leftists were substantially weakened. But China's most prominent hard-liner, Premier Li Peng, who had been the point man in the suppression of the Tiananmen demonstrators, kept his position as a member of the Party Standing Committee. Then, at the National Party Congress in March 1993, he was reappointed for another five-year term as premier of China. Deng wished to keep Li Peng within the top power structure of the party and the government as a warning to intellectuals, students, and others that any revived attempts to criticize and challenge the party would not be tolerated. Reaffirming his basic philosophy after assuming power in 1978, Deng hoped to ensure the future role of the party and the well-being of the country by creating a power structure that would continue economic reform but prevent the rise of Western-type political processes that could lead to power struggles and instability. Deng's greatest fear was that without firm party leadership, based on Leninist rule from above, China would go the way of the former Soviet Union. Other members appointed or reappointed to the Party Standing Committee in October 1992 reinforced Deng's attempt to ensure a smooth succession after his departure through a balance of economic reformists, moderates, and hard-liner Li Peng.[29]

The Third and Fourth Generations

Based on past struggles in China, a smooth succession from the second (Deng) to the third (Jiang) and fourth (Hu and Wen) generations was considered unlikely. The party had lost legitimacy as a result of both the Cultural Revolution and the crackdown at Tiananmen Square. The party lost the support of the students, who were energized in efforts to reform it during the Cultural Revolution and again in Beijing in 1989. Many analysts expected that it would only be a matter of time before the younger generation, supported by intellectuals and others who had lost faith in the party, again sought to take matters into their own hands. The analysts, once again, were wrong. Succession politics were relatively smooth. China's intellectuals, students, and workers are leery of promoting instability, and for the time being, growing prosperity has bought the party time. The increasing political adeptness and sophistication of China's leaders has also helped them maintain power. Jiang

Zemin and Li Peng held on to power until 2003 and then smoothly transferred the reins of government to the next generation.

Jiang Zemin (born in 1927) was considered a moderate and a balance between different factions. Called to Beijing from his native Shanghai by Deng Xiaoping after the Tiananmen Square demonstrations—Jiang had effectively quelled protests in Shanghai without bloodshed—he was appointed party secretary, chairman of the Central Military Commission, and president. Deng Xiaoping apparently hoped that Jiang's simultaneous holding of three of the key leadership positions would enable him to survive the struggles of succession. Jiang handed over power to the "fourth generation" in 2002–2003, although he ensured his continued grip on power through promotion of his "three represents" thought (the party must always represent the requirements of the development of China's advanced productive forces, the orientation of the development of China's advanced culture, and the fundamental interests of the overwhelming majority of the people in China), through his continued role in the Central Military Commission, and through his placement of Shanghai protégés in positions of power throughout the party and especially in the Politburo. Despite early doubts of his abilities, Jiang's legacy is considerable: economic growth, some degree of political stability, increased prominence in the international community, and a smooth succession.

In 2002, Hu Jintao (born December 1942) became general secretary of the CCP and in 2003 he became president of the PRC. Wen Jiabao (born in September 1942) is the new Chinese premier. As premier,

> Wen has emphasized more egalitarian distribution of wealth along with other social goals such as public health and education. In addition, the Chinese government under Wen has begun to focus on the social costs of economic development, which includes damage to the environment and to workers' health. Wen's broad range of experience and expertise, has been important as the "fourth generation" seeks to revitalize the rural economy in regions left out by the past two decades of reform. Wen has appeared to make great efforts to reach out to those who seem left out by two decades of stunning economic growth in rural and especially Western China. Both Wen and Hu hail from, and have cultivated their political bases in, the vast Chinese interior.[30]

Hu and Wen's political skills were put to the test almost immediately. In the winter of 2002 and spring of 2003, Chinese political leaders had first ignored the advent of a strange new flulike disease. Then they tried to hide the severity of the disease and the degree to which it had spread. Only when SARS spread to Hong Kong, Taiwan, Vietnam, and Canada was China forced to admit that the disease had originated in Guangdong province, that it was serious and that the political and medical leadership had misled their people and the world. During the 2003 SARS crisis, many predicted that the disease would be "China's Chernobyl," leading to increased pressure on the CCP and perhaps a fundamental political change. Instead of losing power or authority, however, the party used mobilization techniques long held in its repertory to prevent the further spread of the disease. When SARS finally receded, the party emerged relatively unscathed. Predictions of its demise or reform were greatly exaggerated.

What are the keys, then, to the relatively smooth transition process? Deng succeeded in outfoxing and outliving his more conservative opponents. By the time Deng died, the question was not how to reform the economy but how to make China grow, both economically and as a major power in East Asia and the world. These were goals that virtually the entire party could agree to promote. For the time being, there were no burning issues to fight over and no outsize personalities to challenge Jiang Zemin, Hu Jintao, or Wen Jiabao. If the Chinese economy continues to grow without overheating, the current leadership would seem to be secure. If, however, economic strains—such as potential inflation, unpaid bank loans, infrastructure problems, and supply shortages—continue and grow, political stability may again be affected.

▨ Policy Options

China's decisionmakers, like those in other large contemporary societies, are greatly limited in their domestic policy choices by the availability of resources and the complex structures that restrict their ability to change existing policies. In China, governmental, economic, and social groups at the national, regional, and local levels, by their very existence, place severe constraints on policy choices. Compared with the limited options available in many third world countries and former communist states, however, China's leaders may have many more opportunities and choices.

The following analysis of options is based on the assumption that the CCP leadership seeks to retain its power and influence to control events inside China and maintain its ability to conduct relations with other states. If this is the case, then all party factions would logically support the continuation of the following policies:

1. Maintain a monopoly of political power by trying to prevent the formation of any groups dedicated to questioning or overthrowing the party's authority.
2. Maintain party control over public security forces, the military, and the police.
3. Maintain control over the mass media so that the party can frame the parameters within which public debate takes place.
4. Keep the struggle for power among the various party factions an internal affair, outside of the public arena.

Option 1: Promote Nationalism

Creating pride in the unity of the Chinese nation, along with accompanying policies, can help achieve the overall objective of promoting nationalism. China is more fortunate than most large contemporary states in that its ethnic, racial, and religious minorities are limited to relatively small groups, mostly in peripheral areas. Beijing's current policy of sending large numbers of the Han majority ethnic group to outlying regions, which is likely to continue, will in time make minority groups strangers within their own land. If Beijing wishes to ameliorate outside criticism of human rights conditions in these outlying regions, however, it would be logical to combine population migration with protection of personal freedoms, social well-being, and cultural rights of minority groups, so long as these do not lead to challenges to political authority. In addition, virtually no Chinese want to see their country follow the same course as the Soviet Union, where "Balkanization" was the direct result of the collapse of communist rule. Promotion of Chinese nationhood is a policy the party can use to rally the people. Appealing to the past grandeur of China's Middle Kingdom strikes a responsive chord among the Chinese people.

Option 2: Use Persuasion Rather Than Force in Creating a Greater China

How the party chooses to pursue its goal of unifying the Chinese nation by resuming political control over Hong Kong, Macao, and Taiwan will also help determine its future credibility. Rather than pressing for political reunification or threatening military measures to achieve reunification, as has been the official policy since 1949, the party could continue to allow the de facto economic integration that is already occurring to continue and strengthen. Growing Taiwanese nationalism or political protests against Chinese rule in Hong Kong could, however, so threaten the Chinese leaders that they might choose to intervene politically or militarily. In the case of Taiwan, the upheaval could be extremely dangerous, because both sides have been making great efforts to upgrade their military forces.

Option 3: Combine Nationalism with Military Modernization

China's leaders could choose to emphasize combining nationalism with military modernization, stressing the military's role in guarding China from foreign enemies. This might involve taking limited steps to restore China's ancient sphere of influence in neighboring regions. Although China's involvement in external conflict may strengthen nationalist feelings and rally support to the regime, Beijing will have to orchestrate patriotic desires carefully for the restoration of Chinese influence in areas such as the South China Sea. Any major increase of Chinese military activities in such regions could trigger regional arms races in Asia. This could threaten China's relations with neighboring Asian nations and with the international community.

Option 4: Restore Party Legitimacy

Reformist leaders in China recognize that the party can survive only if it maintains its credibility among the people. This is predicated on a positive perception of the party and its cadres, particularly among the peasantry. To achieve this credibility, the party will have to change its own ethical standards, which increasingly seem to be based on personal enrichment and corruption rather than service to the people and society. Development of a just society, many argue, also depends on establishment of a legal system that administers justice on an equitable basis to peasant and cadre, merchant and scholar. The party cannot put itself above the law.

Option 5: Promote Greater Cooperation Between Different Levels of Government and Regions

As greater decentralization takes place, economic disparities have increased between the "have" provinces and the "have not" provinces. The "trickle down" theory is based on the idea that the poorer, interior provinces will be pulled into the orbit of their richer neighbors eventually. Many argue, however, that wealth does not migrate automatically and that the regime will have to force the richer provinces to contribute to infrastructure development in the poorer provinces. Unless the party can develop ways through which local, regional, and national officials can interact and bargain to promote national well-being, then the bottlenecks and inequities created by further disparities in economic growth may in time overwhelm China's existing social, economic, and political structure, including the party itself.

▓ Discussion Questions

1. To what extent do the Chinese people and their leaders now believe in the teachings of Marx, Lenin, and Mao?
2. How do the Chinese people view Mao Zedong and his accomplishments today?
3. How is the Chinese Communist Party seeking to continue its "Mandate of Heaven" to rule China in the future?
4. With the passage of time, how are the people of China likely to view Deng Xiaoping's contributions to China?

5. Compare and contrast how the Cultural Revolution and the events at Tiananmen Square have affected the relationship between the Chinese people and the CCP.
6. What changes have occurred in Hong Kong since 1997?
7. What are the prospects for Tibet becoming an independent nation-state?
8. Discuss the alternative scenarios for Chinese-Taiwanese relations in the future.
9. In what ways are feelings associated with cultural identity and the idea of the Middle Kingdom a source of unity or disunity inside contemporary China?
10. Would Western-type democratic reforms be more beneficial or harmful to the well-being of China and its people at the start of the twenty-first century? Is it feasible to create a legal system in China that guarantees the basic rights of individuals and corporate entities while at the same time maintaining the leading role of the CCP?
11. What problems facing China may be associated with its rapid rate of economic development (8–9 percent)?
12. What forces inside China might eventually lead to a political structure of empire, federation, or decentralization in the twenty-first century?
13. What is the relationship between the PLA and the CCP? What role might the PLA play as the nature of CCP control over the nation adapts to the future?
14. How are internal developments within China likely to affect its foreign relations?

Suggested Readings

Clough, Ralph N. *Cooperation or Conflict in the Taiwan Strait?* Lanham, Md.: Rowman and Littlefield, 1999.

Dickson, Bruce J., and Chien-min Chao, eds. *Assessing the Lee Teng-hui Legacy in Taiwan's Politics.* Armonk, N.Y.: M. E. Sharpe, 2003.

Dreyer, June Teufel. *China's Political System: Modernization and Tradition.* 4th ed. Boston: Allyn and Bacon, 2004.

Finkelstein, David M., and Maryanne Kivlehan, eds. *China's Leadership in the Twenty-First Century: The Rise of the Fourth Generation.* Armonk, N.Y.: M. E. Sharpe, 2002.

Friedman, Edward, and Barrett L. McCormick, eds. *What If China Doesn't Democratize? Implications for War and Peace.* Armonk, N.Y.: M. E. Sharpe, 2000.

Gamer, Robert E., ed. *Understanding Contemporary China.* 2nd ed. Boulder, Colo.: Lynne Rienner, 2003.

Gladney, Deru C. "Xinjiang: China's Future West Bank?" *Current History* (September 2002): 267–270.

Gurtov, Mel, and Byong-Moo Hwang. *China's Security: The New Roles of the Military.* Boulder, Colo.: Lynne Rienner, 1998.

Han Minzhu, ed. *Cries for Democracy: Writings and Speeches from the 1989 Chinese Democracy Movement.* Princeton: Princeton University Press, 1990.

Kau, Michael Ying-Mao, and John K. Leung, eds. *The Writings of Mao Zedong, 1949–1976.* Vol. 2. Armonk, N.Y.: M. E. Sharpe, 1993.

Kau, Michael Ying-Mao, and Susan H. Marsh, eds. *China in the Era of Deng Xiaoping: A Decade of Reform.* Armonk, N.Y.: M. E. Sharpe, 1993.

Kent, Ann E. *China and Human Rights.* New York: Oxford University Press, 1992.

Kim, Samuel S., ed. *China and the World: Chinese Foreign Relations in the Post–Cold War Era.* Boulder, Colo.: Westview, 2000.

Lampton, David M., ed. *The Making of Chinese Foreign and Security Policy in the Era of Reform, 1978–2000.* Stanford: Stanford University Press, 2001.

Lieberthal, Kenneth. *Governing China: From Revolution to Reform.* 2nd ed. New York: Norton, 2003.

Lilley, James, and David Shambaugh, eds. *China's Military Faces the Future.* Armonk, N.Y.: M. E. Sharpe, 1999.

Lin, Bih-jaw, et al. *The Aftermath of the 1989 Tiananmen Crisis in Mainland China.* Boulder, Colo.: Westview, 1992.

Lin, Nan. *The Struggle for Tiananmen: Anatomy of the 1989 Mass Movement.* Westport, Conn.: Praeger, 1992.

Liu Binyan. "The Long March from Mao: China's De-Communization." *Current History* (September 1993): 241–244.

Ogden, Suzanne. *Inklings of Democracy in China.* Cambridge: Harvard University Press, 2002.

Oksenberg, Michael, Marc Lambert, and Lawrence H. Sullivan, eds. *Beijing, Spring 1989: Confrontation and Conflict—The Basic Documents.* Armonk, N.Y.: M. E. Sharpe, 1992.

Patten, Christopher. *East and West: China, Power, and the Future of Asia.* New York: Random House, 1998.

Perry, Elizabeth J., and Mark Selden, eds. *Chinese Society: Change, Conflict, and Resistance.* New York: Routledge, 2000.

Saich, Tony, ed. *The Rise to Power of the Chinese Communist Party: Documents and Analysis.* Armonk, N.Y.: M. E. Sharpe, 1993.

Schram, Stuart R., ed. *Mao's Road to Power: Revolutionary Writings, 1912–1949.* Vol. 1. Armonk, N.Y.: M. E. Sharpe, 1993.

Shambaugh, David. *Modernizing China's Military: Progress, Problems, and Prospects.* Berkeley: University of California Press, 2003.

Wasserstrom, Jeffrey N. "China's Brave New World." *Current History* (September 2003): 266–269.

Notes

1. Ma Licheng, "New Thinking on Sino-Japanese Relations," *Japan Echo* (June 2003): 35. The article is translated from "Waga Chugoku yo, han-Nichi kodo tsushime," *Strategy and Management* no. 6 (December 2002).

2. Perry Link, *Evening Chats in Beijing* (New York: Norton, 1992), p. 29.

3. For the Chinese viewpoint on Tibet, see Dai Yannian, Edna Driscoll, Yen Qinghong, and Zhu Yuan, eds., *China in Focus—Tibet: Myth and Reality* (Beijing: Beijing Review, 1988); and see *Tibetans on Tibet* (Beijing: China Reconstruction Press, 1988). Refer also to the Chinese Embassy website: www.china-embassy.org.

4. Bradford Trebach, *New York Times,* May 19, 1992, p. A14.

5. See http://www.cia.gov/cia/publications/factbook/geos/hk.html, updated May 11, 2004.

6. T. L. Tsim, "Hong Kong: The Middle of the Journey," *Yale China Association China Update* 2, no. 3 (Fall 1991): 4.

7. Sheila Tefft, "Even Chinese Who Liked British Rule Are Irked over Hong Kong," *Christian Science Monitor,* April 21, 1993, p. 2.

8. Joseph Kahn, "A Democratic China? Not So Fast, Beijing Leaders Say," *New York Times,* April 8, 2004, p. A3.

9. "China-Taiwan Trade Soars on IT," *South China Morning Post,* February 5, 2004, http://www.asiamedia.ucla.edu/article.asp?parentid=7338.

10. United Press International, Taipei, January 1, 1993.

11. Wei Jingsheng, quoted in Uli Schmetzer, "Chinese Dissident Optimistic," *Chicago Tribune,* October 10, 1993, sec. 1, p. 12.

12. For an analysis of the Chinese democracy movement and the events leading up to Tiananmen Square, see George Black and Robin Munro, *Black Hands of Beijing: Lives of Defiance in China's Democracy Movement* (New York: John Wiley, 1993); Susan Ogden et al., eds., *China's Search for Democracy: The Student and Mass Movement* (Armonk, N.Y.: M. E. Sharpe, 1992); Roger V. Des Forges, Luo Ning, and Wu Yen-bo, eds., *Chinese Democracy and the Crisis of 1989: Chinese and American Reflections* (Albany: State University of New York Press, 1993); and Theodore Han and John Li, *Tiananmen Square Spring 1989: A Chronology of the Chinese Democracy Movement* (Berkeley: Institute of East Asian Studies, 1992).

13. For the significance of the events at Tiananmen Square and their consequences, see Bin-Jaw Lin et al., eds., *The Aftermath of the 1989 Tiananmen Crisis in Mainland China* (Boulder, Colo.: Westview, 1992); Timothy Brooks, *Quelling the People: The Military Suppression of the Beijing Democracy Movement* (New York: Oxford University Press, 1992); Lee Wei-chin, "Read My Lips or Watch My Feet: The State and Chinese Dissident Intellectuals," *Issues and Studies* 28 (May 1992): 29–48; "China's Sort of Freedom," *The Economist,* October 17, 1992, pp. 39–41; Richard A. Hartness and Guilian Wang, "The Problem of Culture: The Clash Between Gerontocrats and Paedocrats in the 1989 Spring Uprising in China," *Asian Profile* 20 (April 1992): 97–107; Anthony P. B. Lambert, "Post-Tiananmen Chinese Communist Party Religious Policy," *Religion, State, and Society* 20, nos. 3–4 (1992): 391–397 (in this article the author notes that "the downfall of Marxist regimes in Eastern Europe . . . aroused fears of a similar mass movement taking hold among China's working class, and suspicions that both the Catholic and Protestant churches in China could become bases for political subversion"); Andrew Scobell, "Why the People's Army Fired on the People: The Chinese Military and Tiananmen," *Armed Forces and Society* 18 (Winter 1992): 193–213; and Martin King White, "Prospects for Democratization in China," *Problems of Communism* 41 (May–June 1992): 58–70.

14. See Lee Wei-chin, "Crimes of the Heart: Political Loyalty in Socialist China," *Studies in Comparative Communism* 25 (September 25, 1992): 228–241.

15. See Sheila Tefft, "Prison Letters Reveal Plight of Chinese Dissidents," *Christian Science Monitor,* March 4, 1993, p. 1.

16. Nicholas D. Kristof, "Beijing Journal: Three Years After Tiananmen Protests, Who Among Chinese Remembers," *New York Times International,* June 5, 1992, p. A4.

17. The Carter Center, http://www.cartercenter.org/documents/nondatabase/chinavillagefactsheet.pdf, viewed April 14, 2004.

18. Kathy Chen, "China Eases Its Grip on Media," *Wall Street Journal,* April 8, 2004, p. A14.

19. Quoted in Howard W. French, "China Tries Again to Curb Independent Press in South," *New York Times,* April 15, 2004, p. A14.

20. Maria Hsia Chang, "China's Future: Regionalism, Federation or Disintegration," *Studies in Comparative Communism* 25 (September 1992): 211–227.

21. See Ann Scott Tyson and James L. Tyson, "As Party Declines, Who Is in Charge?" *Christian Science Monitor,* August 12, 1992, pp. 9–12.

22. Ibid., p. 9.

23. These developments were reported in a survey by Asian Watch, "Continuing Religious Repression in China," which was released on May 28, 1993, and is discussed in the *Chicago Tribune,* May 30, 1993, sec. 1, p. 14.

24. "International Religious Freedom Report 2003," released by the Bureau of Democracy, Human Rights, and Labor, http://www.state.gov/g/drl/rls/irf/2003 /23826.htm.

25. Joseph Kahn, "Martial Law Declared as Nearly 150 Die in Central China," *New York Times,* November 1, 2004.

26. See Luc Chartrand, "Hong Kong's Reverse Takeover," *World Press Review* 39 (September 1992): 42; Cindy Fan, "Regional Impacts of Foreign Trade in China, 1984–1989," *Growth and Change* 23 (Spring 1992): 129–159; James L. Tyson and Ann Scott Tyson, "Chinese Reforms Widen Gap Between Coast and Hinterland," *Christian Science Monitor,* July 22, 1992, pp. 9–12; Ting Wai, "The Regional and International Implications of the South China Economic Zone," *Issues and Studies* 28 (December 1992): 46–72; and Chris Bramall, *Legacies of Maoist Economic Development in Sichuan* (New York: Oxford University Press, 1993).

27. U.S. Department of State Reports on Human Rights Practices, 2003, released by the Bureau of Democracy, Human Rights, and Labor, February 25, 2004, http:// www.state.gov/g/drl/rls/hrrpt/2003/27768.htmCountry.

28. See Roderick MacFarquhar, "Deng's Final Campaign," *New York Review,* November 19, 1992; Chiang Chenchiang, "The Influence of the Old Guard in Mainland Chinese Politics," *Issues and Studies* 28 (July 1992): 25–34; Chenpang Chang, "A New Round of Power Struggle in Peking," *Issues and Studies* 28 (April 1992): 109–111; Chong-Pin Lin, "The Coming Chinese Earthquake," *International Economy* 6 (May–June 1992): 50–57; David Shambaugh, "Regaining Momentum Deng Strikes Back," *Current History* 91 (September 1992): 257–261; Ross Terrill, "Rocking the Old Guard," *World Monitor* 5 (May 1992): 24, 26–28; Nicholas D. Kristof, "Chinese Shake Up Top Party Group; Free Market Gains," *New York Times,* October 20, 1992, pp. A1, A6; and Lena H. Sun, "A Last Hurrah for China's Old Guard," *Washington Post Weekly Edition,* September 21–27, 1992, p. 18.

29. See "New Party Leadership," *Beijing Review* (November 2–8, 1992): pp. 13–17; and Kristof, "Chinese Shake Up Top Party Group."

30. FreeDictionary.com, http://encyclopedia.thefreedictionary.com/wen%20jiabao, viewed April 15, 2004.

The Ascendancy of
Adam Smith over Karl Marx

It was really unimaginable. I didn't dare to dream about it. Before my house
was made of clay. Now I have a brick house. These two decades have seen
an incredible change.

—Guo Hai Wang, a farmer in Inner Mongolia[1]

I was laid off in 1998 from Angang Steel Works. . . . I have to pay rent, water,
electricity. Before I was laid off all of this was paid by the factory. I used to
have health insurance when I worked at the factory, but now I have nothing.
. . . I don't have money to go to the doctor, I can't afford it. There's no money
to send my parents to the doctor either when they are ill. . . . My wife wants
a divorce, she wants to leave me and take the child with her, and I feel terrible about it.

—Li Chunhai, former steel
factory worker, Liaoning province[2]

The sweeping reforms introduced by Deng Xiaoping are the basis of China's
remarkable economic development since the 1980s. To bring about these reforms, China's leaders have turned to the outside world for investment, aid,
trade, and technology. Although the formal decisionmaking process on the
surface seems as tightly controlled as in the past, beneath the surface several
different policymaking processes are evolving that have helped make these
economic reforms possible, reaching down from the leaders in Beijing to the
local village and township governments in China's vast rural hinterland. In reality, decentralization of economic decisionmaking is affecting the way in
which political decisions are being made at all levels of Chinese society. Current economic policy, in turn, is based on remarkable changes in Chinese economic thought, which went through a number of dramatic stages in the twentieth century.

In this chapter we will look at the remarkable economic changes brought
about first by Deng Xiaoping and his followers, which have occurred at all
levels of society, and note the relationship between changing economic practices and the evolution of the decisionmaking process, especially at the local
level and in rural areas. Although authoritarian trappings remain in place,

under the surface there has already been substantial movement toward differ-ent decisionmaking processes. We will look at the results of this new econ-omy: new models in technology, markets, and education; economic revolution in rural China; joint ventures and special economic zones (SEZs); trade and tourism; and finally the relationship between economic liberalism, political freedom, and human rights.[3] Deng Xiaoping himself used a modified rational actor approach in which, after weighing the costs and benefits of different economic practices beyond China's shores, he announced and then imple-mented radical changes in Chinese economic practice. He did this years be-fore Gorbachev and his followers began to think about such changes toward economic liberalism, which have yet to be carried out effectively in parts of the former Soviet Union.

▓ The New Economics: Deng Xiaoping and the Open Door

Deng Xiaoping, after defeating a number of rivals to succeed Mao, faced the unenviable task of saving China's communist system and the power of the Chinese Communist Party (CCP), both of which had been damaged almost beyond repair by the Cultural Revolution. Deng sought pragmatic solutions to China's problems. In principle, Deng supported Marxist theory. In practice, he modified many of Mao's policies, especially in the production and distribu-tion of goods and in China's economic relations abroad. As Deng reportedly said, he did not care if the cat was black or white, so long as it caught mice.

The evolution of Marxist, neo-Marxist, and Leninist principles within China may be divided into three periods. The 1920s up to 1949 saw the fol-lowing:

- emphasis on nationalism,
- anti-imperialism, and
- rural class struggle and revolutionism.

The period from 1949 to 1977 saw a shift toward

- Leninist principles of revolution and rule,
- emphasis on nationalism and anticapitalism,
- anti-imperialism,
- rural revolution and communes,
- the Great Leap Forward,
- the Cultural Revolution,
- neo-Marxism,
- autarky, and

- Leninist and Stalinist rule.

From 1978 to the present, China has witnessed

- nationalism,
- a dual economy,
- empowerment of the rural population,
- the Open Door policy,
- entry into the global economic system,
- partial shift from Leninist to authoritarian rule, and
- emphasis on basic economic and social, but not political, rights.

The Cultural Revolution had damaged China's infrastructure and educational system, as well as the country's ability to advance science and technology. By 1978, Deng and his followers realized that drastic changes were needed. Stagnation and disillusionment, brought about by the Cultural Revolution, needed to be replaced by new approaches that would allow the people to work together toward a brighter future.

Deng, no supporter of capitalism, was a pragmatist. He observed the successes of China's neighbors, such as Japan and the Four Little Tigers (South Korea, Taiwan, Hong Kong, and Singapore), three of which had Chinese populations. Though Deng may have believed that the capitalists of the West sought to exploit third world countries, he also recognized that even in protesting this exploitation, third world countries, acting through the United Nations, were no longer rejecting the global capitalist system but seeking to make it more equitable and fair to the poor countries of the world.[4] Beginning in 1978, Beijing took a similar approach. Whereas Mao had practiced economic autarky, Deng believed that China's future depended not only on its joining the international economic system, which is based on marketplace capitalism, but also on actively participating in the different economic regimes that make up the global system, such as the World Bank, the International Monetary Fund, and the General Agreement on Tariffs and Trade. Thus Deng and his followers abandoned self-reliance in favor of the Open Door policy, which Deng introduced in late 1978. Instead of isolating China from the international system, Deng sought to use the capitalist system and its market incentives to bring about immediate improvement in China's economy by introducing capitalist practices and trade with the West.

In fact, Deng and his followers took advantage of China's disillusionment with Maoist policies to introduce new approaches that the people would welcome. He first carried out reform in the countryside, releasing the energies of the peasants by allowing them to farm their own land and create rural industries. Private production and distribution of goods were first allowed in the countryside and then gradually extended to the cities. At the same time, a dual economic system was maintained. New enterprises created new jobs, greatly expanding China's economy, but the old public sectors were also maintained to avoid the displacement of existing jobs, with their socialist benefits. Thus, part of the iron rice bowl was retained. Only gradually has the Beijing leadership cut back on subsidies to the public sector; it has done so in order to give the public sector time to adjust to market incentives, including the possibility of bankruptcy.

In effect, the public production and service sectors must compete with the more efficient private sectors or face bankruptcy and reorganization if they are unable to keep up with private competitors. However, a Western diplomat has observed that the problem of reforming state enterprises is that they are "more like enormous feudal villages than modern corporations. They have to provide housing, recreation, hospitals, parks, and all manner of services, sometimes for hundreds of thousands of employees and their families."[5]

In spite of all the difficulties, the proof of China's success in moving toward an economy of global importance is visible through the results. According to the World Bank, conditions in the Chinese countryside have improved remarkably, especially in comparison with third world countries like India (see Table 3.1). According to a study conducted by Pranab Bardhan, professor of economics at the University of California,

> Over the last three decades official data suggest that the average annual rate of growth of per capita income was about 7 per cent in China and 2.5 per cent in India. Productivity per hectare in agriculture (say, in rice) has been much higher in China for centuries, but the relative progress in manufacturing in recent decades has been phenomenal. In the early fifties the total GDP [gross domestic product] in manufacturing in India was slightly below that in China, in the late nineties it was less than a quarter of that in China. In 1999 the manufacturing share of GDP was 38 per cent in China, while it was 16 per cent in India. Indian labour productivity in manufacturing was about 71 per cent of that in China in 1952; in 1995 it was 37 percent. Compared to India, total electricity use per capita is twice as high in China and teledensity (the number of telephones per thousand people) is several times higher. In 1999 the share of world trade (exports plus imports) in goods was 3.3 per cent for China, 0.7 per cent for India; in services the corresponding percentages were 2.1 and 1.2. The total amount (in dollars) of foreign direct investment in China was 18 times that in India in 1999. In the same year gross domestic saving as a proportion of GDP was exactly twice as high in China as that in India.[6]

The World Bank estimates that over the past twenty years, China has been able to lift 400 million people out of poverty.[7]

Should China be able to continue this trend in the twenty-first century, its economic growth rates could exceed those in most other countries and match the economic miracles that occurred in Japan in an earlier era, followed by

Table 3.1   A Comparison of Chinese and Indian Poverty Rates

		Population Below Poverty Line				Population Below Percentage of International Poverty Line (U.S.$1/day)
	Survey Year	Rural Percentage	Urban Percentage	National Percentage	Survey Year	
China	1996	7.9	< 2.0	6.0	2000	16.1
	1998	4.6	< 2.0	4.6		
India	1993–1994	37.3	32.4	36.0	1999–2000	34.7
	1999–2000	30.2	24.7	28.6		

Source: World Bank, *World Development Indicators, 2003,* http://www.worldbank.org/data/wdi2003/pdfs/table%202-6.pdf.

similar miracles in recent years in South Korea, Taiwan, Hong Kong, and Singapore. In the twenty-first century, barring unforeseen circumstances, China, with its huge population, could have markets and production rivaling not only Japan, but also North America and Europe. To reach this goal, however, China will have to confront serious issues. First, China will need to maintain stability and order during an era when popular aspirations are even greater than the opportunity to fulfill these demands. Second, because the population continues to grow at a rate of nearly 15 million a year, ways must be found to provide more jobs outside traditional agriculture, especially through the creation of light industrial and service jobs in China's rural hinterland. Third, China's strained infrastructure and energy supply must be improved. Transportation and electricity are inadequate to meet current demand, much less support an economy that has been growing at the rate of over 9 percent during the past two decades. Finally, support from the global economy must continue, including increased investment and Chinese exports at a time when other regions either are in recession or are experiencing very low growth rates.

Technology, Markets, and Education: The Western or the Japanese Model?

China's post-Mao reformers knew that the existing system was not working. But there were a number of other different possibilities based on the experience of other countries and regions, all of which, from the Chinese perspective, had both advantages and disadvantages. In the end, Deng and his followers adopted some practices while rejecting others based on U.S., European, Japanese, and other Asian systems.

The U.S. Model

Beijing's reformers admired U.S. technology. Beginning with Deng's Open Door policy, thousands of Chinese students were sent to the United States, many with Chinese government assistance, to learn about science and technology as well as new business and administration techniques. Ideally, they would then bring this knowledge back to China and help China catch up with the West. Because the United States in 1978 was an informal Chinese ally in resisting Soviet influence in Asia, Beijing also hoped to get help from the United States in modernizing China, including the military.

Furthermore, Beijing sought technology and capital from the United States by encouraging U.S. corporations to invest in China, both through joint ventures and by creating U.S. subsidiaries in China. Ideally, these investors would then export their goods back to the United States and other Western countries and provide hard currency through the sale of labor-intensive products such as shoes, textiles, clothes, Christmas-tree light bulbs, greeting cards (including the musical kind), toys, and glassware. These measures succeeded beyond anyone's imagination. But other parts of the U.S. model have had little appeal to Beijing. The U.S. government has practiced a hands-off policy in regard to the U.S. economy, whereas Beijing's reformers continue to support a dual economic system. The Chinese central government owns and subsidizes large industries, and the private market and system of production have been allowed to grow alongside the public economy. Beijing's leaders also dislike the extreme disparity of wealth in the United States. Although they want to increase the well-being of the people, they also have held on to their socialist egalitarian values, in which government is supposed to use its power to enhance the well-being of all segments of society. In practice, however, Chinese economic reforms have substantially undermined China's social services. The burden of education, health care, pensions, disability, and unemployment benefits has been increasingly shifted to the local government level. In the past, agricultural collectives and state enterprises provided these services, but now most of the growing private sector does not provide them, and local government is hard-pressed to find revenues to meet these needs.

Beijing was also concerned with the role of special interests and the public in the U.S. political system. Deng and his followers did not believe that marketplace reforms would have to be followed by political reforms in which the people and organized economic interests would replace the dominant role of the CCP. Deng and his supporters believed that the Chinese Communist Party could orchestrate the creation of a private sector while maintaining a large public sector, something that is almost totally absent in the U.S. economy. Furthermore, Deng and his economic reformers were convinced that the energy of the people could be utilized in supporting these new private enterprises, in which the appeal would be enrichment and a better life; at the same time, the party and government would continue to manage the changing economy by using the party-controlled media and its monopoly of power to prevent any organized opposition to party policies.

The Western European Model

Deng sought to diversify China's relations with the West in order to gain more investment capital and trade, but also to avoid too much dependence on any single country, such as the United States. Beijing, however, has been less successful in opening up the European Community market to Chinese goods than in increasing its sales to the U.S. market. Still, the European model, with greater government assistance and regulation of the economy, appeals to Beijing's leaders, especially the government planning and assistance aimed at increasing production and the distribution of wealth. With privatization in the countryside, however, China's governmental units provide much less than European governments in the way of social services such as health care, educational benefits (especially above the primary school level), unemployment benefits, and old-age benefits. Larger state enterprises in China are supposed to provide such benefits, although some have not fulfilled wage, pension, and other commitments to their workers, but employees in the private sector are largely on their own unless they can persuade local enterprises and governments to help take care of these needs. As production has increased in China's coastal provinces and economic export zones, tax resources have gravitated to the regional and local levels.

The Japanese Model

The Japanese model has both virtues and dangers from the Chinese perspective. Beijing is quite aware of how Japan's authoritarian leaders were able to impose reform from above beginning in the 1860s. The Meiji reforms were directed by a transformed Japanese aristocracy, which shifted its rural power base to the new capitalist economy based on industry, finance, and trade. In sending hundreds of thousands of students overseas, mainly to Western countries, Beijing has emulated the Japanese practice of sending its sons and daughters to Western Europe and the United States to learn the latest Western technology. However, approximately 70 percent of Chinese students, especially since Tiananmen Square, have avoided returning to the Chinese mainland. Like the Meiji reformers, China offers incentives and good positions to entice the students to come back and assume key jobs in economics, government, elite structure, research, and the educational system, but with limited success.

A major difference between the Japanese and the Chinese models relates to investment. Japan's ruling elite, from the time of the Meiji reforms to the present, has severely restricted overseas investment. Unlike in China, nearly all Japanese capital has been generated within Japan or through overseas trade in other countries, not through outside investment or loans. Today, Beijing's leaders have mixed feelings about Japanese investment in China and other parts of Asia. They want the technology and the capital, but they are concerned about Japanese domination of the Chinese and other Asian economies, more so than the danger of domination by investors from North America and Europe. They remember all too well Japan's desire for a "coprosperity sphere" in Asia during World War II. In the future, China and Japan may become competitors for Asian resources. Yet China needs Japanese investment to develop its own resources, especially energy, including oil, natural gas, and new solar technologies. Japan's low-technology investments in China and its reluctance to transfer its more advanced technology, especially technology that could be used to modernize China's military, raises suspicions in Beijing that Japan wishes to exploit China's resources, cheap labor, and markets while preventing the upgrading of its military capability.

The Four Little Tigers and the Overseas Chinese

In China's search for development models as well as capital investment, the greatest source of help has come from Chinese living outside mainland China (who number over 55 million if Chinese from Taiwan and Hong Kong are included) and more recently from South Korean investment. In both Taiwan and South Korea, land reform was successfully introduced in the 1950s, resulting in the breakup of large estates into small private farms, which were then assisted by the government. Cheap loans, availability of inputs such as low-priced fertilizer, hybrid seeds (part of the green revolution), market transport, and market structures based on competition all contributed to a revolution in the countryside. Increased agricultural production then provided capital to help industrialize Taiwan and South Korea. Beijing's leaders could look to the Korean model as an example of how to build large capitalist corporate operations, such as shipbuilding and heavy industry, and they could look to the Taiwanese model as an example of how to create small light industries based on intensive labor.[8] Deng and his followers first carried out their land reforms based in part on the South Korean and Taiwanese models. Then they introduced small factories in the countryside, based on light industry and cheap labor and patterned after the Taiwanese model.

China's utilization of its overseas citizens may be its secret weapon in making it one of the world's leading economies in the twenty-first century. Hong Kong Chinese have provided the largest single source of capital for mainland China. Hong Kong business leaders are employing over four times as many workers in manufacturing operations inside China as they are in Hong Kong itself, where wages are at least ten times as high as on the mainland. But investment has also come from overseas Chinese in other parts of Asia as well as North America.

Ethnic Chinese throughout Southeast Asia (see Table 3.2) are a key part of the business community, conducting family businesses that make up a major portion of manufacturing, marketing, trade, and finance in countries such as Thailand, Malaysia, Vietnam, Singapore (which is three-quarters Chinese), the Philippines, and Indonesia. Along with Chinese from Hong Kong and Taiwan, they are accustomed to avoiding politics while at the same time working with authoritarian systems, in which business relationships are conducted on the basis of personal contact and influence (*guanxi*). Because overseas Chinese have many family ties and personal relationships with Chinese mainlanders and they also understand the culture and requirements of doing business back home, they have many advantages over other outside investors, such as those from Japan and Europe as well as non-Chinese from North America. Although Japan has been considered the leading investor in Asian countries, the combination of Chinese ties throughout Asia, North America, and inside China is creating an interdependent Chinese economy without borders. Hong Kong is the chief service center (now rivaled by Shanghai) for these activities, with the largest amount of capital coming from Hong Kong and Taiwan. However, the network of Chinese contacts is creating interdependency and informal relations in which business transactions are conducted on a highly personal basis, with mainland China becoming the chief location for manufacturing operations. With Deng's Open Door policy, overseas Chinese flooded into the mainland as tourists and on business. They established contacts through relatives and friends, as well as with local government and

Table 3.2   Ethnic Chinese Outside Mainland China (in millions)

Taiwan	21.0
Indonesia	7.2
Hong Kong	6.0
Thailand	5.8
Malaysia	5.2
Singapore	2.0
Myanmar (Burma)	1.5
Vietnam	0.8
Philippines	0.8
Rest of Asia and Australia	1.8
United States	1.8
Canada	0.6
Latin America	1.0
Europe	0.6
Africa	0.1

Source: The Economist, July 18, 1992, p. 2. The data come from the *Overseas Chinese Economy Yearbook.*

party officials, all of whom worked closely with them in setting up a growing number of business operations. Already, in the areas of Guangdong province in southern China adjacent to Hong Kong and Macao, living standards have risen dramatically as the countryside becomes integrated with the Hong Kong economy.

As for Chinese mainlanders, through both government and private investors they have in turn invested in the economy of Hong Kong and Guangdong province, which has become the financial and service center for economic activities throughout southern China. Operations involving overseas Chinese investment extend beyond China's special economic zones in Guangdong and Fujian provinces (the latter is adjacent to Taiwan) and are now reaching into China's hinterland and rural areas. There, the use of personal family ties and cooperation, with local officials willing to make deals, are resulting in the integration of most of southern and southeastern China into a single international market network. Investment comes from overseas Chinese, light manufactured goods are produced with cheap mainland labor, and the goods are then trucked to Hong Kong or other ports for shipment to overseas markets.

Economic Revolution in Rural China: Life in the Chinese Village

Deng Xiaoping's greatest contribution to the future development of China was probably his radical agrarian reform. Mao's farm collectives and communes were largely a failure because China's farmers, lacking incentive and reward, were unable to reap the fruits of their own labor. Rural populations felt exploited and longed to have control over their own land and to make the decisions that would enable them to receive the benefits of their efforts. Deng Xiaoping correctly observed how returning the land to the peasants in South Korea and Taiwan helped to initiate the economic miracles in those countries, providing both capital and labor for later industrial development. Today in China, household production units can lease their land, and these leases can be inherited.

Realizing that the breakup of the communes and increased efficiency in farm production would also release millions of peasants who would then become surplus labor, Deng and his reformers also carried out a second rural revolution, creating the incentives and opportunities for the establishment of millions of rural industrial and service enterprises. These would be created through the efforts of the rural people themselves, who under the new township and village rules would be allowed to create private and collective enterprises; these enterprises would then sell their products and services in the marketplace and use most of the profits for improvement in living standards or reinvestment.

Local Communist Party cadres directly benefited from both increased agricultural and rural industrial production. Because they controlled power structures at the lowest level of government, they were able in many cases to have household farmland assigned to themselves and to participate in the ownership and management of rural industries and services. The newly created wealth resulting from a dramatic increase in production could then be either taxed through local governmental structures, allegedly to provide locally needed social services, or siphoned off through corrupt deals, in which the rural entrepreneurs gave rewards and favors to party cadres for contracts and necessary arrangements in order to produce and market their products.

According to Premier Li Peng:

> The township and village enterprises were a great invention of the Chinese farmers made in the reform process. In the 1980s, these enterprises of different types mushroomed rapidly, giving employment to various townships and preventing a rush of surplus rural labor to the cities. Now, in the total value of rural production, the output value of the township and village enterprises and tertiary industry has exceeded that of agriculture. This is of major significance to the improvement of the farmer's livelihood and the stability of the rural areas and the society as a whole.[9]

Town and village enterprises were created to mop up excess agricultural labor, keep people in the countryside, and generate local income. The overall results have been truly astounding, creating growth rates exceeding those in most other rural regions of the world, whether in developed or less developed countries. By 1992, 18.5 million new rural enterprises employed 96 million people and accounted for one-fourth of China's gross national product (GNP).[10] This was in addition to agricultural production, which reached 441 million metric tons of grain in 1992, enough to feed nearly all of China's people and provide certain types of surpluses for export. By 1992, China had become a major exporter of corn and oilseeds, even though it continued to be a major importer of wheat. From 1978 to 1992, township and village enterprises (TVEs) were responsible for two-thirds of the growth in Chinese exports. In 1998, they contributed 28 percent of the nation's GDP. At the same time, they employed over 100 million former agricultural workers.[11]

Yet these increases in both rural enterprises and farm production were highly uneven, occurring mainly in China's more fertile and highly populated coastal and central regions. And in the twenty-first century, growth of TVEs is slowing. From 1991 to 1995 they grew at the rate of 42 percent, but from 1997 to 1999 they grew at the rate of only 17 percent. According to Joseph Fewsmith, a specialist in Chinese economics, there are four possible reasons: intensive growth is replacing extensive growth, some TVEs have essentially been privatized, obtaining financing is difficult, and close relations with government entities are actually hindering good business practices.[12]

The rapid growth of both agricultural and industrial production in rural China has also been accompanied by a number of political and economic problems that will need to be resolved if China's rural economic miracle is to continue. Politically, the self-sufficient communes of the Mao era have been replaced by the township, which now is the basic unit of government throughout rural China. Depending on population density, a typical township may have as many as 50,000 people, with greater numbers in China's rich coastal provinces, such as Guangdong and Fujian. Typically, there are now elective councils at the township level, with both party cadres and local dignitaries, who are often successful in business, serving for three-year terms. Throughout most of rural China, however, many of these elective positions remain uncontested. In effect, local party cadres both control the bureaucratic structures and have decision-making power with regard to authorizing the creation of economic enterprises, controlling tax revenues of the townships, and providing channels for obtaining needed resources that often are not available to local enterprises through the free-market system. In China's dual economy, prices and resources through the state structure are much cheaper, but party officials down to the local level are able to decide who gets these materials, giving them personal influence with local enterprises that are dependent on their favors.

Villages, which are below the townships, have developed a certain amount of autonomy in local decisionmaking parallel to decentralization of economic decisionmaking since Deng's rural reform began. In the past, the local party secretary at the village level was the key decisionmaker, but with the growing desire of the local population to control local government decisions, the party secretary has become vulnerable to outside influence in the local village. In the village council, two or three persons now frequently run for office. Even if party cadres are elected, they must take into consideration the needs of local enterprises, which are the source of wealth for the cadres, local bureaucracy, and everyone else. Increasingly, townships and villages are dependent on local financial resources, not only for providing the capital for new agricultural or industrial undertakings, but also for local services such as education, health care, and infrastructure for road maintenance, irrigation, and water supplies. Because local party cadres are also farmers and participate in local enterprises, if they do not have the support of the people, they might receive unfavorable treatment after they have completed their term of office on village councils.[13]

Several different types of economic structures coexist at the village and township levels. In addition to the household land leases for agricultural production, there are private enterprises, collectives, and public enterprises. Most private enterprises tend to be rather small, often initiated by individual families and friends. Collectives, on the other hand, are composed of community businesses in which the participants are shareholders. Because party rules give a number of privileges to collectives that are not always available to private enterprises (for example, tax breaks and sometimes the availability of resources at cheaper prices from the controlled public sector), these economic units have expanded very rapidly in rural areas. In fact, many collectives are in reality private undertakings that are structured as collectives to take advantage of their special privileges. Public enterprises are often able to compete only because they receive even more privileges from government, such as access to loans from government and state-controlled financial institutions that are unavailable to the private sector. The maintenance of public sector enterprises, however, is frequently very important as a major source of employment in rural regions, where there may be little opportunity to develop other types of successful enterprises. China's rural areas are very uneven in resources, infrastructure, and market opportunities, and the local party cadres and rural population have to rely largely on their own initiatives and alternate forms of economic structures to provide a livelihood and for basic needs. Since China undertook its economic reforms, however, the most rapidly growing sector of industrial production has been that of nonstate enterprises.

Although China's rural revolution has produced remarkable results, there has been controversy within the CCP over what role party and government should play in rural China at the local level. In 1988, even prior to the Tiananmen protests, the party conservatives sought to slow down the transition to private control, fearing that the party would lose its influence in China's townships and villages. Then, when students demonstrated at Tiananmen Square against party corruption throughout China, the conservatives seized the initiative. For the next three years, they sought not only to slow down privatization in the countryside, but also to reverse the process by taking over the more successful private enterprises and converting them to state ownership. According to one local official, "Officials seize[d] rural enterprises in order to squash the supposed threat to communism from industries flourishing outside the direct control of bureaucrats and party officials." However, "they were driven by nothing more than bureaucratic gluttony."[14] The people would again be dependent on favors from local party officials, since they would no longer have control over the production and distribution of wealth. The reformist wing in Beijing, however, was opposed to these conservative efforts, even though the Tiananmen events tilted the balance of power temporarily in favor of those who wanted to resist privatization. Deng Xiaoping's famous January 1992 visit to the Gold Coast in southern China signaled a resurgence of the reformists in Beijing and a renewal of economic reform and support for the "socialist economic market," an expression used to identify socialism with marketplace reforms. Though the Gold Coast SEZs received new approval from Deng and his supporters, his public relations trip to the south also signaled full support for market and investment reforms throughout China, and China's rural reforms at the township and village levels were the heart of these reforms. In October 1992, the reform wing further strengthened its party leadership at the Fourteenth Party Congress, and the conservative wing was essentially defeated.

Ten years later, to solidify structural changes in rural China, the National People's Congress adopted the Rural Land Contracting Law. According to Brian Schwarzwalder, of the Rural Development Institute, the law will accomplish three things:

> First, by enshrining 30-year land rights in law, by requiring that they be confirmed by contracts, and by prohibiting any readjustments or interference by local officials, the law provides farmers with a long enough tenure period to recover the value of long-term investments. Second, the law establishes a "framework for the development of markets for rural land use rights." This will have two beneficial consequences: it will "allow voluntary, gradual reallocation of land rights to the most efficient farm households"; and the "higher productivity and new wealth" that will result from such exchanges will stimulate rural economic development. Third, it will "strengthen the rule of law in the countryside," by inflicting strict penalties on local officials who transgress on farmers' land use rights.[15]

The official view, that of Li Peng, is that "the law has great significance for the protection of farmers' fundamental interests, the promotion of agricultural development and the maintenance of social stability in rural areas."[16]

Strengthening of the household (private) farm and private and collective enterprises (collectives really operate much like private factories) did not mean smooth sailing for the private sector. But the party cadres would now have to take into account the wishes of the rural population. In the twenty-first century, contested elections on the local level are leading to greater or lesser degrees of official accountability, if not yet to grassroots democracy. The social, economic, and political structures that are already transforming life in the townships and villages will continue to evolve as the demands of the new Chinese economy dictate greater flexibility, openness, and accountability.

Another problem, also involving the future role of the party cadres in rural China, needs to be resolved if the harmony and well-being of the people are to be ensured. In the past, party cadres have often been above the law at the township and village levels. With the new contracts creating private, collective, and other enterprises, as well as inheritable household leases on farmland, a new legal system is needed in rural China. Contracts should not be subject to the personal whims of political and bureaucratic officials, whether party cadres or others. While China has been developing a new system of law and order, including training lawyers and judges, contracts and rights are still sometimes flouted in courts of law depending on the political delicacy of the case. Because over two-thirds of China's population continues to live in rural China and their loyalty and well-being depend on fair treatment and protection of hard-earned wealth from corrupt officials, an independent court system capable of impartially providing due process of law is urgently needed.

Joint Ventures and Special Economic Zones

The inner face of China's economic reforms has been the remarkable level of change in the Chinese village. The outer face has been China's dramatic opening to outside investment and trade, keyed by joint venture investments in China's special economic zones. The first zones were created in the province of Guangdong, which borders Hong Kong. Shenzhen, the most famous SEZ, is located next to Hong Kong on the Zhu River Delta. Other SEZs include Zhuhai, adjacent to Macao; Shantou, in Guangdong; and Xiamen, in Fujian province. China's SEZs are patterned after Taiwan's SEZs, in which foreign investors were given special privileges, including special rights to import resources and export finished products with a minimum of regulations and taxes. Joint ventures, in which foreign investors enter into contracts with Chinese counterparts, have been the principal form of corporate structures, but other arrangements have also been made available. The Deng reformists sought to attract new technology, capital, and production of goods, which then could be exported for hard currency. These resources, in turn, could be used to speed up modernization and development. Initially, China's SEZs were not designed to serve the domestic market, and restrictions were placed on how much of a joint venture's production could be sold inside China.[17] The phenomenal growth of the Shenzhen SEZ typifies the success of Deng's outward reach for new investment and capital, which have been attracted by China's cheap and disciplined labor. From a population of 70,000 in 1980, Shenzhen grew to nearly 4 million permanent residents in 2004, with another half million migrants living illegally inside Shenzhen in a shadowy existence. Wages in the city rose to three times the wages in surrounding regions; however, regions surrounding Shenzhen also began creating their own light industries and, combined with other SEZs and adjacent territories, are now providing 100 million additional jobs for the Chinese people, mostly migrants from rural China.

Shenzhen, the center of these developments in southern China, is rapidly becoming another Hong Kong as it shifts from light industry to finance and other service industries. A visitor to Shenzhen and the other SEZs is overwhelmed by the sound of the jackhammers that accompany endless construction sites with bamboo scaffolding. New factories, highways, sewer and water lines, and apartment complexes are being built as far as the eye can see. Traffic jams seem to be everywhere as bicycles, trucks, and buses (but few cars) patiently wait their turn to weave through the construction bottlenecks. To speed up transport between Guangzhou and Hong Kong (almost 100 miles to the south), a new four-lane superhighway was built that cut travel time in half.

Following the student demonstrations at Tiananmen, Western investment in China temporarily slowed down. But investments from overseas Chinese, as well as from South Korea and Japan, did not slow down at all. Another SEZ has been established on Hainan Island in the South China Sea (especially to attract investment from Southeast Asia), and Beijing is creating SEZs in other regions. By 1992, China was again strongly encouraging further overseas investment. Additional provinces opened up new special industrial zones, in some cases providing even more advantages than those created in southern China. Shenzhen expanded its free trade zones, and new ones were created along China's eastern coast at Shanghai and Tianjin. Investment was at the same time further encouraged by allowing more foreign currency exchange, the lack of which had been a major constraint limiting new investment. Beginning in 1991, foreign corporations were also permitted direct leasing of land. Additional Yangtze River ports located at Wuhan, Jiujiang, and Wuhu were opened up to foreign ships, and foreign banks were allowed to open branches in a number of China's major cities. Previously, this had been permitted only in Shenzhen. From 1992 onward, the Chinese government has created a number of additional free trade zones, as well as industrial and technology development zones. Shanghai's Pudong is perhaps the most visible and successful of all these. The goal, of course, is to encourage more regionally integrated economic development.

Because of increased investment in both rural and urban regions from both domestic and international sources, the Chinese economy has grown at a rate of approximately 9 percent annually. Although Beijing's leaders wished to slow this rate down at various periods in order to prevent an overheated economy, they are and have been interested in seeking large overseas investments that will bring in new types of technology and balance the light industry in China's rural economy and special economic zones. Beijing wishes to avoid too much dependence on any one source of capital, whether from Asia, North America, or Europe.

From the point of view of the West, the resurgence of Beijing's commitment to the Open Door policy may be reassuring, but China's growing interdependence with the outside world poses serious problems for Beijing. In the SEZs and in the coastal areas, lifestyles are rapidly changing. In Shenzhen, with its many discotheques, lifestyles are closer to those found in Hong Kong than those found in Beijing or even Shanghai. In Macao, Chinese gamble using Hong Kong dollars. This has allowed the revival of old ills, such as crime and prostitution, which the Communists had claimed to have eradicated from China. All of these things are disturbing to the party, which fears cultural pollution from the West but realizes the impossibility of returning to the past.

Enterprise in China: State-Owned and Private

State-owned enterprises (SOEs) are the albatross of the Chinese economy. Since 1978, a third of state enterprises, mostly huge industrial complexes, continue to lose money. Beijing's leaders are committed to making the SOEs function more rationally—that is, at a profit—but the social ramifications of such a policy are immense. For many years SOEs functioned as part of the welfare state. Marginally skilled workers were kept on the payroll whether or not they were actually needed or productive. As part of the state-owned enterprise, workers were entitled to benefits ranging from housing to health care to pensions. Moreover, many SOEs have not been efficiently managed. Profit was not a motive, and the losses multiplied. Concerned about the ramifications of allowing too many SOEs to in effect declare bankruptcy, the Chinese government has helped prop them up. Foreign investment in SOEs is encouraged, and Chinese banks have been directed to issue loans to SOEs. Not surprisingly, many SOEs have not met their repayment schedule and many of these loans have had to be written off.

Even with Beijing's go-slow approach to reform, employment in SOEs fell from 112 million to 86 million, a reduction of 23 percent, from 1996 to 2000.[18] The World Bank's International Finance Corporation believes that SOE reform is proceeding well. It cites the following factors: "80–90% of small and medium SOEs have been transformed," the large SOEs are changing, monopolies in the "strategically important infrastructure and energy sectors" are being broken up, and the government has also "nurtured over 20 giant corporations and conglomerates that have proven competitive in the international market."[19]

At the same time, private enterprise slowly gained ground, with the government finally allowing bank lending to nonstate enterprises and the promulgation of a business environment more favorable to the private sector. According to Kellee Tsai of Johns Hopkins University, "From 1990 to 2000 the average annual growth rate in the number of private enterprises was 32.8 percent; the sector now employs 22.7 percent of the work force and accounts for one third of the gross domestic product; and the 'creation of new private sector employment' is greater than the total for the state and collective sectors."[20] The growth of China's nonstate economy is illustrated in Table 3.3.

Employment and Unemployment

China must create, depending on who is doing the estimating, 10–20 million additional jobs each year to mop up unemployed rural and urban workers, as well as deal with underemployed SOE workers. The unemployed include displaced farmers, rural workers with no jobs and no prospects (who often become part of the migrant "floating population"), and urban workers dismissed from failing state-owned enterprises. Despite China's phenomenal growth, it has not been able to create enough new jobs annually, and the unemployment rate—officially around 4 percent and unofficially 8–10 percent—has been in-

Table 3.3   China's Nonstate Economy, 1989–1998

	Nonstate Economy (in U.S.$ millions)	Percentage of Total Economy
1989	21.51	—
1990	23.35	8.6
1991	26.59	13.9
1992	29.14	9.6
1993	36.46	25.1
1994	50.45	38.4
1995	63.20	25.3
1996	69.95	10.7
1997	76.52	9.4
1998	87.01	13.7

Source: Joseph Fewsmith, "The Political and Social Implications of China's Accession to the WTO," *China Quarterly* 167 (September 2001): 583.

creasing. Rising unemployment frequently leads to increasing social instability. Particularly if China's economy slows, the leaders in Beijing will become increasingly nervous about the lack of work in their socialist market economy.

China's Comparative Advantage

There are many industrial products in which other Asian countries have a clear comparative advantage over China. Because China's economy is expanding at a rapid rate, with greater maturity it could gain comparative advantage in other products. However, this would require much greater efficiency in the production of a wide range of products. China would also need to overcome a number of basic problems relating to energy shortages, transportation bottlenecks, state and party interference in the running of enterprises, excessive and unpredictable regulations, excessive taxes, employment of unneeded workers, lack of incentive to make a profit, and the presence of a dual economy in which many products are unavailable at reasonable prices or are available only through bribery of party cadres or government officials. Other problems that may greatly hinder China's future development and ability to compete in world markets relate to extreme variations in living standards and economic development and the immature nature of the market system. In addition, planning at the national, provincial, or local level is often inconsistent or may even work at cross-purposes. There is also a shortage of capital available to the national government to overcome many constraints as China's overall economy continues to grow.

Key Elements of a
Knowledge-Based Economy

China must encourage its organizations and people to acquire, create, disseminate, and use knowledge more effectively for greater economic and social development. The four pillars of a knowledge-based economy are:

1. An economic and institutional regime that provides incentives for the efficient use of existing knowledge, the creation of new knowledge, and entrepreneurship.
2. An educated and skilled populace that can create and use knowledge.
3. A dynamic information infrastructure that can facilitate the effective communication, dissemination, and processing of information.
4. An effective innovation system comprising a network of firms, research centers, universities, think tanks, consultants, and other organizations that can tap into the growing stock of global knowledge, assimilate and adapt it to local needs, and create new knowledge or technologies.

Source: Carl J. Dahlman and Jean-Eric Aubert, "China and the Knowledge Economy: Seizing the 21st Century," World Bank, 2001, http://www .worldbank.org/wbi/knowledgefordevelopment/docs/chinaoverview_0917 .pdf.

Economic Liberalism, Political Freedom, and Human Rights: What Relationship?

Beijing's leaders, after the death of Mao, were well aware of some of the dangers of opening China to interdependence with the global system by opening markets at home. The other alternative looked worse, however, and few in the party leadership were willing to defend the economic policies of the past. The example of the Soviet Union precluded any defense of stringent central planning.

China's leaders have adopted an incremental approach to economic change, combined with a negative approach to political change. Yet China's future economic development and its role as a leading member of the global community in the next decades may depend not on incremental changes but on a rational, systematic political and economic restructuring guided by a vigorous leadership. Incremental change may well lead eventually to economic and political instability that could undermine China's global position. These structural problems include the following:

- China's dual economic system: inefficient state versus efficient private industry.
- Party and government officials: increasing personnel costs and rising corruption.
- Growing disparity in wealth and income: the poorer interior regions versus the richer coastal regions.
- Iron rice bowl: the need to provide a mechanism to give social benefits formerly provided by the state.

These problems were a major complaint of student demonstrators at Tiananmen Square, who were also joined by workers from many other sectors of society. Following the demonstrations, party leaders sought to improve living conditions, but to no avail. Underemployment and unemployment continue to be problems. Disparities in wealth and social benefits are increasing, even as GNP continues to rise at an annual rate of over 9 percent. The national government is operating at a large deficit, and there are no funds available to help the poorer provinces and local communities, even as the national military budget is being increased. Without solutions to these problems, the Communist Party leadership may have great difficulty in holding on to power over the long term. But what are the alternatives? What kind of political, economic, and social reforms are required, and how can they be implemented?[21] From the Chinese perspective, an authoritarian political system based on party leadership seems essential to ensure China's rapid transition to a "socialist market economy" while at the same time maintaining order and stability. China's leaders seem convinced that overseas investors, as well as tourists, will go where there is political stability, regardless of whether the regime is authoritarian or democratic. In fact, China's leaders probably believe that Western investors, given a choice, might prefer investing where there is political stability with an authoritarian government, so long as there is legal protection and a guarantee of the investor's contracts entered into in good faith with Chinese officials and coinvestors. Some of these Western investors may in fact, from the Chinese perspective, see greater opportunity to make a profit in an authoritarian society such as China than in a democratic society such as the United States.

China's leaders, to a greater or lesser degree depending on the political situation, do allow the media to discuss economic and social change while prohibiting them from discussing basic change in the political system. But the lack of discussion does not mean that political change is not taking place. Even with a reemphasis on central political control following the 1989 demonstrations, a certain amount of grassroots democracy began to emerge in the 1990s, especially in China's rural areas, including villages and townships. In local rural communities, party cadres are actively involved in interacting with nonparty interest groups, increasingly on a cooperative basis rather than through a strictly dominant-subordinate relationship. In addition, with the growing number of small businesses in rural areas, party cadres are often partners in these operations, in which they share in the profit making. Although there has been little publicity about grassroots democracy in rural China, party cadres and non-Communist local dignitaries are increasingly running against each other in competitive elections for council seats in villages and townships. By supporting grassroots democracy in rural China, the CCP may in the future be an important part of the emerging political system. By helping to support, on an incremental basis, greater meaningful participation of the people in electing and removing political leaders at the local level based on popular appeal, the Chinese Communists might avoid the fate of their counterparts in Eastern Europe and the former Soviet Union.

> **Changes to the PRC Constitution, March 14, 2004**
>
> "The State protects the lawful rights and interests of the individual and private sectors of the economy, and exercises guidance, supervision and control over individual and private sectors of the economy." Revised to: "The State protects the lawful rights and interests of the non-public sectors of the economy such as the individual and private sectors of the economy. The State encourages, supports and guides the development of the non-public sectors of the economy and, in accordance with law, exercises supervision and control over the non-public sectors of the economy."
>
> Article 13: "The State protects the right of citizens to own lawfully earned income, savings, houses and other lawful property. . . . The State protects according to law the right of citizens to inherit private property." Revised to: "Citizens' lawful private property is inviolable. . . . The State, in accordance with law, protects the rights of citizens to private property and to its inheritance. . . . The State may, in the public interest and in accordance with law, expropriate or requisition private property for its use and shall make compensation for the private property expropriated or requisitioned."

China in the World Trade Organization

To fulfill its goal of becoming a major player in the international economic arena, China campaigned to become a member of the World Trade Organization (WTO). Beijing was successful, and China acceded to the WTO in 2001 after agreeing to the following reforms:

- The elimination of import quotas by 2006.
- The elimination of import tariffs on computers, semiconductors, and related products by 2005.
- Reduction of import tariffs on agricultural products.
- Reduction of import tariffs on industrial products.
- Reduction of import tariffs on motor vehicles and parts.
- Up to 50 percent foreign ownership in telecommunications and insurance industries.
- Permission for importers to own domestic distribution networks.
- Full market access for foreign banks.[22]

In other words, China agreed to open its internal markets to foreign competition. It did so despite considerable internal debate about the wisdom of the WTO agreement and the effect of globalization on Beijing's ability to control its economy. According to one commentator:

> The U.S. controls the regulations that have been formulated in the international economic organizations; all are designed to accord with the interests and needs of the institutional model of the strong capitalist states. As soon as China joins the WTO, the U.S. can at any time find an excuse to interfere in, sanction and intimidate our country into accepting so-called "international norms" that do not accord with our national characteristics. And to help the multinational companies to control China's industrial and financial lifelines, it [the United States] will usurp our economic sovereignty and force us to carry out suicidal reforms just as it has in Latin America, Russia, South-East Asia and elsewhere.[23]

Why, after decades of protecting its industries (even after initiating economic reforms) would China agree to such far-reaching changes to its internal economy? To China's leaders, membership in the WTO confers the international prestige they desire and verifies the success of their economic reform efforts. WTO membership also allows China access to foreign capital and investment on an even larger scale. While the presence of foreign entities may increase competition, particularly with domestic manufacturers, Beijing believes that the best domestic entities will survive and prosper. According to Nicholas Lardy, an analyst of China's international economy:

> The real market opening in China that is going to occur as a result of membership in the WTO is going to be additional investment liberalization and investment in sectors that have been relatively closed, and these are all in the services sector. Investment in telecommuncation, financial services and distribution will be the most important liberalizations that will occur. . . . There are big gains for China. . . . There is the provision of additional services in telecommunications, which are still under-provided. Foreign capital will help in increasing the penetration rates. The opening of distribution services

is extremely important for many joint venture companies that want to expand their presence in the market.[24]

A more open economy, according to China's leaders, will lead to a stronger and more diversified economy.

Moreover, China's exports will benefit. For example, with the WTO-mandated elimination of textile quotas in 2005, U.S. manufacturers fear that Chinese textile exports will deal their industry a death knell.[25] They are up in arms and demanding that part of China's WTO agreement be invoked, a clause that allows member countries to impose limits on imports of products that cause market disruptions. According to the American Manufacturing Trade Action Coalition, "Every national textile association in this coalition faces a three-dimensional threat from China's highly subsidized export machine. . . . Coalition members face the loss of significant market share in their own domestic market, in first-world markets and in critical developing-world markets."[26]

China's admission into the World Trade Organization in 2001 is a major step in its acceptance and integration into the global trade system. China claims it is ready to assume full responsibility in meeting WTO obligations, under which members agree to abide by all the multilateral rules. With its membership, Beijing will be obligated to restructure its regulations for importing many types of goods into China. But there will be new opportunities for China to use its comparative advantage in labor-intensive goods by exporting to existing and new markets, as well as to other states.

Whither China, Boom or Bust?

In the early twenty-first century, China has become the nexus of the world's economy:

> China has become a manufacturing hub for the rest of the world in low-end labour-intensive goods—and the rest of the world is becoming a manufacturing hub for China in high-end, capital intensive goods. . . . China may be a threat to certain parts of the global supply chain that rely on low cost labour, but it represents an even greater opportunity via production efficiency gains, economic welfare gains and long-term dynamic potential. Its booming exports are more than matched by booming industrial imports and foreign investment opportunities. It has become the new engine of global growth.[27]

Given this level of economic interdependence, the health of the Chinese economy is of tremendous concern internationally. In the early twenty-first century, China's fast-paced growth has won plaudits but also caused concern. Beijing itself has been concerned, as commodity shortages are developing, infrastructure is becoming strained, and inflation is rising. Amid internal and external discussions over whether Beijing will be able to engineer a "soft landing," the government is seeking to rein in the economy's expansion.

Though China's leaders have important economic, social, and legal choices involving political considerations, most changes are likely to be incremental and gradual. If so, power may remain in the hands of the CCP, especially at the provincial and national levels. Whether Adam Smith will finally triumph over Karl Marx remains problematic, even though China seems committed to moving further in the direction of marketplace capitalism. China's leaders seem unconvinced that Western-style democracy is necessary, or even desirable, as China seeks development of its "social market economy," increasingly based on government by law rather than by people, but not based on political change. Yet Beijing is not likely to succeed over the long term without accelerating both economic and political change. According to Yasheng Huang, a professor at the Massachusetts Institute of Technology's Sloan School of Management and a former professor at the Harvard Business School:

> In the next revision of the constitution, the fundamental change will be a political one. . . . [Chinese officials] have got to be committed to private-property rights. They have to trust the market. They have to create a nurturing environment with neutrality of regulations and equal treatment. You have to have fair rules of the game. You have to have transparency. China needs exactly the same things you would advocate for any country in the world. After 25 years of economic reforms, China needs a fundamental institutional change in order to move reforms forward. . . . FDI will only do so much. The main changes ought to come internally.[28]

Policy Options

Beijing's leaders are aware of the contradictions in their dual economic system, which will cause increasing difficulties in furthering development. But they are also worried about inflation and overheating of the economy.

Option 1: Maintaining China's Current High Rate of Economic Development

Although the majority of China's leaders support rapid economic development at home and an Open Door policy abroad, there are growing contradictions resulting from this rapid development that pose serious problems, even threatening China's social and political stability. In order to continue China's rapid economic growth, it will also be necessary to deal with the following developments, which are closely related to China's economic reforms:

- China needs more effective legal protection for property and investors. Traditionally, Chinese prefer to settle disagreements through personal negotiation or mediation, which often means rewarding those who are in a position to help protect one's interests. Growing corruption and danger of confiscation can no longer be handled effectively through these traditional procedures, and there is a need for impartial commercial law that deals with individual and corporate property rights. However, there is little Chinese tradition for this type of formal legal system. Under Confucianism, as well as in contemporary China, justice relies more on the ethical behavior of people in positions of responsibility than on legal restraints on those in power.

- In order to increase economic efficiency and eliminate corruption, China may need to either phase out its dual economic system (both a large public sector and large private sector) or else make the public sector subject to marketplace discipline (elimination of double pricing and unlimited ability of public enterprises to borrow without concern for bankruptcy). But the public sector is a major source of party wealth. By controlling goods from the public sector, priced much lower than they would be in the open market, party officials can personally sell these goods at open market prices and pocket the markup. Further, because of the shortage of certain resources available only through the public sector, party officials are in a position to channel these resources to purchasers who are willing to make the highest side payments.

- China needs to eliminate crime and corruption through greater appeal to community pride and public morality. The emphasis on getting rich has spurred new efforts to produce wealth, but it has also brought corruption both inside and outside government, as people seem more concerned about personal enrichment than the well-being of society. The renewed efforts at Marxist indoctrination that were reinstituted after Tiananmen Square were a failure. If China's future is to be ensured, then ways must be found to balance the desire for personal gain with dedication to the well-being of the community.

- Ways must be found to meet the basic needs of hundreds of millions of Chinese who seem to have fallen through the cracks since the implementation of Deng's economic reforms. In the Maoist era, the iron rice bowl provided the basic needs of the people, such as food, clothing, employment, disability payments, old-age benefits, education, housing, and health care, all of which were the responsibility of one's public work unit, whether rural or urban. With increasing privatization, millions of people may be better off, but millions of others no longer have access to these social and economic benefits. Logically, because the central government has no funds to provide these services, local authorities should provide them through taxation. But it is very difficult to raise taxes, especially in interior provinces that have not experienced the rapid growth of the coastal regions.

- China must more fully utilize human resources. With privatization and pressures on families to have only one child, discrimination against women in both education and job opportunities has increased. Preference is given to males, who have opportunities for better education and jobs, whereas women work long hours at low wages in China's labor-intensive light industries. But if China is to continue its rapid economic development, ways must be found to train and utilize the talents of Chinese women fully.
- Ways must also be found to provide more energy and better transportation, as well as obtain needed resources such as timber and iron ore, which are in short supply inside China. China also needs more food production just to keep up with its population growth. However, reliance on coal for energy, continued rapid cutting of China's forests (with only partial replacement of trees), and more intensive cultivation of China's limited cropland all place further stress on the environment. One solution may be greater imports of cleaner energy as well as timber, food, and other crucial commodities. But this will require greater exports or risk an unfavorable balance of payments.

Option 2: Slowing Down China's Rate of Economic Growth

High growth rates create inflation if there are shortages of goods and services such as transportation and electricity. High growth rates also create greater inequities and discontent because many people and regions do not share in the newly created wealth. Discontent can bring instability and protest. Two of the major causes of the Tiananmen demonstrations were inflation and corruption, both stimulated by China's rapid economic change. Party hard-liners believe that corruption, crime, breakdown in morality, and decreasing social responsibility can all be traced to China's rapid economic change, especially changes associated with Western cultural and materialistic consumer values. Slowing down growth may solve some of China's growing problems:

- Slower growth rates may lessen pressure for basic structural reforms, which are creating serious bottlenecks, for example, in transportation and energy. Less demand for these resources makes it easier to correct these deficiencies on a long-term basis.
- Slower growth rates will mean less pressure on the dual economy. China's leaders need time to make adjustments in the public sector to

make it more efficient and responsive to the marketplace. Virtually all party leaders seem dedicated to pragmatic adjustments within the dual economy rather than elimination of the public sector (the latter might further undermine party authority and power). There is also fear that without central regulation and control of key industries and services such as finance, communications, and transportation, China could become divided into economic regions.

- Slower growth rates may reduce temptations for a further buildup of China's military at a time when China faces fewer external threats than at any time in the modern era. Economic necessity was a major factor that induced the superpowers to bring the Cold War to an end. If China grows more rapidly than its neighbors, Beijing may be tempted to use military buildup as an instrument of foreign policy. This could stimulate an arms race in East and Southeast Asia. Rapid growth could also speed up China's efforts to find new oil reserves in the South China Sea to alleviate its growing energy shortages, even though countries in Southeast Asia may take measures to counter Chinese military domination of these territories, which they also claim.

- Slower growth rates may help create an atmosphere in which China's people are less addicted to get-rich schemes and more willing to seek careers based on service to community needs. With 1.2 billion people, there is a limit to consumerism patterned on countries such as the United States and those in Western Europe.

- Slower growth rates may help China avoid vulnerabilities in the global economy that might undermine Chinese stability and well-being. Should recession continue outside China (for example, in Japan and Western Europe), many countries may face overwhelming pressures to practice protectionism in trade and jobs. Slower growth inside China could give its leaders greater flexibility in avoiding outside leverage to extract concessions from the country as a condition of trade and investment.

Option 3: Working More Closely Together

China's leaders at the national, regional, and local levels need to work closely together to share and more effectively divide responsibilities if domestic trade wars and inefficient use of resources are to be avoided. Already, provincial authorities are husbanding scarce resources and protecting their own industries at the expense of interregional trade and the economic benefits of comparative advantage. In the past, the Chinese Communist Party has been able to use its unity to carry out economic policies made in Beijing, but increasingly, ways must be found to promote cooperation based on the mutual self-interest of the different regions, especially if the resources of China's vast interior are to be utilized effectively:

- Because the central government is losing its power to extract revenue while the richer provinces are gaining increased revenue, basic social services must largely be provided by local government. Richer provinces must be persuaded to share their newfound wealth with their poorer neighbors, or else they will be inundated with hundreds of millions of Chinese seeking better services and opportunity by migrating to coastal provinces such as Shandong, Fujian, and Guangdong.
- With its limited resources, the central government must concentrate on what it can do best, such as conducting foreign policy and opening up greater opportunities for trade and investment. However, even these efforts will require greater cooperation with regional and local authorities.
- The central government should also concentrate on ways to speed up the development of the interior and eliminate internal trade barriers that, if not corrected, could lead to economic disintegration and regional trade blocs inside China.

Discussion Questions

1. Is China fully committed to creating a capitalist-type market economy?
2. Are making money and improving living standards much more important to the Chinese than attaining Western-type political rights?
3. Do capitalists prefer to invest in a society with a Western-type political system rather than one with an authoritarian-type political system?
4. To what extent is the protection of human rights essential to attracting tourists to China and increasing Chinese exports to Western democracies?
5. What are the prospects for improving political rights inside China?
6. Is a Western-type legal system essential to the development of a capitalist market system?
7. To what extent is China committed to creating a legal system based on government by law, rather than government by people who are above the law?
8. What is the relationship between economic liberalism, political freedom, and human rights?
9. To what extent has Adam Smith triumphed over Karl Marx in China?
10. How have Hong Kong, Taiwan, Japan, and South Korea each made special contributions to the economic development of China?
11. How has economic development changed life in China's rural villages and townships?

12. What are the advantages and disadvantages of maintaining a dual economy in China?
13. What can be done to promote economic development in China's interior provinces?
14. How have China's economic reforms changed the relationship among national, regional, and local government in China?
15. Would China be better off by trying to maintain or slow down its current rate of economic development?
16. How is the question of women's rights related to China's future economic development?
17. How have economic reforms affected Chinese social values concerning such issues as crime and dedication to community service?
18. How will China's membership in the World Trade Organization affect it economically? Politically?
19. How has China's tremendous growth rate affected the international market for raw materials such as petroleum products and steel?

Suggested Readings

Dickson, Bruce J. *Red Capitalists in China: The Party, Private Entrepreneurs, and Prospects for Political Change.* Cambridge: Cambridge University Press, 2003.

Goodman, David S. G., and Gerald Segal, eds. *China in the Nineties: Crisis Management and Beyond.* New York: Oxford University Press, 1991.

Gregory, Neil, Stoyan Tenev, and Dileep Wagle. *China's Emerging Private Enterprises: Prospects for the New Century.* Washington, D.C.: International Finance Corporation, 2000.

Hale, David, and Lyric Hughes Hale. "China Takes Off." *Foreign Affairs* (November–December 2003): 36–53.

Howell, Jude. *China Opens Its Doors: The Politics of Economic Transition.* Boulder, Colo.: Lynne Rienner, 1993.

Huang, Yasheng. *Selling China: Foreign Direct Investment During the Reform Era.* Cambridge: Cambridge University Press, 2003.

Langlois, John D. "The WTO and China's Financial System." *China Quarterly* 167 (September 2001): 610–629.

Lardy, Nicholas R. *China's Unfinished Economic Revolution.* Washington, D.C.: Brookings Institution, 1998.

———. *Integrating China into the Global Economy.* Washington, D.C.: Brookings Institution, 2002.

Lin, Justin Yifu, Fang Cai, and Zhou Li. *The China Miracle.* Hong Kong: Chinese University Press, 1996.

Solinger, Dorothy J. *China's Transition from Socialism.* Armonk, N.Y.: M. E. Sharpe, 1993.

Steinfeld, Edward S. *Forging Reform in China: The Fate of State-Owned Industry.* Cambridge: Cambridge University Press, 1998.

White, Gordon, ed. *The Chinese State in the Era of Economic Reform.* Armonk, N.Y.: M. E. Sharpe, 1992.

▦ Notes

1. Guo Hai Wang, quoted in LifeOnline, *The Real Leap Forward,* http://www. tve.org/lifeonline/index.cfm?aid=1406, viewed May 23, 2004.

2. BBC News, *Voices from Modern China,* http://news.bbc.co.uk/1/shared/spl/hi/asia_pac/02/china_party_congress/voices/html/li_chunhai.stm.

3. See Suzanne Ogden, "The Changing Content of China's Democratic Socialist Institutions," *In Depth: A Journal for Values and Public Policy* 3, no. 1 (Winter 1993): 237–256. Ogden described the growth of pluralistic decisionmaking processes at the local level. The struggle for succession in the 1990s created caution and hesitancy to use the rational actor decisionmaking model. This reinforced the bureaucratic-organizational model, which preserved the privileges of both the new private sectors and also the remaining public sectors of the economy. However, Ogden pointed out that there was clearly a growth in grassroots democracy, and these developments indicated the growing importance of a pluralistic decisionmaking process in the 1990s. She also noted that China's people felt in the 1990s that they had more personal freedom than at any time in their memory.

4. Third world countries proposed that a new international economic order be established in the 1970s. Third world economic issues are dealt with through the UN Conference on Trade and Development.

5. Quoted in Brenton Schlender, "China Really Is on the Move," *Fortune,* October 5, 1992, p. 118.

6. Pranab Bardhan, *Crouching Tiger, Lumbering Elephant: A China-India Comparison,* http://globetrotter.berkeley.edu/macarthur/inequality/papers/bardhancrouching. pdf, viewed May 23, 2004.

7. World Bank, *World Development Indicators 2004,* press release, April 23, 2004, http://www.worldbank.org/data/wdi2004.

8. For an analysis of the contrasting South Korean and Taiwanese industrial models, see Tun-jen Cheng, "Distinctions Between the Taiwanese and Korean Approaches to Economic Development," *Journal of East Asian Affairs* 7, no. 1 (Winter–Spring 1993): 116–136.

9. Premier Li Peng, January 31, 1992.

10. Ann Scott Tyson and James L. Tyson, "China's Villages, Part 2: Rural Entrepreneurs Take Root," *Christian Science Monitor,* July 29, 1992, pp. 9–12.

11. Joseph Fewsmith, "The Political and Social Implications of China's Accession to the WTO," *China Quarterly* 167 (September 2001): 578–579.

12. Ibid.

13. For an analysis of changing political relations at the village level in the 1980s–1990s, see Tyrene White, "Reforming the Countryside," *Current History* (September 1992): 273–277.

14. Quoted in Tyson and Tyson, "China's Villages, Part 2," p. 12.

15. Brian Schwarzwalder, "Off the Beaten Track: Rural China in Transition," *China in Transition: A Look Behind the Scenes,* September 25, 2002, http://www. ncuscr.org/public_education/sept%2025%20conference%20report.htm.

16. Wu Bangguo, "Rural Land Contracts Should Be Protected," *People's Daily Online,* September 30, 2003, http://english.peopledaily.com.cn/200309/20/eng 20030920_124589.shtml.

17. David Wall suggests that because of imports of duty-free resources into the SEZs as an incentive for investment, as well as a diversion of a large proportion of production in the SEZs to the domestic market (which is highly profitable and carried out through guanxi-type deals in which officials allow the diversion of production from in-

tended overseas markets), China's SEZs may in fact be a net drain on China's hard currency reserves. David Wall, "SEZs in China: The Administrative and Regulatory Framework," *Journal of East Asian Affairs* 7, no. 1 (Winter–Spring 1993): 226–260.

18. Fewsmith, "The Political and Social Implications," p. 579.

19. *China in Transition: A Look Behind the Scenes,* September 25, 2002, Conference Report by Samantha Blum, http://www.ceip.org/files/pdf/china_092502_summary.pdf, viewed January 13, 2004.

20. Ibid.

21. Most Western observers are convinced that China's leaders will continue economic reform, but they also believe that Adam Smith's laissez-faire economics will in time lead to greater civil and political rights, not just social and economic rights. In David S. G. Goodman and Gerald Segal, eds., *China in the Nineties: Crisis Management and Beyond* (New York: Oxford University Press, 1991), see David Kelly, "Chinese Marxism Since Tiananmen: Between Evaporation and Dismemberment," pp. 30–34; Anita Chan, "The Social Origins and Consequences of the Tiananmen Crisis," pp. 64–86; and Ann Kent, "Human Rights: The Changing Balance Sheet," pp. 105–130. In analyzing the evolution of Marxist values since Tiananmen, some argue that there has not been a mass movement toward popular democracy. Instead, critics inside China have shown more interest in party reform, as well as greater individual opportunity to engage in meaningful dialogue, on the basis of political interaction among the articulate elements of Chinese society, not on the basis of mass participation by the peasants, who currently make up about 70 percent of China's population. Furthermore, even many of the Tiananmen demonstrators were and are strong supporters of political order.

22. International Finance Corporation (IFC), *China's Emerging Private Enterprises: Prospects for the New Century* (Washington, D.C.: IFC, 2000), p. 3.

23. Shao Ren, a Beijing-based scholar, quoted in Joseph Fewsmith, "The Political and Social Implications of China's Accession to the WTO," *China Quarterly* 167 (September 2001): 586.

24. Nicholas R. Lardy, "The Economic Future of China," speech to Rice University and the Texas Asia Society, April 2002, http://www.asiasociety.org/speeches/lardy.html.

25. As a result of the Uruguay Round Agreement on Textiles and Clothing, a full integration of textiles and textile apparel manufactured in countries that are members of the WTO will commence on January 1, 2005. This is the fourth and final phase of the integration. On the aforementioned date, all textiles and textile apparel manufactured in a WTO country and exported on/after January 1, 2005, will no longer be subject to quota restrictions.

26. "Eurocoton, FTA Endorse Istanbul Declaration," *Textile World News,* May 2004, http://www.textileindustries.com/news.htm?cd=2389&id=7155.

27. Glen Hodgson and Mark Worrall, economists at Export Development Canada, quoted in David Hale and Lyric Hughes Hale, "China Takes Off," *Foreign Affairs* (November–December 2003): 46.

28. Knowledge@Wharton, *A Contrarian's View of What's Behind Foreign Direct Investment in China,* http://knowledge.wharton.upenn.edu/index.cfm?fa=view article&id=806, viewed May 27, 2004.

China and Russia

Observe developments soberly, maintain our position, meet challenges calmly, hide our capacities, bide our time, remain free of ambitions, and never claim leadership.
—Deng Xiaoping on the Chinese Communist Party's
response to the crisis of world socialism

Our region is getting integrated into the Asia-Pacific, there is no alternative to that process. . . . We are not choosing our neighbors and we have to maintain friendly relations with China.
—Viktor Ishaev, governor of Khabarovsk Krai[1]

Traditional Rivalries: Qing China and Romanov Russia

China and Russia have one of the longest common borders in the world. Since the seventeenth century, this border, which extends from Afghanistan in the west to Korea in the east, has been the cause of conflict and of diplomatic contact and negotiation. How to determine where Russia meets China has been the theme of Sino-Russian relations for 300 years as an ascendant Russia steadily expanded its sphere of influence into areas claimed by Qing, Nationalist, or Communist China. Even after the establishment of the People's Republic of China (PRC) in 1949, during the era of fraternal relations among communist countries, Chinese fears of Soviet encroachment both into its territory and into its affairs undermined the relationship and led directly to the Sino-Soviet split in 1960. In the 1990s, long after arguments over communist ideology became obsolete, Russian and Chinese diplomats were still meeting to settle acrimonious border issues. Only in 1997–1998 did the two nations finally demarcate their border and normalize relations.

China, in effect, entered into the international system because of its border with Russia. The Treaty of Nerchinsk, signed by Russia and China in 1689, was China's first formal border treaty. Relations were to some degree formalized by this treaty and later agreements, so much so that by 1850 trade had ex-

"Before and after the campaign for the liberation of Nanking, there were some well-meaning friends, both within and without the country, who said that we should be content with separate regimes in North and South China and should not provoke the intervention of imperialism, especially of American imperialism" (written by Kuo Mo-jo; the term *friends* refers to Stalin; quoted in Stuart Schram, *Mao Tse-tung* [Baltimore: Penguin, 1975], p. 245).

panded to the point where almost half of Russia's exports of manufactured goods were going to China.[2] At the same time, however, the Qing dynasty was quickly losing its mandate to rule, allowing England, France, and other Western nations to encroach on Chinese sovereignty. Russia also took advantage of Chinese weakness to expand its political and economic influence in the border areas and particularly in Manchuria. Although the Qing dynasty was increasingly apprehensive of Russian expansion into areas it considered to be part of the Chinese empire, by the mid–nineteenth century it had too many enemies, which prevented it from fighting the Russians vigorously. The Sino-Russian Treaty of Peking, signed in November 1860, opened the entire northern frontier to Russia's political and commercial influence.[3] Inexorably, the czars acquired tracts of land that the Qing empire also claimed. Russia had succeeded in its quest—not dissimilar from that of Europe and the United States in southern China—of creating its own enclaves within China's border areas.

Revolutionary Relations: The Bolsheviks and the Chinese Communists

The Chinese Revolution in 1911 caused hardly a stir in Russia, which had its own political problems. A world war and a revolution similarly prevented Russian interference in Chinese politics. But a Soviet Union led by the Bolshevik Party was dedicated to world revolution against the capitalist powers, whether in their home territories or in their colonies. China, which in the early 1920s was ruled by a jumble of rival military leaders and by foreign powers, seemed to the Bolsheviks to be ripe for revolution.

Lenin and the Third Communist International therefore sought to help China throw off the influence of the imperialist powers and thereby advance international communism. In 1920 the Soviet Union announced that it would relinquish the special privileges, including extraterritoriality, that czarist Russia had acquired through its "unequal" treaties with Qing China. This voluntary abrogation of its special status aroused much admiration for Lenin and the Soviet Union among the growing numbers of nationalist Chinese who sought to end foreign penetration of their country.

Even Sun Yat-sen, the "George Washington of China," was willing to accept help from Moscow. By 1923, the Soviet Union had engineered an uneasy alliance with Sun Yat-sen and his Nationalist (Kuomintang [KMT]) Party. The Soviets believed that Sun was the most likely to succeed in reunifying China and ridding it of foreign influence. To that end, Moscow sent money, advisers, and military equipment. A Nationalist army was organized for the first time, with the assistance of Soviet advisers, and the Nationalist Party was reorganized on the principles of democratic centralism, which guided it well into the 1980s.

The formation of the Chinese Communist Party (CCP) in 1921 did not alter Soviet strategy, which was to ally itself with the group most likely to gain control of China and drive out the capitalist nations. Communist ideology was far less important to Moscow than its ability to damage the imperialist system and to attack the weak links in the imperialist chain that controlled the world's economy. CCP members were therefore required to become members of the Nationalist Party and to submit to its discipline. Zhou Enlai even taught at the Nationalist Party military academy headed by Chiang Kai-shek. The first united front between the Nationalists and Communists barely outlived Sun's death in 1925, however, and the rise of Stalin in Russia and Chiang in China ensured its quick demise.

Chiang began to take control of the Nationalist Party in the mid-1920s and rid it of Communists. Through a series of bloody purges he succeeded, and the Chinese Communists were driven into the interior mountains in the late 1920s. Stalin had advocated a policy of promoting urban revolution through Communist Party activities in China's urban areas. Chiang's victories showed that this policy had been a dismal failure, and by the mid-1930s Mao Zedong had taken control over the CCP on a platform that advocated fomenting agrarian revolution through organizing the peasants first, before moving into the cities. Mao's theory of revolution was the antithesis of Stalin's, and until their dying days each resented the other's claim to know how best to implement a communist revolution in China.

By the late 1930s, the Communists had survived the Long March and were a political power in Yenan. They had succeeded in evading Chiang's troops and were winning plaudits for their campaigns against the Japanese invaders. Stalin was presented with a quandary that he initially tried to solve by urging (with the United States) another KMT-CCP united front, this time to fight the Japanese. The second united front ended in another split, and the Chinese Communists began to gain strength on their own without any substantial aid from the Soviet Union. In any case, the Soviet Union was desperately fighting the Nazis and therefore unable to help either the Nationalist

Party or the CCP in any substantive way. At the end of World War II, after Stalin finally declared war on Japan, Soviet armies moved into Manchuria to drive out the Japanese. Arms confiscated by the Soviets from the Japanese were given to the Chinese Communists, Stalin's only major contribution to the CCP war effort; yet Stalin's order that Manchuria's industrial facilities be dismantled and shipped back to the Soviet Union enraged the Chinese, Communists and Nationalists alike.

Stalin's ineptness in managing Soviet relations with China from the late 1920s through the end of World War II actually strengthened, rather than weakened, Mao Zedong and the Chinese Communists. Mao had carefully cultivated a Communist Party that was beholden to him rather than Stalin, thereby making it more attractive to nationalist Chinese who would support any group whose charter called for expelling all foreign powers from China. Of course, Stalin did not appreciate such independence. During the civil war that followed the end of World War II, as Mao's troops fought the Nationalists for control over all China, some observers came to believe that Stalin preferred a Nationalist China or a China split between Nationalists and Communists to a China controlled by Mao's independent, nationalist Communist Party. A divided China was a weak China, and Stalin's preference for weak neighbors was well known.

Even Stalin, therefore, may have greeted the establishment of the People's Republic of China with mixed emotions. Whereas the outside world was unnerved by the world's most populous nation joining the international communist movement, Stalin feared that so potentially powerful an ally as the Chinese Communists could upset the movement's balance. The PRC was established in 1949, in the same year that Yugoslavia consolidated its maverick status in the international communist movement in an almost cocky manner: "The Communist chieftain of a primitive Balkan country with a population of only 16 million said no to Stalin, chased out Soviet minions, imprisoned Soviet partisans, and dared the Soviet bloc to do its worst."[4] Mao's CCP likewise was beholden to none and was not likely to follow Stalin's every order. The Chinese Communists had achieved the victory hoped for by Lenin and the Bolshevik Party, but at what cost to the international communist movement?

▓ Two Communist Superpowers

After the establishment of the People's Republic of China, Mao chose to "lean to one side," that of the Soviet Union. Washington's anticommunist rhetoric and a common Marxist-Leninist ideology made an alliance between China and the Soviet Union more attractive to Mao than any sort of entente between the United States and China. Mao also hoped a Sino-Soviet alliance would provide some security for his infant regime, especially against Japan, which the Chinese still feared.

So Mao traveled to Moscow in late 1949, and after enduring Stalin's disrespectful treatment, the Sino-Soviet Treaty of Friendship, Alliance, and Mutual Assistance was signed in February 1950. Stalin, according to Mao, "was not willing to sign a treaty. . . . After two months of negotiations he at last signed."[5] The terms of the Sino-Soviet alliance bear out Stalin's reluctance to accord the PRC equal status, rather than the satellite status accorded to the Eastern European nations. China was given the equivalent of $300 million in credits for five years, which it would have to pay back with raw materials at a 1 percent interest rate. Poland received more aid from the Soviet Union than China! In addition, Mao had to accept Soviet control over two major ports in Manchuria and over the Chinese Eastern Railway. Soviet-Chinese joint stock companies were created to exploit mineral deposits in western China and thereby to ensure Soviet economic penetration into the country.[6] Mao had achieved an alliance with the Soviet Union, but at great cost to his personal pride and the pride of the Chinese state. Once again, Russia's traditional goal of expanding its control in the border regions and of controlling its neighbors was more important than a common ideology.

Winter clouds are heavy with snow, which flies like willow catkins,
The myriad blossoms have all faded, and flowers are rare for the moment,
High in the heavens frozen currents whirl imperceptibly,
Only the hero dares pursue the tiger,
Still less does any brave fellow fear the bear,
The plum blossoms rejoice in the snow that fills the sky,
Small wonder that the cold should kill the flies.

In this poem by Mao Zedong, the tiger is U.S. imperialism and the bear is the Soviet Union. Quoted in Stuart Schram, *Mao Tse-tung* (Baltimore: Penguin, 1975), p. 306.

Relations between China and the Soviet Union continued to be difficult, especially after the outbreak of the Korean War in June 1950. Although Mao was probably informed—most likely by the Soviets—of the North Korean decision to invade South Korea prior to the beginning of the campaign, he probably had little input into the decision. Neither Mao nor Stalin expected the commitment of U.S. troops (under the UN umbrella) to fight the North Koreans, and when General Douglas MacArthur began to march north toward the Chinese border, Mao made the agonizing decision to send the China People's Volunteers to North Korea.[7] Three years of bitter fighting led to a stalemate, and not until after Stalin died in 1953 was an armistice finally signed. Mao and Chinese military leaders would not forget, however, that Stalin did not commit Soviet troops to the struggle. Their bitterness at bearing the burdens of the Korean War would not be easily overcome.

To the outward world, however, Sino-Soviet ties appeared to be flourishing. The Soviets provided additional economic aid to China in the form of loans, credits, technical assistance, and training. By 1960, about $2 billion worth of Soviet credits had been extended to China.[8] The Soviets also made some efforts to equalize the political relationship. Nikita Khrushchev visited China in 1954, and he agreed to return to Chinese control the ports, railroad, and joint stock companies that were included in the Sino-Soviet friendship treaty. Just as important to the Chinese was the 1957 Sino-Soviet treaty for nuclear technology cooperation, under which the Soviet Union was to provide China with a sample atomic bomb and technical data on its manufacture.[9] After the death of Stalin, the Soviet leaders appeared to be treating Mao and the People's Republic as their equals rather than as another satellite regime.

However, by the summer of 1960, the Soviet advisers in China—nearly 10,000 people—were called home. To add insult to injury, they were ordered to bring home with them all blueprints and plans. The Chinese were left with Soviet-designed factories and military equipment for which they had no design information. This withdrawal of advisers signaled to the world that the two Communist giants were no longer partners. Although many in Washington came late to an acceptance that the Sino-Soviet split was not a hoax, relations between China and the Soviet Union deteriorated markedly throughout the decade, to the point where they engaged in border skirmishes in the late 1960s.

The reasons for this deterioration in relations were numerous. Some ascribe the origins of Sino-Soviet distrust to the traditional Russian distrust of the Chinese.[10] Others look to historical resentments that turned the Chinese against the Soviets, especially Stalin's lukewarm support for the Chinese Communist Party in its early days. (Soviet economic aid of $2 billion to the People's Republic sounds impressive until one realizes that it was only 40 percent of the aid the United States gave to Taiwan during the same period.[11]) Ideological differences also created tensions. Although Mao resented the way Stalin treated him, he did not approve of Khrushchev's denunciation of Stalin in 1956 or of his de-Stalinization campaign. In particular, Khrushchev's condemnation of the cult of personality hit too close to home for Mao Zedong. The Soviets, for their part, condemned Mao's Great Leap Forward, especially its claim to lead China into pure communism at an accelerated rate. The Soviet Union, after all, was the birthplace of communism and would, Moscow believed, be the first nation to pass through Marx's dictatorship of the proletariat into communism. Foreign relations also played a part in the Sino-Soviet split. China's claims of third world leadership were bound to annoy the Soviets, as Khrushchev's attempts to improve relations with the United States in the late 1950s annoyed China. Khrushchev's handling of the Cuban missile crisis, during which the Chinese believed he caved in to the United States, and Soviet support for India during the Sino-Indian border war—both in 1962— only inflamed the already uneasy relationship.

By the time that the Soviet Union signed the Atmospheric Limited Test Ban Treaty in 1963 (which prohibited nuclear testing in the atmosphere, in outer space, and underwater), after reneging on its promise to aid China's nuclear development, relations were irreparably ruptured. Some even claim that the Soviet Union and the United States considered a joint strike against China's nuclear facilities before China completed work on its own nuclear bomb.[12] A preemptive strike never happened, however, and in October 1964 the PRC exploded its first nuclear bomb. What had been a falling out over historical and ideological issues now became a potentially devastating security threat for the Soviet Union, China, and the world.

Why did the Sino-Soviet alliance degenerate into the Sino-Soviet split in little more than a decade? Instead of being considered a limited economic and security partnership, as exists in most alliance systems, the Sino-Soviet alliance was conceived in broad terms based on a common ideology. Because of the presumed congruence of interests, no mechanism was established to resolve disputes. Neither the Soviets nor the Chinese could admit that serious problems might arise. Disagreements therefore escalated into personal power struggles.[13] Neither Khrushchev's successors nor Mao would compromise. The Sino-Soviet split continued through more dangerous and more passive phases until 1989, when the Soviet Union was on the verge of disintegration.

The Brezhnev Doctrine

Leonid Brezhnev, Khrushchev's successor, consolidated his power as China was descending into the chaos of the Cultural Revolution. Soviet horror at Mao's deliberate decimation of the Communist Party apparatus, offices, and personnel was acute. That the chaos could be curbed only by army control of several provinces exacerbated the Soviet reaction. In Marxist-Leninist societies, the Communist Party was supposed to be the vanguard, leading the masses and controlling the military. That the People's Liberation Army had to be called in to rescue the Chinese regime was anathema to communist doctrine. The Soviet Union, a society that had come to value order and stasis above all else, could not comprehend Mao's ultimately self-destructive drive for a complete revolution in the party and in society.

Brezhnev, of course, had problems closer to home. Czechoslovakia, too, was experimenting with forms of communism that deviated from the Soviet model. The consequences were disastrous for the Czechs and Slovaks, as Soviet tanks rolled into Prague in 1968. The proclamation of the Brezhnev Doctrine, which averred that the Soviet Union had the right to invade any fraternal communist state that did not meet Moscow's expectations, sent a chill through

The Brezhnev Doctrine

"There is no doubt that the peoples of the socialist countries and the Communist Parties have and must have freedom to determine their country's path of development. However, any decision of theirs must damage neither socialism in their own country nor the fundamental interest of the other socialist countries nor the worldwide workers movement, which is waging a struggle for socialism. This means that every Communist Party is responsible not only to its own people but also to all the socialist countries and to the entire Communist movement. Whoever forgets this in placing sole emphasis on the autonomy and independence of Communist Parties lapses into onesideness, shirking his internationalist obligations" (Joseph L. Noggee and Robert H. Donaldson, *Soviet Foreign Policy Since World War II*, 3rd ed. [Elmsford, N.Y.: Pergamon Press, 1984], p. 247).

not only Eastern Europe but also the Asian communist nations. By 1969, the Soviet Union could not get even five of the fourteen ruling communist parties in the world to attend an international communist conference in Moscow. China, North Korea, North Vietnam, Albania, and Yugoslavia boycotted the proceedings. The conference communiqué illustrated the weakness of international communism. It did not censure the Chinese Communists, as the Soviets had hoped it would, and it observed that there was "no leading center of the international communist movement."[14]

This was further proven later in 1969 when Soviet and Chinese armed forces fought in the border areas. Some, notably Henry Kissinger, then the U.S. national security adviser, believed the Soviets were responsible for the confrontations.[15] Most believed, however, that forces loyal to Lin Biao, China's defense minister, initiated hostilities as part of the struggle for leadership going on in Beijing and throughout China during the Cultural Revolution. Tensions continued to mount in the 1970s, especially after the Vietnamese, who were Soviet allies, invaded Cambodia, and after the Soviets invaded Afghanistan. Indeed, despite military needs on the southern and western borders of the Soviet Union, U.S. intelligence experts estimated that nearly one-quarter of all Soviet military forces were aligned against China in the 1970s.[16] The Soviet Union obviously felt the need to contain the Chinese, a tremendous drain on its military and economic resources that became insupportable within a decade.

Indisputably, the greatest impact of the Sino-Soviet border clashes, coming so soon after Soviet tanks rolled into Prague, was that they illustrated to all communist nations and to the entire world that international communism was a chimera. From 1969 onward, it was evident that only military force, and not ideology, bound the nations of Eastern Europe to the Soviet Union. For China, the Soviet Union's military strength became a source of great fear, so much so that rapprochement with the United States, the capitalist enemy, seemed preferable to nonalignment with either side in the Cold War. The progression of the Sino-Soviet split into open hostilities was seen as irrefutable proof by many that traditional power relations continued to be overriding determinants of state-to-state relations, never to be superseded by ideological beliefs or other "low" political factors.

Even the world's greatest military powers cannot afford to practice broad-scale containment for an extended period of time, however, and by the early 1980s both Soviet and Chinese leaders were issuing statements calling for a lessening of tensions. In 1979, the Chinese announced their conditions for a normalization of relations: reduction of Soviet troops in the border areas, Soviet withdrawal from Afghanistan and Mongolia, and an end to Soviet support for Vietnam's invasion of Cambodia.[17] Leonid Brezhnev responded in his Tashkent speech of March 1982 by calling for normalization of relations. The Soviet quagmire in Afghanistan, its economic problems, and its isolation from the third world combined to make it less of a threat to the Chinese. In addition, with President Ronald Reagan assuming office in the United States after an election campaign in which he promised to review U.S. relations with Taiwan, Beijing became nervous about U.S. intentions and was therefore more willing to explore ways to reduce tensions with the Soviets.[18] At the same time, the Soviets became more and more anxious to reallocate their resources from the border with China to other, more pressing areas. Full Sino-Soviet normalization of relations would not come quickly, however, because old antagonisms were not easy to overcome and because of the stasis in the Soviet political system as one leader after another died in office.

Gorbachev and Sino-Soviet Relations

Finally, in 1986, a new Soviet leader called for a new China policy. Mikhail Gorbachev, the new secretary-general of the Soviet Communist Party, was eager to reduce Sino-Soviet tensions so he could reduce military spending. He was also eager to find economic partners, particularly to furnish the consumer goods in such short supply in the Soviet Union. In a speech in Vladivostok, which is in the Soviet Far East and abuts China, Gorbachev called for an end to a China encirclement policy. As a direct result of Gorbachev's Vladivostok speech, talks began in 1987 between the Soviets and the Chinese on issues including demarcation of the frontier. Sino-Soviet economic interactions also expanded dramatically. Trade between Heilongjiang province and the Soviet

Union increased 95 percent between 1986 and 1987, and trade between Xinjiang province and the Soviet Union increased 75 percent during the same period. Even more startling, the Chinese Communist Party sent a delegation to Moscow to attend the celebration of the seventieth anniversary of the Bolshevik Revolution, and Chinese officials in Beijing held a reception to honor the occasion.[19]

Mikhail Gorbachev's thoughts extended beyond Soviet relations with China alone to a conceptualization of an East Asian security system. In a 1988 speech in Krasnoyarsk, in Central Asia, Gorbachev included a seven-point proposal that he reiterated throughout his tenure. Gorbachev called for the following steps to reduce tensions in East Asia: discussions relating to a freeze on nuclear weapons in the region; balanced reduction of naval and air forces in the area and limits on their activities; further actions to reduce the risk of incidents at sea and in the air; and opening security talks between the Soviet Union, the United States, and the People's Republic.[20] Gorbachev could not achieve an East Asian security system, or even a multilateral security conference, but he did convince the Chinese that a Soviet Union that practiced glasnost and perestroika was a less threatening neighbor than a Soviet Union that espoused the Brezhnev Doctrine.

Gorbachev's efforts to fulfill China's three prerequisites for a normalization of relations bore fruit. On May 15, 1989, Gorbachev arrived in Beijing for a summit meeting, the first visit by a Soviet leader since Khrushchev visited China in the 1950s. Ironically, Gorbachev arrived in Beijing just as China was being riven by demonstrations in Tiananmen Square against corruption in the Chinese Communist Party and for more openness in society. The students and workers who took to the streets knew that the world press would be in Beijing for the summit meeting and planned their protests for maximum coverage from foreign television networks. No real decisions could be made at the summit—when Deng

"The still uneasy nature of Sino-Soviet relations in 1989 was illustrated in Foreign Minister Qian Qichen's review of the People's Republic's foreign relations. Qian wrote of 'Soviet big-power chauvinist performances . . . breaching contracts, withdrawing experts, pressing for the repayment of debts, deploying heavy concentrations of troops along the border and provoking clashes. In the following decades [1960–1980], not once did the Soviet Union abandon its military threat against China'" (Allen S. Whiting, "China's Foreign Relations After 40 Years," in Anthony J. Kane, ed., *China Briefing, 1990* [Boulder, Colo.: Westview, 1990], pp. 70–71).

Xiaoping did not even control the streets of Beijing and Gorbachev had to enter the Great Hall of the People through a back door—but the point had been made. China and the Soviet Union had finally opened a dialogue after nearly thirty years of unremitting hostility.

Over the next two years Soviet and Chinese delegations met frequently and increasingly profitably, although the Chinese leaders were not happy with the Soviet decision not to interfere with the revolutions in Eastern Europe in late 1989. Paradoxically, China had been a leading critic of the Brezhnev Doctrine in 1968. In 1989, when Gorbachev decided to let Eastern Europe go its own way, the Chinese leaders were equally discomforted by the wholesale rush to abandon communism. Although Deng Xiaoping offered a cautious response, the implications for the remaining communist regimes in the world were obvious and unsettling. Nevertheless, realist politics and economic imperatives again triumphed over ideological differences. As Li Peng told a German magazine, "This normalization does not apply to the ties between the two communist parties; only the relations between the two sides have again returned to normal."[21] In other words, China and the Soviet Union were moving toward state-to-state relations that would be considered normal between a superpower and a large regional power. Issues of Communist Party relations, ideological differences, and the like, were not a part of the equation.

This was best illustrated by the series of moves that ensued to improve military relations. Gorbachev had demobilized 200,000 troops, reduced the Soviet Pacific fleet by one-third, withdrawn Soviet troops from Mongolia and Afghanistan, and destroyed the intermediate-range ballistic missile force east of the Urals.[22] By May 1990, Chinese fears of the Soviet military had abated to the point that Central Military Commission vice chairman Liu Huaqing visited Moscow to discuss Chinese purchase of Soviet weapon systems and technology.[23] On May 16, 1991, Party Secretary Jiang Zemin visited Moscow to witness the signing of an agreement on border issues by the foreign ministers of the Soviet Union and the People's Republic, nearly 300 years after the first Russo-Chinese border treaty. China even extended $1 billion in commodity credits to Russia.

Ironically, a rift that began at least partially over interpretations of communist ideology outlived the birthplace of communism itself. The border agreement, which was initially agreed to by the Soviet Union and China, was ratified by the Russian Supreme Soviet in February 1992. In March 1992, the foreign ministers of Russia and the People's Republic exchanged the instruments of ratification.[24] Not only had the Sino-Soviet split officially ended, but the Soviet Union had also officially ended. Relations between Russia and China would henceforth be based on the same political, military, and economic factors that govern relations between most nation-states in the post–Cold War international system.

▩ The End of Communism

The unthinkable occurred in August 1991. After a coup attempt against Gorbachev failed, he was forced to dissolve the Soviet Communist Party and, by December, to announce the end of the Soviet Union. China had become the largest and (with the exception of small nations such as Cuba, North Korea, and Vietnam) virtually the only communist nation left in the world. Understandably, the Chinese Communist leaders were nonplussed. With the rest of the world, they had watched Gorbachev's moves with a mixture of fascination and dread, and they were as surprised as everyone else by the precipitate collapse of the entire Soviet political and economic apparatus.

Chinese preferences in the battle over Soviet reform were never expressed openly, but it is clear that most leaders in Beijing preferred Soviet hard-liners to the reformers. In 1989, Chinese leaders regarded Gorbachev as a class traitor who let Eastern Europe succumb to capitalist encroachment. By 1991, however, with the rise of Boris Yeltsin, the Chinese Communist Party supported Gorbachev, especially because Gorbachev was increasingly forced to rely on more hard-line supporters.[25] Gorbachev had become the lesser of two evils.

The coup attempt therefore seemed to the Chinese leaders to be a godsend, an opportunity for orthodox Communists to restore the Communist Party of the Soviet Union to its correct role. Indeed, the coup leaders, realizing that they would have a sympathetic audience in Beijing, may have warned China's leaders of their plans beforehand. Army chief of staff Chi Haotian met with Soviet defense minister Dimitri Yazov in Moscow on August 12, and when Chi returned to Beijing he reported to an enlarged Politburo meeting on August 18, the day before the coup attempt. When the coup began, the Chinese press carried many articles, mostly favorable, that were perhaps prepared ahead of time.[26] Chinese disappointment at the failure of the coup attempt was acute, although in accordance with Deng Xiaoping's guidance regarding the CCP response to the crisis of world socialism, the public response was muted.

Within party circles, however, the mood was bitter. The official line was that the Soviet Union had collapsed because glasnost had been carried out too far and perestroika not far enough. Gorbachev, according to this school of thought, had erred in managing the reform process rather than dealing with the structural defects of the Soviet system. He had also erred in his precipitate introduction of political and economic reforms in a nation suffering from an "excessive centralization of political and economic power [that] fostered bureaucratism, personal arbitrariness, patriarchy, lifelong official tenure and all sorts of privileges and corruption."[27] Gorbachev's reforms undermined the Communist Party of the Soviet Union, leaving him no base of support.[28]

Others attributed the collapse of the Soviet Union to a more sinister motive: a U.S. policy of peaceful evolution. The United States, according to this school of analysis, seeks to undermine the values of socialism through economic, political, and cultural penetration of socialist states accompanied by Western assistance and commerce.[29] Gorbachev, by opening up the Soviet Union to Western influences, some Chinese leaders believed, had allowed a pernicious anticommunism to invade and destroy the Soviet Union.

Whichever theory they espouse to explain the collapse the Soviet Union, all of Beijing's leaders were badly frightened by the events in Eastern Europe and the former parts of the Soviet Union. China's leaders are now even more convinced that they were right in suppressing the Tiananmen student demonstrations in light of the mass demonstrations that led to the collapse of communist regimes in Eastern Europe. At the same time, they congratulate themselves on China's successes in avoiding Soviet economic mistakes, which they attribute largely to the reforms introduced by Deng Xiaoping and his followers.

Since 1989, overt political opposition in China has been stifled, and therefore Chinese civil society today has few organized forces capable of challenging the ruling CCP. Chinese leaders are convinced that the retention of party rule and authoritarian government is also essential for the development, well-being, and stability of the Chinese nation, as well as the avoidance of all the political turmoil and splitting apart of states that has occurred in the former communist world. Perestroika without glasnost has therefore become the modus operandi of the Chinese leaders.

The Four Modernizations Versus Glasnost and Perestroika

The end of Soviet communism gave rise to a debate that will undoubtedly last for generations. What did Deng Xiaoping do right in his attempts to reform Chinese communism? What did Mikhail Gorbachev do wrong? Why did Deng's reforms bring China to the verge of economic "takeoff," whereas Gorbachev's reforms only deepened the Soviet economic crisis? How did Deng Xiaoping manage to survive the massive demonstrations at Tiananmen Square, whereas Gorbachev's Soviet Union could not outlast a bumbling coup attempt? What were the critical differences?

When analyzing what was wrong with their systems, Deng and Gorbachev came to completely opposite conclusions. Deng concluded that communism would be preserved in China only if the living standards of the people improved, and he concluded that this could happen only if the economy were liberalized and private enterprises were encouraged. Because Deng's purpose was preservation of the communist system he had wrested from the ashes of the Cultural Revolution, political reform was not his goal; rather, he sought to preserve power for those he had appointed to office since returning from political exile. A combination of an open economy and a strong Communist Party, Deng believed, was the best insurance of a wealthier and more powerful China.

Gorbachev approached the Soviet Union's problems from a diametrically opposed perspective. He viewed the Communist Party apparatus, which had not been shaken up since the horrors of Stalin's purges, as the cause of the Soviet Union's problems. The *apparatchiki* were, Gorbachev believed, interested only in preserving their own perquisites and were unalterably opposed to any changes, even if these changes would benefit the Soviet people. So Gorbachev tried to restructure the Communist Party apparatus first through allowing public criticism of its defects and by replacing Khrushchev- and Brezhnev-era cadres with his own appointments. No overarching plan for economic change was ever developed, and the proposals for economic restructuring that Gorbachev put forth were either extremely limited in scope, proposed but never implemented, or implemented in such a halfhearted fashion that they were bound to fail.

Deng and Gorbachev, of course, faced different obstacles. Deng had to restructure a political system that had collapsed. Gorbachev had to shake up a system that had become desiccated. Deng wanted to effect change in a country where 80 percent of the people were still peasants after forty years of communism and where state-owned industries were still responsible for an overwhelming percentage of the gross national product. Gorbachev had to cope with work habits formed by seventy years of communism. Although the Soviets had successfully transformed their people from illiterate peasants to educated comrades, a large percentage of the people worked for the party, for the state, or in state-owned industries that barely functioned. After Stalin's brutal collectivization of agriculture, Soviet agricultural workers on state farms and collectives had adopted the same attitudes and work habits as their industrial comrades. Deng could begin simply by allowing China's peasants to sell some of the crops they produced on their plots of land. Gorbachev had no such simple option to initiate economic change.

Similarities Between China and the Soviet Union

Some argue that too much is made of the differences, that actually many similarities existed between China and the Soviet Union. For example, Marshall Goldman, an expert on the Soviet economy, argues that Chinese agriculture suffers from the same capital deficiencies as did Soviet agriculture; yet the Chinese increased their output and shipments to urban areas with only a modest increase in storage facilities and without building new ones. They did this through allowing the peasants to operate on their own,[30] something Gorbachev now regrets not doing. In January 1993 Gorbachev said, "I consider it my biggest miscalculation that we did not take agriculture as the starting point of the reform process and that we stopped halfway."[31] Goldman extends his critique of Gorbachev's methods of economic reform:

> Several important lessons arise out of China's experiences. Build institutions such as private businesses—banking and manufacturing first, or at least simultaneously. Agricultural reform, and the creation of private agriculture in particular, is crucial. Peasants, service personnel, and workers should also be encouraged to dabble in handicraft work and manufacturing. Economic incentives should be designed to tempt large numbers of people into becoming entrepreneurs.[32]

Closer analysis of the purported differences also reveals many similarities in terms of politics. Gorbachev's attempts to reform the Communist Party structure through opening it to criticism mortally wounded the party instead of revitalizing it. New and vigorous appointments could not reinvigorate a system that only a few old believers still had faith in. In China, the Communist Party apparatus survives, but it, too, is mortally wounded. Instead of the party imploding as it did in the Soviet Union, the Chinese Communist Party is becoming increasingly irrelevant. It is already despised by the Chinese people for its corruption. The new generation of entrepreneurs either ignore the party or bribe its cadres, and the best and the brightest join the party only if forced into it or given special privileges. Few believe that the CCP will maintain its vanguard role for many more years. Instead, many believe that the CCP will either transform itself into a totalitarian ruler backed by the military or wither away as did the Communist Party of the Soviet Union. Thus Deng's victory may be a pyrrhic one. The Chinese Communist Party still rules, but with little support from the masses and few prospects for the future.

How to Preserve Communism in China?

Despite the reluctance of many Chinese leaders to admit it, China was even more open to Western economic penetration than was the Soviet Union. The demonstrations at Tiananmen Square illustrated that values borrowed from the West, especially the value of democracy, were already affecting China's student population. Two groups argued over the approach the Chinese Communist Party would have to take to ensure that it, too, did not end up in the dustbin of history. Party conservatives argued that the collapse of the Communist Party of the Soviet Union showed that China should mount a class struggle and a vigorous campaign against bourgeois ideology. Deng Xiaoping, however, argued that the Soviet Communist Party's problems were caused by a lack of the sort of change he spearheaded in China. Poverty, Deng asserted, would lead to demands for change. Only continued reform and opening could save China.[33] Deng triumphed, and economic reform and growth became the guiding principle of the CCP in the post–Cold War era. The question that Deng's successors will have to face is whether economic reform and growth are enough to sustain a ruling Communist Party. It was not enough to sustain the Soviet Communist Party, the most powerful one in the world. Will the fate of the CCP be any different?

Russia and China in the Twenty-First Century

China's relations with Russia in the post–Cold War era are governed by the same dynamics that govern all interstate relations in the international system. Issues of state sovereignty, interdependence, and balance of power dominate China's policymaking with respect to Russia, the other states of the former Soviet Union, and the rest of the world. China and Russia continue to be the dominant military powers in East Asia by virtue of their size and their possession of nuclear weapons. The United States and Japan also play prominent roles. Their interactions with each other and with the other nations of East Asia will determine the nature of security issues in the region. And there are many security issues that have to be addressed.

The Chinese may be among those who rue the end of the Cold War and the certain sort of security that a bipolar world system offered. Now, many Chinese balance a fear of a unipolar world led by the United States with an equally great fear of a nationalist, obstreperous Russia. Equally frightening to the Chinese is the possibility of Russian political instability, which could spill over into Central Asia and thereby threaten Chinese security. Both of these scenarios—an aggressive Russia or a state that is dissolving into further political and economic chaos—would threaten Chinese security, so much so that China might consider once again "tilting" toward the United States despite fears of U.S. hegemony.

Alternatively, Russia may overcome its current political and economic instability and develop a centrist foreign policy such that Russia and China will work together to solve East Asian security issues, thereby working toward their goal of a multipolar rather than a U.S.-dominated

> ### Li Peng on Sino-Russian Relations
>
> China and Russia "share long borders which should be peaceful and friendly ones. . . . The economies of the two countries are strongly complementary and their economic and trade relations have experienced rapid development in recent years. . . . Both China and Russia should proceed from reality to explore new ways for further bilateral cooperation" (BBC, *Summary of World Broadcasts,* February 25, 1994).

unipolar international system. Elements of this type of foreign policy were already put into place by the Yeltsin government and have been continued by President Vladimir Putin. To that end, the Shanghai Cooperative Organization (SCO)—comprising China, Russia, Kazakhstan, Kyrgyzstan, Tajikistan, and Uzbekistan—was established in 1996 to enhance regional security, preserve stability, and contain separatist groups and religious extremists. And China, Russia, and the United States, in the wake of the September 11, 2001, terrorist attacks in the United States as well as the Chechen attacks in Russia, have a huge incentive to closely monitor potential terrorist organizations; yet China and Russia also fear the expanded U.S. military presence around the world, particularly in Afghanistan and the Middle East. Indeed, in August 2003, China, Russia, Kazakhstan, Kyrgyzstan, and Tajikistan held joint antiterrorist exercises on the Chinese border, the first time China had participated in multilateral joint military maneuvers.

Economic Relations

Bilateral Chinese-Russian trade in 2003 reached $15 billion, up from $12 billion in 2002. This total, while a tiny percentage of China's foreign trade, was actually larger than that for U.S.-Russian trade during the same years. Despite the relatively low volume of trade, at least from the Chinese perspective, economic relations have progressed steadily from virtually nil to barter trade to cross-border trade in low-level consumer goods to high-level discussions regarding major energy projects. As with Chinese-Russian political relations, Chinese-Russian economic relations are becoming routine, and transactions are more closely following international trade norms. China values access to Russian energy resources[34] and Russian arms, while Russia seeks to develop the economy of its eastern provinces. Currently, China sells Russia footwear, garments, foodstuffs, electronics, and machinery, while Russia sells China fertilizer, rolled steel, refined oil, aluminum, and timber. According to a Russian international affairs adviser, "Our joint ventures [with China] now exceed those with Japan, South Korea and the United States combined, mostly in trade, timber and

> The Sino-Soviet Treaty of Friendship, Alliance, and Mutual Assistance, signed by Mao and Stalin in 1950, created a joint-stock company that was to exploit Xinjiang's natural resources, ostensibly for the benefit of both nations. Very much resented by the Chinese, Khrushchev renounced any Soviet interest in the joint-stock company. Even this could not prevent the downward spiral of Sino-Soviet relations in Xinjiang. In the late 1960s, the two nations fought several times at their borderline and nearby.

wood processing."[35] Nevertheless, the traditional mistrust—as evidenced by the xenophobic reaction to limited Chinese immigration into the Russian Far East in the 1990s—combined with the low level of trade in actual terms and the focus of the international trade system on the United States, Europe, and Japan, has led many analysts to believe that trade will not become the major factor in stabilizing Chinese-Russian relations in the near future.

China and Russia also hope to increase trade with their Central Asian neighbors. Member states of the Shanghai Cooperative Organization, initially established with a security mission, are now discussing the establishment of a SCO free trade zone. China can provide cheap consumer goods of relatively high quality, which are in short supply and in great demand in former communist countries and Soviet republics. These countries, in turn, have many natural resources that are badly needed in China and capable of being exploited through joint ventures. The desire to serve as a successful model of economic reform in communist societies may also be a force driving China to increase economic interactions; indeed, Russian economic reformers have visited China's special economic zones. Although trade between China and the SCO states will undoubtedly increase and diversify, trade relations with the United States, Western Europe, Japan, and the Four Little Tigers will continue to be more important. Only those countries can provide China and Russia with the capital and the technical know-how needed to develop their economies successfully.

Military Relations

In November 1993, Russia and China signed a five-year military cooperation agreement that would provide China with military technology. According to the U.S. Department of Defense, "Beijing reportedly purchased approximately $1.0 billion worth of Russian weaponry a year on average during the 1990s, accounting for about one-quarter of total Russian arms sales. . . . These sales have increased in the late-1990s. Russian leaders are not expected to reduce significantly their sales effort in China even under pressure. Similarly, improved U.S.-Russian relations after the September 11 terrorist attacks are unlikely to cause Moscow to scale down arms transfers to Beijing."[36] As China modernizes its armed forces, it has relied on upgrading its armaments with Russian imports, which are compatible with the resources it acquired during the period of Sino-Soviet friendship. With the deterioration of the Russian military, the clear superiority of U.S. weaponry, and China's desire to develop its own research and development infrastructure, in all likelihood Russian arms sales to China will become less important over time.

Yet the balance is delicate for all parties engaged in the arms trade. The United States is unnerved by signs of Russo-Chinese military cooperation, and Washington has urged Russia not to sell China aircraft and certain long-range bombers.[37] This complicated military interchange among the United States, Russia, China, and Taiwan illustrates well the complexities of the post–Cold War world. Will Russia and China continue to expand military ties, or will a nationalist revival in Russia force China to improve relations with the United States? How will China deal with its fears of a bloc of Muslim states in Central Asia? And will Russian and U.S. relations with Taiwan alarm the Chinese sufficiently to provoke them into action?

How to Deal with Central Asia?

Five Central Asian republics have emerged from the wreckage of the Soviet Union: Kazakhstan, Turkmenistan, Uzbekistan, Kyrgyzstan, and Tajikistan. Together these republics have a population of 50 million indigenous peoples who adhere to Islam. But there is also a large Russian minority. Three have a common border with the province of Xinjiang in northwestern China. The non-Han residents of Xinjiang have far more in common with their brethren in the new Islamic republics (sometimes even close relatives) than they do with the Chinese leaders in Beijing. Always a source of tension, the Xinjiang border area is becoming more fluid and at the same time potentially more volatile. Formerly, Xinjiang abutted the Soviet Union, and no other outside influences were allowed. Now Turkey, Saudi Arabia, Iran, and Pakistan are all competing to win friends in the Islamic areas of the former Soviet Union.[38]

What are China's policy choices in dealing with the newly independent Central Asian republics? Although the status of these republics might seem to be a stimulus to demands for independence in Xinjiang, long an extremely sensitive issue in Beijing, China's leaders will not allow any such eventuality. Since the era of the Sino-Soviet split, China has exerted strong control over Xinjiang, and it has been careful to settle the province with Han Chinese loyal to Beijing. Rather, the greatest danger to regional security is probably the danger of civil war within the republics. Fighting in Tajikistan from 1992–1997 illustrates the fragility of the new nations.

Beijing's leaders are united in their desire to keep a low profile in Central Asia while trying to establish regular lines of communication. China's interests in the area are defensive, as it seeks to prevent any instability in the region from reaching its borders. U.S. scholars believe that Beijing's Central Asia policy is shaped by four principal sets of interests: strategic positioning, national security, border stability, and economics and trade.[39] In order that its political, economic, and military resources not be diverted from China's primary international and domestic goals, Beijing seeks to maintain stability in Central Asia. If that requires working with Russia, acquiescing to the presence of U.S. troops in the region, and forming a regional security organization, the benefits to China will come in the form of preventing separatism, working together to combat terrorism, developing trade, and securing access to new energy sources. According to Bates Gill, a China specialist at the Center for Strategic and International Studies in Washington, D.C., "The Chinese are sending people all the time to meet prime ministers and presidents and generals and all the way down the diplomatic ladder. . . . This is all about soft power, and strategic and diplomatic relationships. . . . Central Asia is a fantastic lens or model for what China is trying to do all over its periphery: reaching out and settling old scores, and trying to establish a benign kind of hegemony."[40]

Foreign Policy Decisionmaking

Before Russia and China can develop a comprehensive, long-term approach to security issues in East Asia, both sides will have to decide how they wish to develop the policymaking framework. In Russia today, the foreign policy establishment is in the midst of a debate over what principles will guide it over the next few decades. Should Russia adopt a Sino-centric policy favoring ties with China, a Nippon-centric policy favoring ties with Japan, or a pragmatic and flexible balance-of-power approach[41] that would balance Japanese economic strength through economic ties to China and balance Chinese military strength through ties to Japan, the United Nations, and others? The discussion over how to direct a proposed oil pipeline from Russia, whether to Japan or to China, illustrates this conundrum.[42]

China's leaders are asking similar questions. What are their foreign policy and security goals? First, they would like to avoid any spillover of disorder in neighboring regions into China's periphery regions. Although contact cannot be cut off between people with similar cultural traits on both sides of the border, Beijing seeks to maintain formal diplomatic relations with its neighbors based on the principle of noninterference in each other's affairs. Second, even though China's leaders can be highly critical of the present leadership in former communist countries, particularly those that have joined the North Atlantic Treaty Organization (NATO) and supported U.S. intervention in Iraq to oust Saddam Hussein, they realize that open antagonisms in the current situation serve no purpose, and they have therefore sought to establish correct relations with the nations of Eastern Europe and the former Soviet republics. Third, both China and its former communist neighbors have reason to cooperate politically to solve continuing problems, such as border issues that have poisoned relations in the past, as well as ideological disagreements. To that end, despite some misgivings, China has generally been supportive of the former Soviet Republics in Central Asia as a source of stability and a protection against further spread of disintegrative nationalism.[43] It serves no purpose to create political and ideological tensions or to support particular groups in neighboring states during the rapid and uncertain transition both inside China and in the former communist world. A chronological listing of important events in Russian-Chinese rapprochement is included in Table 4.1.

Table 4.1   Normalization of Chinese-Russian Relations, 1992–2003

September 1992	Decree on the Russian Federation's relations with China	Russia agrees to not establish official relations with Taiwan
December 1992	Boris Yeltsin visits China	First summit meeting between Russia and China results in a joint statement on the foundation of mutual relations
September 1994	President Jiang Zemin visits Russia	Russia and China agree not to be the first to use nuclear weapons or target nuclear missiles against each other; western sector of the China-Russia border is demarcated
May 1995	Jiang visits Russia to attend the fiftieth anniversary ceremonies of the World War II victory	Russia confirms its opposition to Taiwan joining the UN; China supports Russia's membership in the Asia-Pacific Economic Cooperation
April 1996	Yeltsin visits China	China supports Russia's concerns about eastern expansion of the North Atlantic Treaty Organization; trade increases; establishment of the Shanghai Cooperative Organization
April 1997	Jiang visits Russia	Jiang expresses concern about a unipolar world
November 1997	Yeltsin's third visit to China	Demarcation of the eastern border; establishment of a biannual meeting at the prime ministerial level
May 2003	Hu Jintao visits Russia, his first foreign visit after becoming president	Chinese and Russian foreign ministers meet twelve times and hold ten telephone talks; seventy Russian and forty Chinese delegations at or above the deputy minister level visit each other's countries during 2003

Sources: Yu Bin, "Living with Normalcy," *Pacific Forum CSIS Comparative Connections: An E-Journal on East Asian Bilateral Relations,* 4th Quarter 2003, p. 7, http://www. csis.org/pacfor/cc/0304qchina-rus.html; and Chen Qimao, "Sino-Russian Relations After the Break-Up of the Soviet Union," in Gennady Chufrin, ed., *Russia and Asia-Pacific Security* (Stockholm: Stockholm International Peace Research Institute, 1999), pp. 129–130, http://www.projects.sipri.se/russia/.

As China's leaders look to the north and northwest, the former republics of the Soviet Union pose opportunities and dangers. Conservatives and reformers alike are still trying to recover from the shock of seeing the Soviet Union come apart, and they will do whatever is necessary to try to prevent similar happenings in China by avoiding the mistakes they think were made in Moscow. The collapse of the Soviet Union changed the geopolitical power structure, ended the Cold War, and for the foreseeable future, reduced any major security threat to China from its neighbors to the north and northwest. Yet Putin's realpolitik, which in one sense Chinese policymakers approve, has also unnerved them, as his understanding of U.S. primacy has led to Russian compromises on NATO, the antiballistic missile treaty, and other multilateral issues that Chinese conservatives believe have weakened Moscow's international position. China, with its successful market developments, believes it provides a model, which may have many lessons for its former communist neighbors, on how to develop and modernize their societies through adopting market capitalism. But "Russian pessimists assess China as a potential threat to Russia and advocate avoidance of measures that would strengthen China, including arms and technology transfers. Optimists believe that China is stable, which is in Russia's interest and that China's military modernization is not offensive in nature, with the possible exception of Taiwan."[44]

Policy Options

China's leaders observed the collapse of communism with some disquiet, but Beijing's relations with the former communist world are as good or better than during the height of the Cold War. China's policy options in its relations with the former communist world and with the few remaining communist states are far more varied than at any time since the founding of the People's Republic.

Option 1: Pursuing Nonalignment

China and Russia seek to maintain good relations based on the five principles of peaceful coexistence, while at the same time taking advantage of opportunities to cooperate on specific issues. Both Beijing and Moscow share a common interest in creating stable security conditions in Asia, especially in Northeast Asia, because this would reduce Japan's temptation to rearm. Beijing and Moscow also have an interest in increasing trade and good relations among countries in Southeast Asia because regional arms races could lead to a resurgence of U.S. military activity in Asia as well as a rapid militarization of Japan.

Option 2: Chinese-Russian Military Cooperation

Although it is not in Beijing's or Moscow's interest to seek formal military alignments in the post–Cold War era, both nations are already benefiting by sharing military technology and trading weapons for hard cash or consumer goods. The two nations also have a common interest in maintaining stability and preventing conflict in Asia. Continued military cooperation, however, must be carried out in ways that do not alarm Japan, the United States, and other nations in Asia. Moreover, China and Russia will have to overcome over two centuries of distrust and tension that in the past have led to military engagements. China and Russia's strategic partnership "offers both countries the opportunity to overcome possible isolation in international affairs and helps them to assert their specific national interests vis-à-vis uncooperative Western nations":[45]

- Current Russian arms sales to China benefit both sides. Moscow gets hard currency for sales of advanced military aircraft and cheap Chinese consumer goods for sales of other weapons. The military complexes of both countries benefit from joint ventures to produce arms. These transactions are a major source of trade, involving billions of dollars of arms, consumer goods, and hard cash. China's arms purchases from the Russians are essential to the modernization of its military forces, especially because the United States, Japan, and other nations restrict sales of military technology to China.
- Both Beijing and Moscow share a common interest in creating stable security conditions in Central Asia. China seeks to squash separatist groups on its western borders, and both China and Russia fear the rise of fundamentalist influence in the Muslim populations in Central Asia. To prevent regional arms races and increasing U.S. influence in Central Asia, another fear shared by China and Russia, both nations also have an interest in helping create a stable Central Asia.

Option 3: Promoting Trade and Investment

In the economic realm, Moscow and Beijing have growing opportunities to increase both trade and investment. Beijing would like to diversify its trade, which is still heavily oriented toward the United States, Japan, Hong Kong, and Taiwan. The Russian market seems one obvious choice for expansion of Chinese trade. China may also serve as a model of reform to Russia as Moscow seeks to marketize its economy:

- Beijing views Russian Siberia as a potential source of raw materials just waiting to be developed through joint ventures involving China,

Russia, and other Asian countries. The proposed oil pipeline project, which China wants developed through its territory rather than through Russia to Japan, is the best example of this policy.

- China could provide skilled and disciplined labor for joint ventures while South Korea, Hong Kong, and Taiwan could provide the capital. Siberian raw materials, such as timber and minerals, could then be exported to all these countries in exchange for consumer goods.

Option 4: Promoting Multipolarity

At the multilateral, global level, geopolitical realities dictate that in some instances Moscow and Beijing will have complementary interests while at other times they will be in conflict. Both nations, however, will have a vested interest in promoting multipolarity. With the United States being the sole remaining superpower, fear of U.S. hegemony in the international system will drive both China and the Soviet Union to promote shifting alliances as a tactic to encourage a balance of power:

- Both nations seek to preserve their veto privileges and special rights as permanent members of the UN Security Council. Chinese and Russian leaders believe that other arrangements are likely to strengthen Western or third world domination of the global security system at their expense. China and Russia oppose UN intervention inside states, whether to promote basic human rights or to encourage regime compliance as in the case of Iraq. China and Russia agree that such intervention is a violation of the sovereign rights of states and the five basic principles of peaceful coexistence; moreover, they fear U.S. dominance of the UN agenda.
- Chinese-Russian rivalries continue even in the post–Cold War world. Both nations are competing for trade, economic assistance, and technology transfer from global economic regimes such as the World Bank and the International Monetary Fund, as well as from the United States, the European Union, and Japan.
- Should radical changes take place inside Russia that lead to nationalist irredentism, China is likely, for geopolitical reasons, to join with the West and other regions in using global security structures to restrain Russian expansionism into the former Soviet Union.

Option 5: Promoting a Peaceful
Balance-of-Power System in Central Asia

Beijing is likely to continue its current policy in Central Asia of supporting a balance of power among the Central Asian states and their neighbors. This seems preferable to the future unification of the five Islamic states in the region. At the same time, Beijing may work to lessen tensions in the area, because the most destabilizing and threatening scenario to China would be the rise of fundamentalist Islamic forces; such a scenario might promote instability among the indigenous Islamic groups inside Xinjiang, China's northwestern province. By working closely with both Iran and Pakistan, Beijing hopes to maintain some type of balance within the region, lessening the danger that overt hostilities will spill over into China's western border areas.

Discussion Questions

1. What were the reasons for cooperation between China and the Soviet Union in the 1950s?
2. From the Chinese perspective, what were the sources of conflict between China and the Soviet Union during the Cold War years?
3. From the Russian perspective, what were the sources of conflict between the Soviet Union and China during the Cold War years?
4. From the perspective of China's leaders in Beijing, what were the reasons for the collapse of communism in Eastern Europe and the Soviet Union?
5. Why are relations between China and the former communist countries better after than during the Cold War years?
6. How has the collapse of the Soviet Union affected the balance of power in Asia?
7. How do Chinese leaders view Gorbachev, Yeltsin, and Putin?
8. How relevant are current Chinese political and economic domestic developments as a model to be followed by Russia and the former parts of the Soviet Union?
9. In what ways are the Chinese and Russian governments working together to create peace and stability in Northeast Asia?
10. Although there is no official Sino-Russian military alliance, why is military cooperation between the two countries increasing?
11. How does Beijing seek to deal with current developments taking place inside Russia and other former communist countries? Explain the reasons for China's current position on developments inside former communist countries.
12. How does Beijing view Russia's role in the United Nations in the post–Cold War era?
13. How did the September 11, 2001, terrorist attacks on the United States affect both Chinese-Russian relations and Chinese and Russian relations with the mostly Muslim former Soviet republics of Central Asia?
14. A leading U.S. scholar of the Soviet Union has stated, "A great weakness of the current Russian-Chinese relationship is the virtual absence of the multidimensional societal connections that, for example, connect China

and the United States even during periods of great stress."[46] What issues underlie this assessment of Chinese-Russian relations?

15. What policy toward the newly emerging former communist states in Central Asia would best promote Chinese national interests?

▓ Suggested Readings

Chufrin, Gennady, ed. *Russia and Asia-Pacific Security.* Stockholm: Oxford University Press/Stockholm International Peace Research Institute, 2000.

Cohen, Warren I., and Akira Iriye, eds. *The Great Powers in East Asia, 1953–1960.* New York: Columbia University Press, 1990.

DeLisle, Jacques. *Asia's Shifting Strategic Landscape: Long-Term Trends and the Impact of 9/11.* FPRI Conference Report. November 2003.

Dittmer, Lowell. "China and Russia: New Beginnings." In Samuel S. Kim, ed., *China and the World: New Directions in Chinese Foreign Policy.* Boulder, Colo.: Westview, 1993, pp. 113–127.

———. *Sino-Soviet Normalization and Its International Implications, 1945–1990.* Seattle: University of Washington Press, 1992.

Fletcher, Joseph. "Sino-Russian Relations, 1800–1862." In John Fairbank, ed., *The Cambridge History of China,* vol. 10, *Late Ch'ing, 1800–1911,* pt. 1. Cambridge: Cambridge University Press, 1978, pp. 318–350.

Floyd, David. *Mao Against Khrushchev: A Short History of the Sino-Soviet Conflict.* New York: Praeger, 1963.

Gill, Bates, and Matthew Oresman. "China's New Journey to the West: China's Emergence in Central Asia and Implications for U.S. Interests." Report of the CSIS Freeman Chair in China Studies, Center for Strategic and International Studies. August 2003.

Klintworth, Gary. *Sino-Russian Detente and the Regional Implications.* Canberra: Strategic and Defense Studies Centre, Australian National University, 1992.

Lukin, Alexander. "Russia's Image of China and Russian-Chinese Relations." CNAPS Working Paper. May 2001. http://www.brookings.edu/fp/cnaps/papers/lukinwp_01.htm.

Moltz, James Clay. "Regional Tensions in the Russo-Chinese Rapprochement." *Asian Survey* 35, no. 6 (June 1995).

Nelsen, Harvey W. *Power and Insecurity: Beijing, Moscow, and Washington, 1949–1988.* Boulder, Colo.: Lynne Rienner, 1989.

Newell, Josh. *The Russian Far East: A Reference Guide for Conservation and Development.* 2nd ed. McKinleyville, Calif.: Daniel and Daniel, 2004.

Ross, Robert S., ed. *China, the United States and the Soviet Union: Tripolarity and Policy Making in the Cold War.* Armonk, N.Y.: M. E. Sharpe, 1993.

Stuart, Douglas T., and William H. Tow, eds. *China, the Soviet Union, and the West: Strategic and Political Dimensions in the 1980s.* Boulder, Colo.: Westview, 1982.

White, Stephen. *Gorbachev and After.* 3rd ed. New York: Cambridge University Press, 1992.

Woodrow Wilson International Center for Scholars. *Sino-Russian Strategic Partnership: A Threat to American Interests?* Asia Program Special Report no. 99. September 2001. http://wwics.si.edu.

Notes

1. Ishaev, who is cited as often critical of China, is quoted in Jeanne L. Wilson, "Prospects for Russian-Chinese Relations: Whither the Strategic Partnership?" Asia Program Special Report no. 99, September 2001, p. 18.

2. Joseph Fletcher, "Sino-Russian Relations, 1800–1862," in John Fairbank, ed., *The Cambridge History of China*, vol. 10, *Late Ch'ing, 1800–1911*, pt. 1 (Cambridge: Cambridge University Press, 1978), p. 335.

3. Ibid., p. 347.

4. Adam Ulam, *The Rivals: America and Russia Since World War II* (New York: Penguin Books, 1980), p. 138.

5. Ross Terrill, *Mao: A Biography* (New York: Harper and Row, 1980), p. 201.

6. Ibid., pp. 201–202.

7. Allen S. Whiting, *China Crosses the Yalu* (Stanford: Stanford University Press, 1968).

8. Steven I. Levine, "Soviet Asian Policy in the 1950s," in Warren I. Cohen and Akira Iriye, eds., *The Great Powers in East Asia, 1953–1960* (New York: Columbia University Press, 1990), p. 308.

9. Stuart Schram, *Mao Tse-tung* (Baltimore: Penguin, 1975), p. 291.

10. Harold C. Hinton, "Sino-Soviet Relations: Background and Overview," in Douglas T. Stuart and William H. Tow, eds., *China, the Soviet Union, and the West: Strategic and Political Dimensions in the 1980s* (Boulder, Colo.: Westview, 1982), p. 9.

11. Terrill, *Mao*, p. 202.

12. Gordon H. Chang, "JFK, China, and the Bomb," *Journal of American History* 74, no. 4 (March 1988): 1287–1310.

13. Levine, "Soviet Asian Policy in the 1950s," p. 311.

14. Joseph L. Nogee and Robert H. Donaldson, *Soviet Foreign Policy Since World War II*, 3rd ed. (New York: Pergamon Press, 1988), p. 250.

15. Henry Kissinger, *White House Years* (Boston: Little, Brown, 1979).

16. William G. Hyland, "The Sino-Soviet Conflict: A Search for New Security Strategies," in Richard H. Solomon, ed., *Asian Security in the 1980s: Problems and Policies for a Time of Transition* (Cambridge, Mass.: Oelgeschlager, Gunn, and Hain, 1979), p. 40.

17. Chi Su, "China and the Soviet Union: Principled, Salutary, and Tempered Management of Conflict," in Samuel S. Kim, ed., *China and the World: New Directions in Chinese Foreign Policy* (Boulder, Colo.: Westview, 1989), p. 136.

18. Michael Yahuda, "Deng Xiaoping: The Statesman," *China Quarterly* (September 1993): 562.

19. Robert S. Ross, "Foreign Policy in 1987: Independent Rhetoric, Pragmatic Policy," in Anthony J. Kane, ed., *China Briefing, 1988* (Boulder, Colo.: Westview, 1988), pp. 45–46.

20. Robert A. Scalapino, "The China Policy of Russia and Asian Security in the 1990s," in Sheldon W. Simon, ed., *East Asian Security in the Post–Cold War Era* (Armonk, N.Y.: M. E. Sharpe, 1993), p. 161.

21. Allen S. Whiting, "China's Foreign Relations After 40 Years," in Anthony J. Kane, ed., *China Briefing, 1990* (Boulder, Colo.: Westview, 1990), p. 71.

22. David Shambaugh, "China's Security Policy in the Post–Cold War Era," in Steven L. Spiegel and David J. Pervin, eds., *At Issue: Politics in the World Arena*, 7th ed. (New York: St. Martin's Press, 1994), pp. 142–143.

23. John W. Garver, "The Chinese Communist Party and the Collapse of Soviet Communism," *China Quarterly* (March 1993): p. 1.

24. George Ginsburg, "The End of the Sino-Russian Territorial Disputes?" *Journal of East Asian Affairs* 7, no. 1 (Winter–Spring 1993): 261–320.

25. Garver, "Chinese Communist Party," p. 11.

26. Ibid., p. 13.

27. Chai Chengweng, quoted in David Armstrong, "Chinese Perspectives on the New World Order," *Journal of East Asian Affairs* 8, no. 2 (Summer–Fall 1994): 457–458.

28. Marshall Shulman, "Reform and Soviet Collapse Spur Discussions Between American and Chinese Specialists," *United States–China Relations: Notes from the National Committee* (Spring–Summer 1992): 6.

29. Paul H. B. Godwin, "China's Asian Policy in the 1990s: Adjusting to the Post–Cold War Environment," in Simon, *East Asian Security,* p. 127.

30. Marshall L. Goldman, "The Chinese Model: The Solution to Russia's Economic Ills?" *Current History* (October 1993): 321.

31. Ibid.

32. Ibid., p. 324.

33. Garver, "Chinese Communist Party," p. 25.

34. "In order to satisfy energy demand in North China, natural gas or electricity can be directly transferred into the load centers in North China from producing fields and power plants in the Russian Far East if the electricity price is competitive and the investment is possible and valuable." He Xin, an engineer with the State Grid Corporation of China, quoted in James Brooke, "Let a Hundred Russian Kilowatts Bloom," *New York Times,* March 23, 2004, p. W7.

35. James Brooke, "Russia Catches China Fever: Commerce Thrives in Free Trade Zone in the East," *New York Times,* March 28, 2004, pp. W1, W7.

36. "Report to Congress Pursuant to the FY2000 National Defense Authorization Act," *Annual Report on the Military Power of the People's Republic of China,* July 2002, http://www.defenselink.mil/news/jul2002/d20020712china.pdf.

37. Patrick Tyler, "Russia and China Sign a Military Agreement," *New York Times,* November 10, 1993.

38. In a summit conference held in Turkey in 1992, all of the Central Asian republics except Tajikistan met with Turkey and Azerbaijan to consider a proposal by Turkey's president, Turgut Ozal, for a free trade zone and eventual economic union. President Ozal also called for a regional investment bank and pipelines to carry Central Asian oil and natural gas to Europe via Turkey. "Turkey Seeks an Economic Muslim Union," *New Arabia,* November 12–25, 1992, p. 24.

39. Bates Gill and Matthew Oresman, "China's New Journey to the West: China's Emergence in Central Asia and Implications for U.S. Interests," report of the CSIS Freeman Chair in China Studies, Center for Strategic and International Studies, August 2003, pp. viii–ix.

40. Quoted in Howard W. French, "China Moves Toward Another West: Central Asia," *New York Times,* March 28, 2004, sec. 1, p. 1.

41. Mette Skak, "Post-Soviet Foreign Policy: The Emerging Relationship Between Russia and Northeast Asia," *Journal of East Asian Affairs,* no. 1 (Winter–Spring 1993): 152.

42. Although Moscow never officially announced its decision, it is in negotiations with Japan and "the Chinese have said they don't think their project has been competitive." Erin E. Arvedlund, "Russia to Run 2,500-Mile Oil Pipeline in East Asia," *New York Times,* April 21, 2004, pp. W1, W7.

43. Shulman, "Reform and Soviet Collapse," pp. 12–13.

44. Yuri V. Tsyganov, "Russia and China: What Is in the Pipeline?" Gennady Chufrin, ed., *Russia & Asia-Pacific Security,* http://projects.sipai.se/russia.

45. Ibid.

46. Steven I. Levine, "Some Reflections on the Russian-Chinese Strategic Partnership," in Woodrow Wilson International Center for Scholars, *Sino-Russian Strategic Partnership: A Threat to American Interests?* Asia Program Special Report no. 99, September 2001, http://wwics.si.edu.

China and the United States

The United States acknowledges that all Chinese on either side of the Tai-wan Strait maintain there is but one China and that Taiwan is a part of China. The United States Government does not challenge that position. It reaffirms its interest in a peaceful settlement of the Taiwan question by the Chinese themselves.

—*The Shanghai Communiqué*[1]

Historical Background

Sentimental Imperialists

It was Chinese tea that was dumped into Boston harbor in December 1773 to protest British rule over the thirteen colonies. U.S. trade with China in tea, china, spices, silks, and furniture predated even the American Revolution. The history of official Sino-U.S. contacts is nearly as long. In 1844, the United States signed a treaty with China that promised "peace, amity and commerce."[2] The treaty also guaranteed that the United States would be granted the same trading rights as the British, and the Chinese promised to grant automatically to Washington all future privileges given to other Western nations. Thus was born the most-favored-nation (MFN) status, which the Chinese called "jackal diplomacy" and which continues to cause friction in Sino-U.S. relations to this day.

From the earliest Western contacts with China, the myth of the China market prevailed. The idea that the huge Chinese population would want to buy foreign products, creating a huge import market and huge profits for exporters, drove Western powers to demand spheres of influence in China. Those in the United States also believed in the myth, even though U.S. trade with China was only 1 to 2 percent of the total volume of U.S. exports for most of the nineteenth and early twentieth centuries. Still, the hope of expanding markets continued, and Washington viewed the ever-growing number of foreign enclaves with alarm. Successive U.S. administrations were not concerned enough with China to take the trouble to establish a U.S. sphere of influence; however, Washington very much wanted access to the markets in areas controlled by the Western powers. To effect this, in 1899 the McKinley administration sent letters to the great powers, including Britain, Germany, Russia, and Japan, asking that they promise to preserve commercial equality for all nations in any spheres that they controlled. Despite evasive responses, the administration declared the powers had agreed to Open Door status, and secret U.S. contingency plans to establish a U.S. sphere of influence in China never had to be put to the test.[3]

Besides trade, the other great U.S. interest in China was the promotion of Christianity. Along with France, England, and Germany, the United States sent missionaries to China to convert the Chinese and run charitable institutions. Although never successful—only approximately 1 percent of the Chinese population converted—by 1930 half of the 3,000 missionaries in China were U.S. citizens.[4] The Chinese were generally uninterested in adopting a foreign religion, and most were especially resistant to accepting a religion that came to symbolize foreign imperialism in China. Few U.S. citizens at home, however, realized how unsuccessful the missionaries were; rather, most believed that their missionaries were being honored in China for their role in bringing Christianity to the country and for introducing the concept of public charity.

Trade and Christianity became the two factors that determined Sino-U.S. interactions well into China's revolutionary era. Because it did not actually control any Chinese territory, the United States believed that it was behaving in a more benevolent manner than the other Western nations. This notion was particularly reinforced by the U.S. allocation of monies paid by the Chinese government to Western powers for damages incurred during the Boxer Uprising toward educating Chinese students in the United States. The people of the United States were *sentimental imperialists*—they believed they were unlike their more rapacious brethren in Europe and therefore had a special relationship with the Chinese.

Most Chinese, however, failed to notice the difference between the United States and the European powers. After all, the United States demanded the special rights and privileges of the other foreign powers in China, contributed troops to the forces fighting the Boxers in Beijing, and sought to demonstrate the superiority of Christianity to "heathens." To many Chinese, the United States was little different from all the other powers that were eroding China's sovereignty and its pride. Their attitude was perhaps best stated by the Chinese minister to the United States in 1899 (the year of the Open Door) when he protested against "the utter disregard of the American government for the friendly relations that should exist between two governments."[5]

Nationalism and Revolution

To many Chinese, the less than honorable U.S. attitude toward China was demonstrated yet again at the Versailles Conference in 1919. Despite President Woodrow Wilson's previous high-minded statements regarding U.S. respect for Chinese sovereignty, he acquiesced in the transfer of Shandong province from German to Japanese control. The Chinese students and intellectuals who protested did not prevent the transfer, but they did forge a new sense of Chinese nationalism that precluded foreign intervention. U.S. intervention in China was as little appreciated as that of other foreign powers. The fact that the United States refused to give up extraterritorial rights (immunity from Chinese law) for its citizens in China until after World War II had started did not increase respect for the United States in Chinese patriotic circles.

World War II

During the late 1920s and the 1930s, Washington paid only intermittent attention to China. The rise of fascism in Europe was of paramount concern to most of the U.S. people, and China, divided into satrapies controlled by sparring warlords, was only of marginal interest. Even the myth of the China market had been proven false—as late as 1940, $78 million in U.S. exports went to China while $227 million went to Japan.[6]

Only as Japanese expansionism in the Far East continued, with images of the Japanese "rape" of Nanjing indelibly etched in U.S. minds through pictures in *Life* magazine and newsreels, did China come into focus as a component of U.S. security policy. After Japan joined the Axis (with fascist Germany and Italy) in 1940, official and public opinion in the United States began to favor China. The United States then adopted a dual policy toward Japan: an oil embargo and a simultaneous attempt to find a diplomatic solution to the East Asian crisis. For the United States, one condition of any talks was a Japanese pledge to respect Chinese territory and sovereignty, but the Japanese refused to withdraw their troops from Manchuria. On December 7, 1941, the tide turned. Once the United States was at war with Japan, preservation of a free and independent China became a vital component of the U.S. international security agenda.

During World War II, the U.S. policy toward China was complicated by the growing strength of the Chinese Communists in their base areas and the virtual civil war between the Communists and the Nationalists. The primary U.S. goal was to defeat the Japanese invaders in China. To some, Chiang Kai-shek's goal seemed to be to defeat the Communists instead. President Franklin Roosevelt adopted a number of approaches. He sent a U.S. general, Joseph Stilwell, to train the Chinese Nationalist troops to fight the Japanese. But he also sent a group of U.S. diplomats to meet with the Communists to determine if a united front against the Japanese could be arranged. He tried to massage Chiang's and China's pride by treating China as one of the four "global policemen," along with the United States, the Soviet Union, and the United Kingdom (which, with France, are now the permanent members of the UN Security Council).

Nothing seemed to work. Chiang forced Stilwell out, and the morale of the Nationalist troops remained low. The Nationalists and the Communists never effectively cooperated in the anti-Japanese war. And the United States could not create Chinese national pride. Ultimately, neither the Nationalists nor the Communists defeated the Japanese in China. The U.S. troops defeated Japan on its own territory and then faced the monumental task of disarming Japanese troops in China, which they did with the assistance of Chiang's troops, who benefited from the Japanese disarmament.

After 1945, Chiang's forces were free to fight Mao's troops for control of China. Communist and Nationalist troops fought each other with weapons confiscated from the Japanese and with weapons supplied to Chiang's forces by the United States but often appropriated by Mao's troops. U.S. efforts to mediate between the two parties in hopes of creating a coalition government came to naught. Both the Nationalists and the Communists were loath to compromise, and the Communists believed that the United States was partial to Chiang Kai-shek. In January 1947, General George C. Marshall, the U.S. negotiator, left China in disgust after in effect pronouncing "a plague on both your houses."

▩ The Cold War Years

When the Dust Settled

The United States soon came to the decision that the Communists would be victorious, and it tried to limit the anticipated domestic political damage through education. The China White Paper, published in August 1949, was a report authored by the State Department to justify the administration's policy of disengagement to the U.S. public. In the foreword, Secretary of State Dean Acheson attempted to placate supporters of the Nationalists while also making the case that a Communist victory was inevitable no matter what the United States did:

> A realistic appraisal of conditions in China, past and present, leads to the conclusion that the only alternative open to the United States was full-scale intervention in behalf of a Government which had lost the confidence of its own troops and its own people. . . . The unfortunate but inescapable fact is that the ominous result of the civil war in China was beyond the control of the government of the United States. Nothing that this country did or could

have done within the reasonable limits of its capabilities could have changed that result; nothing that was left undone by this country has contributed to it. It was the product of internal China forces, forces which this country tried to influence but could not.[7]

The white paper was not enough to silence critics. In 1949, President Harry Truman had to persuade Congress to lower its allocations for China aid, and he was forced continually to defend his administration from charges (particularly by Republicans) of abandoning the Nationalists to the Communists. The "Who Lost China" debate continued in Washington into the 1960s.[8]

As predicted, the Chinese Communists did soon prevail, largely because of better military leadership, a reputation for incorruptibility, and an appeal to Chinese nationalism. The People's Republic of China was established on October 1, 1949. Defeated, Chiang and his supporters were forced to flee to the southern island of Taiwan, where they established a rump Nationalist regime. Most U.S. policymakers expected that after the Chinese Communists had consolidated control of the mainland, they would then mount an amphibious invasion of Taiwan, thereby finally finishing the bloody civil war. Even the Truman administration reached the controversial decision, which was by no means unanimously accepted, particularly in the military, not to intervene when Chinese forces crossed the Taiwan Straits.

U.S. policymakers in 1949 and early 1950 were initially unsure of how to react to the establishment of the People's Republic. Two options were considered: to recognize the regime or to ignore it because of its communist government. Policymakers opposed to recognition cited the threat to the stability of Southeast Asia posed by a communist China, the degree to which the People's Republic marched in lockstep with the Soviet Union, the danger to the functioning of the United Nations if the Security Council were to have another communist permanent member, and the U.S. obligation to the Nationalist Chinese on Taiwan. Policymakers who favored recognition argued for it in the distant future, and then only because the prerogatives of international law would demand U.S. recognition of a stable communist regime.

This debate between absolutes had not been resolved by mid-1950. After the outbreak of the Korean War on June 25, 1950, recognition of the People's Republic was no longer considered a viable policy option. The invasion of South Korea by Communist troops from North Korea was perceived in Washington to be another example of militant communism driving toward world domination. Prior Soviet and Chinese knowledge of the attack was considered a given.

As a result, the United States reversed its East Asia policy. Washington sent troops to defend South Korea, which had only a few weeks earlier been considered outside the U.S. defense perimeter. The Truman administration also quickly reversed its laissez-faire position by sending the Seventh Fleet into the

Taiwan Straits. No longer would the United States allow the anticipated Communist invasion. Chiang's island regime became a U.S. protectorate.

Chinese entry into the Korean War in October 1950 after U.S. troops marched toward the Korean-Chinese border fulfilled Washington's worst fears of the Chinese Communists. U.S. and Chinese troops fought face-to-face for nearly three years until an armistice was finally signed in July 1953. The legacy of distrust had been transformed into a legacy of hatred engendered by open warfare.

The Eisenhower Administration

Sino-U.S. relations during the administration of President Dwight Eisenhower were punctuated by two episodes of near war, the Taiwan Straits crises of 1954 and 1958. In addition to the Sino-U.S. dispute over Taiwan's status, which threatened world peace, a number of major issues of contention repeatedly arose between the United States and the People's Republic during the Eisenhower administration. These issues, which included recognition, UN membership, trade, China's imprisonment of U.S. citizens,[9] and U.S. retention of Chinese citizens, formed a theme of Sino-U.S. relations from 1953 through 1960. A less important issue, but one that received tremendous press coverage, was how Washington should respond to the Chinese invitation to U.S. news reporters.[10] Not one of these issues was resolved during the Eisenhower administration or, it might be added, the next two administrations.

Taiwan. The Eisenhower administration mounted a complex effort to support the Nationalist regime while at the same time subtly restraining its reckless behavior toward the People's Republic. One of President Eisenhower's first acts after taking the oath of office was to "unleash" Chiang Kai-shek, stating that the U.S. Seventh Fleet would not stand in the way of Nationalist attempts to invade the mainland. The Mutual Defense Treaty of 1954 officially bound the United States to the defense of Taiwan should it be attacked, and Congress endorsed the use of U.S. troops for the defense of Taiwan the next year. At the same time, to curb any tendencies toward recklessness, the administration elicited promises from Chiang's foreign minister that the use of force would be "a matter of joint agreement." In addition, limitations were placed on the use of some of the military equipment supplied to Chiang to prevent employment for offensive purposes.

The first offshore island crisis was by far the more perilous. On September 3, 1954, the People's Republic shelled the island of Quemoy, one of the offshore islands that was held by the Nationalist Chinese despite the fact that it lay no more than a few kilometers from the Chinese mainland and by international law belonged to the People's Republic. Nevertheless, the Nationalists responded by staging raids on the mainland, to which the Communist Chinese responded by bombarding the offshore islands more heavily. The United States supported Chiang's retention of the offshore islands because their loss might have affected the morale of not only the Nationalist government on Taiwan but also the noncommunist governments of Southeast Asia. The U.S. position also lessened pressure from the right wing of the Republican Party.

In January 1955, the situation flared up again when the Communists invaded the Tachen Islands, located 200 miles north of Taiwan. Although the Eisenhower administration had initially counseled the Nationalist Chinese to strengthen their position on these islands, when the situation became dangerous the administration changed its position and urged evacuation because it now regarded the Tachen Islands as indefensible. Subsequently, it supported only Chiang's claims to Quemoy, Matsu, and a small island group in the Taiwan Straits.

Despite pressure from his advisers to retaliate against the Chinese by bombing the mainland, the president counseled caution. The potential escalation of the violence had unnerved U.S. allies and even the administration. Later presidential hints that atomic weapons might be used in the dispute aroused the alarm of U.S. allies, Congress, and the public (not to mention the Chinese) and caused the president unsuccessfully to urge Chiang to withdraw some of his troops from Quemoy. This stalemate was then breached by the Chinese offer to negotiate with the United States, an offer the administration grudgingly accepted. With the advent of the talks, an informal cease-fire was established in the Taiwan Straits that lasted for three years.

In July 1958, the People's Republic announced its intention to "liberate" Quemoy and Matsu, and in August it once again began bombarding the islands. The hostilities sputtered through a number of phases, including debate in the United Nations, abusive letters from Khrushchev to Eisenhower, and abortive Communist cease-fires. Finally, the crisis ended in October with Communist pledges to shell only on alternate days and the development of a U.S. understanding with Chiang that the United States would not assist the Nationalists in any invasion of the mainland. After two major crises in Sino-U.S. relations, crises that many feared could lead to a third world war, the situation in the Taiwan Straits remained virtually unchanged.

Sino-U.S. communication. Sino-U.S. relations during the Eisenhower administration were also characterized by several episodes of reluctant communication, such as the Geneva Conference of 1954 and the Bandung Conference of 1955. These conferences were multilateral, and the Eisenhower administration worked hard to ensure that the participants would not ratify a policy that was soft on communism.

More remarkably, after the Eisenhower administration reaffirmed that it was not according the People's Republic de facto or de jure recognition, the United States accepted the Chinese proposal to begin direct ambassadorial talks. Talks began in Geneva in August 1955. In September, the two nations reached an agreement on repatriation of civilians that was never fully effected; no other agreement was ever ratified during the entire course of the talks, which sputtered on sporadically for another decade.

It was during this period, the mid-1950s, that the Chinese were the most open to the outside world and to substantive negotiations with the United States. Their reasons were pragmatic: a desire for international recognition, a need for trade and credit, and a determination to solve the Taiwan problem in their favor. Domestic politics constrained the Eisenhower administration from discussing the status of Taiwan, however, and it was unwilling to discuss recognition or trade publicly. By 1958, when the administration may secretly have been contemplating a "two Chinas" policy, the People's Republic was in the middle of the Great Leap Forward and was unwilling to compromise with imperialists.

The Kennedy Administration

Sino-U.S. contacts during the administration of President John Kennedy exhibited both the patterns of the previous fourteen years and the start of a new pattern that was to last until the beginnings of rapprochement. Although the rhetoric remained hostile, the threat of direct Sino-U.S. hostilities diminished even as the battle by proxy in Southeast Asia became more intense. The Chinese avoided provocation in the Taiwan Straits, and the United States once again "leashed" Chiang Kai-shek.

Direct contacts continued through the Warsaw talks, which were described by U.S. policymakers as "sterile." Nevertheless, both sides made some effort at introducing an element of freshness in 1961. The Chinese told U.S. representatives that they were waiting with "a great sense of anticipation" for a new U.S. policy at the talks. In response, the United States tried to develop new initiatives on exchanging news reporters, trade, and aid. Nothing came of this, however, and the talks thereafter continued in their familiar unprofitable mode.[11] At the same time, members of the foreign policy decision-making apparatus in Washington openly began to voice their desire for more meaningful contacts, which they hoped might occur in the second Kennedy administration. Not even humanitarian aid—food for the Chinese suffering through a famine—could escape the limits of Cold War sensibilities, Chinese pride, and U.S. domestic politics. No U.S. food aid was sent to China despite general approval of the concept by the administration and the U.S. public.

Washington's recognition of the fact that the Soviets and the Chinese were openly expressing different interests, even if they did not grasp the magnitude of the split, also increased fears. Kennedy and his advisers believed that a split might result in the two communist nations vying for power in Asia and the third world, further destabilizing the international situation. Rather than fighting a monolith, the United States would now have to face two hostile regimes, neither of which had any influence over the other and both of which claimed they would "bury the West."

The Johnson Administration

The Johnson administration's China policy was a mélange of the hard-line (its Vietnam policy), the predictable (finally implementing limited initiatives that had been under discussion in Washington for over a decade), and the unpredictable (President Lyndon Johnson's alleged desire for a summit meeting in Beijing). It was a time of changing paradigms, and nobody in the bureaucracy was entirely sure of how to deal with the change, especially the Chinese leaders, who rejected most of the limited approaches fielded by Washington.

Several initiatives were also fielded through the Warsaw talks.[12] The U.S. representatives asked the Chinese if they would be willing to share meteorological information, exchange scientific data, and exchange seed and plant samples.[13] In addition, the State Department encouraged U.S. colleges to invite Chinese scholars to their campuses, and the U.S. Information Agency invited Chinese journalists to the United States to cover the 1968 election. According to the State Department, these initiatives were rejected.[14]

By 1966, revised passport regulations had been issued.[15] Professional journalists, public health doctors, scientists, scholars, and U.S. Red Cross workers were to be allowed to travel to China, as was any individual who could prove he or she had a valid reason to visit the People's Republic other than tourism. The Chinese, however, issued only a few visas. In April 1967, a license was granted for the sale of drugs and medical supplies. Originally suggested by the State Department, the proposal was approved by the secretaries of state, the treasury, and commerce and by the president in less than two weeks. The Chinese denounced the attempted sale, however, and though other trade initiatives were discussed repeatedly during the Johnson administration, none were implemented.

The rhetoric changed as well during the latter part of the Johnson administration. Official pronouncements on the possibilities of better future relations with the People's Republic grew increasingly explicit during the administration's final years. According to the departments of state and defense, the administration wanted "to induce present and future communist leaders to reappraise US intentions" and to "arouse Peking's interest in developing a more constructive relationship with us."[16]

These administration initiatives were "too little, too late" (or too early), for the Cultural Revolution had erupted in China in June 1966. Any accommodation with the United States was extremely unlikely while millions of the teenage Red Guard were causing chaos in China and while the government of the People's Republic nearly ceased to exist. The administration was dimly aware of this dilemma. Nevertheless, it fielded its cultural and trade initiatives for three reasons: the bomb, Vietnam, and the Cultural Revolution.

China's entry into the nuclear club in 1964 altered the balance of power in Asia to the apparent detriment of U.S. allies on the continent. Encouraging China's entry into the community of nations as a means of preventing potentially aggressive actions became critically important.[17] It became even more important after the United States began bombing North Vietnam, when the world began to worry about a direct Sino-U.S. conflagration. Policymakers in Washington believed that while the United States was acting tough in Vietnam, it could afford to introduce some flexibility into its China policy without appearing weak.

The Cultural Revolution posed a more complex policy problem. President Johnson's advisers well understood that the United States could not determine events on the mainland, and they had no desire to try. They did, however, believe that a new generation of leaders would emerge from the chaos and that the United States should try to impress these men and women with the good intentions of the United States. Without any basis in reality, the U.S. policymakers wishfully believed that the limited changes in policy they had introduced would influence a new generation of Chinese to overcome two decades of nationalist and socialist propaganda. President Johnson could not wait for a new generation, however, and when rapprochement finally came, it was the older generation, both in Washington and Beijing, that spearheaded it.

The Nixon Administration

On July 15, 1971, "without warning to friend or foe,"[18] President Richard Nixon announced that his national security adviser, Henry Kissinger, had recently returned from a visit to the People's Republic and that he himself planned to visit the communist capital. The world was astounded and pleased, particularly because President Nixon's political career was based on vigilant anticommunism. With his television announcement, the People's Republic of China was transformed overnight in the minds of the U.S. public from a "red peril"—if Richard Nixon was willing to visit the capital of the People's Republic of China, it really must be all right—to a fascinating, exotic travel destination. Nixon and Mao, the two former archenemies, were drawn together by a desire to play two sides of the strategic triangle against the third. By opening a dialogue with Beijing, Washington expected it could enhance its security by playing off Beijing against Moscow. But before the United States could play its China card, it had to address the many issues that had prevented a meaningful Sino-U.S. dialogue for so many years. Official recognition was most imperative to the Chinese over the short term, and a resolution of the Taiwan question in favor of reunification was a long-term goal. U.S. goals, in addition to changing the dimensions of Soviet policy, were to lessen tensions in East and Southeast Asia. At a time when the United States was actively engaged in a war in Vietnam, this was no easy task.

In February 1972, President Nixon met Mao in Beijing, "which conveyed to the world that the period of Sino-American hostility was over—indeed, that the two great nations were moving toward cooperation on fundamentals of foreign policy."[19] During Nixon's trip, the two nations replaced twenty-three years of hostility with an uneasy compromise—the Shanghai Communiqué—in which the United States and the People's Republic agreed to disagree about Indochina, Korea, the Indo-Pakistani conflict, and the status of Japan. To achieve "progress toward the normalization of relations between China and the United States," the United States ceased fighting for Taiwan: containment of communism had been replaced as the central tenet governing U.S. policy toward China; Nixon and Kissinger instead adopted the notion of the *strategic triangle,* with all the complex diplomacy that would entail to ensure a balance of power. It worked—the Soviets were soon courting the United States.

Despite President Nixon's promises to withdraw U.S. troops from Taiwan, de jure recognition would take another seven years, primarily because of congressional distaste for the complete abandonment of a longtime ally and because of leadership crises in both countries. Nevertheless, with China's entry into the United Nations in September and with U.S. acceptance of the permanence of the Communist Chinese regime, 1971 marked the end of the international isolation of the People's Republic.

The United States and the People's Republic exchanged official delegations after the Nixon trip, and trade increased drastically between the two countries, but official recognition did not come about until the Carter administration. In 1979, because of fears that the Chinese would not tolerate an unofficial status of quasi-relations for much longer, the United States formally recognized the People's Republic of China, thirty years after its creation. Although late, the results were dramatic. Sino-U.S. trade increased 200 percent between 1978 and 1979, and U.S. tourism in China increased 300 percent.[20] Equally important, U.S. perceptions of China were evolving. Deng Xiaoping's trip to the United States in early 1979, when he visited Washington, D.C., and Disney World, humanized China to millions of U.S. citizens who watched his visit on the nightly news. For a nation that only recently had been portrayed as armed and dangerous to U.S. security, normalization of perceptions was as important as normalization of diplomatic relations.

With full diplomatic relations between Washington and Beijing, the United States no longer recognized the Nationalist government on Taiwan as the government of China. To circumvent this derecognition, the U.S. embassy in Taipei became a nongovernmental agency that hired furloughed State Department employees (who miraculously became State Department employees again after their stint in Taiwan was up). The defense commitment to Taiwan was more difficult to abrogate, even though U.S. troops were withdrawn from

Taiwan. Congress, however, refused to accept Chinese demands for immediate abrogation of the Mutual Defense Treaty of 1954. Rather, it passed the Taiwan Relations Act, which declared, "It is the policy of the United States to provide Taiwan with arms of a defensive character; and to maintain the capacity of the United States to resist any resort to force or other forms of coercion that would jeopardize the security or the social or economic system, of the people on Taiwan."[21]

The Chinese objected, but not too strenuously, because of their desire for leverage against the Soviet Union and, perhaps more important, because of their desire for increased access to U.S. capital and technology. Sino-U.S. relations continued to be difficult, however, particularly in the area of arms sales. The fact that $200 million in U.S. arms were delivered to Taiwan in 1979 and $625 million in 1980[22] confirmed Beijing's worst suspicions—that Washington was in reality trying to implement a two-Chinas policy. With the Soviet invasion of Afghanistan, however, the Chinese began cooperating with the U.S. military and purchasing U.S. arms. Following the visit of the U.S. secretary of defense to Beijing in January 1980, the Chinese even agreed to permit establishment of a joint intelligence listening post in Xinjiang to monitor Soviet military activities.[23] Fearful of Soviet expansionism and worried by their own recent military failure in Vietnam, China's leaders acceded to a de facto two-Chinas policy out of expediency.

The Reagan Administration

In his 1980 presidential campaign, Ronald Reagan adopted the conservative position, lambasting the Carter administration for its abandonment of long-time U.S. ally Taiwan. If elected, he promised he would review Sino-U.S. relations, with the goal of reestablishing relations with Taiwan. Supporters of continued U.S. relations with Beijing greeted Reagan's inaugural as president with great trepidation. China, too, was nervous.

Much to everyone's surprise, particularly many conservative Republicans, President Reagan eventually adopted a China policy that neither Henry Kissinger nor Jimmy Carter could object to. In August 1982, both countries issued the Communiqué on United States Arms Sales to Taiwan. In the communiqué, the Reagan administration agreed to continue the position of the Shanghai Communiqué that Taiwan was a part of China and that unification would be an internal matter. In addition, the United States agreed to not increase its arms sales to Taiwan and to "reduce gradually its sales of arms to Taiwan, leading over a period of time to a final resolution."[24] President Reagan explained his views on China as follows: "Building a strong and lasting relationship with China has been an important foreign policy goal of four consecutive American administrations. Such a relationship is vital to our long-term national security interests and contributes to stability in East Asia. It is in the national interests of the United States that this important strategic relationship be advanced."[25] To prove his point, Reagan visited China in April 1984, his first visit to a communist country.

Though differences over international security issues, human rights, trade, and limitations on U.S. sales of dual-use technology remained, the Reagan administration sought to resolve them through diplomatic discussions. Many felt that Sino-U.S. relations had advanced to the point that, according to then–undersecretary of state Michael Armacost, "we have been able to discuss the most difficult issues without major adverse consequences, while continuing to cooperate and advance our relationship as a whole."[26] Even China's suppression of Tibetan activists and its missile sales to Iran and Saudi Arabia, both in 1987, did not derail Sino-U.S. relations or prevent dramatic increases in U.S. military sales to China (see Table 5.1). Official and public perceptions of China continued to be positive.[27]

Why did Reagan change his China policy so dramatically once he became president? The most cogent explanation is the old adage "Where you stand is where you sit." It was easy for a conservative presidential candidate to argue for abrogation of diplomatic relations with the People's Republic of China in favor of relations with Taiwan, but for a president to do so was far more difficult. A complete rupture of relations with Beijing would have heightened tensions in the Taiwan Straits, and the Chinese might even have responded by putting increased military pressure on Taiwan. The rest of East Asia, too, feared a China not allied to either superpower more than a China with ties to the United States. President Reagan realized that China was strategically, militarily, and politically more important than Taiwan. In view of Reagan's initial belligerent attitude toward the Soviet Union, Sino-U.S. ties were

Table 5.1   U.S. Military Sales to China, 1981–1990

	Total Deliveries (in U.S.$)
1981	0
1982	1,000,000
1983	209,000
1984	8,043,000
1985	46,671,000
1986	55,790,000
1987	37,814,000
1988	88,013,000
1989	106,215,000
1990	3,615,000

Source: Harry Harding, *A Fragile Relationship: The United States and China Since 1972* (Washington, D.C.: Brookings Institution, 1992), p. 371.

important to ensure that the strategic triangle would be organized in a way that was detrimental to Moscow.

The Post–Cold War Era

George Bush, Beijing, and Baghdad

When George H.W. Bush was inaugurated as president in January 1989, Sino-U.S. relations were perhaps better than they had ever been. Even with the continual problems over Taiwan and controversies over trade issues, which increased as trade increased, it seemed that relations between Washington and Beijing had stabilized into a normal pattern characterized by diplomatic interchanges to resolve difficulties. Moreover, George Bush had real China experience; he had headed the U.S. Liaison Office in Beijing for a few years in the 1970s. The future of Sino-U.S. relations looked, if not bright, at least stable.

But any illusions of normalcy in Sino-U.S. relations collapsed on June 4, 1989, as Chinese tanks crushed demonstrations in the environs of Tiananmen Square. The world was outraged, and the U.S. people and Congress called for sanctions. On June 5, 1989, President Bush announced that the following steps would be taken in response to the Chinese military actions against the demonstrators in Beijing:

- suspension of all government-to-government military sales and commercial exports of military materials,
- suspension of exchange visits by U.S. and Chinese military personnel,
- extension of assistance to the Red Cross for its work in China,
- sympathetic review of requests by Chinese students studying in the United States to extend their stay, and
- a review of other U.S.-China programs and activities.[28]

President Bush was reluctant, however, to cut China off completely. Anxious to maintain contact and believing that direct talks would have more influence on China than studious avoidance, Bush sent his national security adviser and deputy secretary of state on a secret mission to Beijing in July 1989 and on another mission in December that was announced to the public after-the-fact. Pictures in the press of two aides toasting the very leaders who had ordered the military to fire on unarmed protesters led to severe criticism of the Bush administration. Why, many critics asked, was it necessary to send secret envoys to China? Why drink toasts to the "Butchers of Beijing"? Would it not have been better to condemn the Tiananmen massacre while at the same time allowing cool but formal contacts through official diplomatic channels, rather than engaging in secret shuttle diplomacy?

Subsequent public and congressional criticisms of President Bush's China policy led to two congressional attempts to legislate conditions on renewal of MFN trading privileges. Both were thwarted only by presidential vetoes. President Bush's philosophy of Sino-U.S. relations, articulated in a 1991 address at Yale University, was that "if we withdraw MFN or imposed conditions that would make trade impossible, we would punish South China . . . that very region where free-market reforms and the challenge to central authority are the strongest."[29]

Perhaps equally as persuasive to President Bush was the fact that he needed China in 1990 and 1991. China could veto any UN Security Council resolution condemning Saddam Hussein's invasion of Kuwait, and twelve resolutions were voted on in the four months following the Iraqi invasion of Kuwait in August 1990. Official U.S. censure of Beijing's handling of the Tiananmen demonstrations was therefore toned down. For this, the People's Republic showed its thanks by abstaining on the vote to use force against Iraq (Resolution 678). China thus had it both ways—it had not approved of the use of force, but it had not disapproved either. It had not angered its African and Asian allies by condoning U.S. intervention, yet it had not incurred U.S. wrath by vetoing the operation. Some call this approach a policy of "maximizing China's rights and interests and minimizing China's responsibility and normative costs."[30]

After defeating Iraq, the Bush administration had perhaps the highest public opinion ratings ever. It seemed that arguments over China policy would be won without difficulty by a president who had demonstrated his foreign policy expertise. And President Bush was still intent on maintaining good relations with China. To that end, Secretary of State James Baker visited Beijing in November 1991, officially ending the suspension of high-level contacts.

During the remaining year of the Bush administration, China and the United States had some good times, some bad. Several agreements were signed that seemed to create a framework for resolving the trade and human rights problems that continued to plague Sino-U.S. relations. On August 7, 1992, the United States and China formally signed a memorandum of understanding to ensure that products made by forced labor in China not be exported to the United States, and both nations signed a memorandum of understanding in which China agreed to reduce controls on imports by December 31, 1993. China also acceded to the Missile Technology Control Regime in early 1992,[31] after having agreed to join the Nuclear Nonproliferation Treaty in 1991. These signs of progress were counteracted, however, on September 2, 1992, when the Bush administration approved the sale of F-16 fighter jets to Taiwan. In a desperate election campaign, President Bush abandoned his many years of promoting U.S. relations with Beijing in favor of courting conservative votes at home. The Chinese, needless to say, were not pleased, and Bush's China policy ended on a sour note. Once defeated, President Bush changed course again.

He ended his presidency by revising his China policy to allow official inter-changes and resume trade and arms sales, allegedly to allow the Clinton administration to begin with a clean slate.[32]

Bill Clinton's Engagement of China

Candidate Bill Clinton severely criticized China's human rights record, and in his first year of office the situation did not improve. The State Department's annual review found that China's "overall human rights record in 1993 fell far short of internationally accepted norms as it continued to repress domestic critics and failed to control abuses by its own security forces."[33] Yet the Clinton administration moderated its campaign position by seeking to step up engagement with China in order to give Beijing an incentive to meet human rights demands before Congress voted to limit renewal of most-favored-nation status. In May 1993, President Clinton determined "that a one-year extension of his waiver authority for China would substantially promote the objectives of the Jackson-Vanik amendment."[34] At the same time, he issued Executive Order 12850, naming the conditions that China would have to meet to continue to receive renewals. China's will to meet these demands, some of which it believed infringed on its sovereignty, was put into doubt during Secretary of State Warren Christopher's visit to Beijing in March 1994, during which time a number of Chinese dissidents were imprisoned. Pushing most-favored-nation renewal through Congress became more and more a political liability for each successive U.S. administration. Table 5.2 shows the differ-

Table 5.2   Illustrative MFN and Full Duty Rates Applicable to Imports from China, 1993

	MFN Rate (%)	Full Rate (%)
Shellfish	Free	Free
Men's trousers (synthetic fiber)	29.7	90.0
Knit women's sweaters, vegetable fiber (excluding cotton)	5.0	45.0
Women's silk apparel	6.9	65.0
Artificial flowers (synthetic fiber)	9.0	71.5
Crude petroleum	0.6	1.2
Audio tape players	3.7	35.0
Hairdressing appliances	3.9	35.0
Luggage and handbags (textile fiber)	20.0	65.0
Plastic handbags	20.0	45.0
Stuffed toys	Free	70.0
Various other toys	6.8	70.0

Source: Vladimir N. Pregelj, "Most-Favored-Nation Status of the PRC," *CRS Issue Brief* no. IB92094, July 23, 1993, p. CRS-4.

ence in MFN and full duty rates on imports from China, highlighting the incentive China has to maintain MFN status.

Trade issues also continued to plague Sino-U.S. relations in the Clinton era. Again, instances of cooperation were followed by acrimonious disputes over the negative U.S. balance of trade and China's limited markets. When China's trade surplus with the United States approached $25 billion per year, second only to Japan's,[35] many blamed it on unfair Chinese trade practices. To discuss trade issues, President Clinton convened the Joint Economic Committee, which had not met since the Tiananmen massacre.[36] Among the agreements reached with China was a textile accord that limited growth in Chinese textile imports to the United States and promised greater enforcement to prevent cheating on quotas.[37]

However, in August 1993, the administration imposed sanctions on an estimated $1 billion in high-technology trade after intelligence indicated that China was shipping missiles to Pakistan in violation of the Missile Technology Control Regime. After announcing the sanctions, the administration also quickly sought to negotiate their end, and by November 1993 it had agreed to allow a U.S. company to sell a supercomputer to China's State Meteorological Administration. Despite Pentagon and congressional misgivings that the supercomputer might be put to military use, the Clinton administration was more concerned with promoting trade and alleviating the U.S. trade deficit with China.[38]

In 1993 the United States and China also agreed to resume contacts between the Pentagon and the Chinese army.[39] In November 1993, high-level Chinese and U.S. military officials met for the first time since Tiananmen. Weapons sales were not discussed, but the two sides agreed to "future dialogue" on topics like international peacekeeping operations and the problems of converting defense industries to civilian use. The U.S. delegate to the talks praised China's peacekeeping record in Cambodia and its diversification of its military industries into civilian areas, but stated that the Tiananmen Square massacre had "taken its toll in terms of mutual understanding."[40]

The two intertwined issues of human rights and trade continued to bedevil Sino-U.S. relations. So long as Beijing's leaders perceived Washington's linking of trade with human rights as an infringement on China's security, they reacted strongly to any admonishments from the United States. Their attitude was never more clearly illustrated than when Secretary of State Christopher visited Beijing in March 1994. Arriving, unfortunately for him, when the National People's Congress was in session, Communist Party leaders perceived the need to take a strong stance against U.S. admonitions on human rights issues because of their need to appear strong to an increasingly disaffected governmental and party bureaucracy. Secretary Christopher was greeted almost rudely by his Chinese hosts and was left with nothing to show for his trip except criticism from home for allowing himself to be humiliated.

The official Chinese position was that "dialogue is beneficial, while pressure is futile."[41]

Bill Clinton came to appreciate the Chinese resistance to pressure by May 26, 1994, when he announced, "I have decided that the United States should renew Most Favored Nation trading status toward China. This decision, I believe, offers us the best opportunity to lay the basis for long-term sustainable progress in human rights and for the advancement of our other interests with China. . . . I am moving, therefore, to delink human rights from the annual extension of Most Favored Nation trading status for China."[42] His only qualification was to ban the import of munitions, principally guns and ammunition, from China.

Why did President Clinton's China policy develop to the point where it was indistinguishable from President Bush's China policy? At the same time that China and the United States were heatedly discussing the relationship of human rights issues to trade, China was expected to spend about $560 billion in infrastructure projects between 1994 and 2000. U.S. companies hoped to contract for some of these projects, and the Chinese leadership was encouraging them. Now that the anti-Soviet rationale for Sino-U.S. relations no longer existed, China's rulers counted on U.S. capitalists to blunt the efforts of human rights advocates to abrogate MFN status, and they were correct in their assessment. The U.S.-China Business Council and other representatives of the U.S. business community mounted a large lobbying effort in favor of MFN renewal. They were joined, paradoxically, by Chinese intellectuals and Chinese entrepreneurs, who feared that termination of MFN status would strengthen hard-liners in Beijing and that increasing foreign trade would be a better lever to liberalize the regime than economic pressure. Ironically, party moderates worked with U.S. capitalists and industrialists, who feared loss of investment in China if MFN status were not renewed, to promote economic development in the People's Republic. Both nations would have suffered: China would have lost an export market for its textiles, toys, and other goods, while the United States would have lost a market for its agricultural and high-technology products. Although dollar estimates of the potential disruption in trade differed, the damage to Sino-U.S. amity would have been immense, and political relations would have been disrupted to an even greater degree than economic relations.

The Second Clinton Term

Chinese-U.S. relations during the second Clinton term were considerably more contentious. From early 1997 through January 2001, the relationship saw highs—including permanent MFN status, a World Trade Organization (WTO) agreement, and arms control agreements—and lows, including the bombing of the Chinese embassy in Belgrade, U.S. allegations of Chinese espionage, and accusations of Chinese involvement in improper fundraising activities.

President Clinton was intent on maintaining balanced relations with China while satisfying domestic constituencies that were suspicious of Beijing. Yet he issued what many perceived to be the strongest statement on Taiwan of any U.S. president since normalization of relations. In June 1998, Clinton said, "I had a chance to reiterate our Taiwan policy, which is that we don't support independence for Taiwan, or two China's, or one Taiwan, one China. And we don't believe that Taiwan should be a member in any organization for which statehood is a requirement. So I think we have a consistent policy."[43] Beijing was certainly delighted by the statement.

Beijing was less than happy, however, when the United States and its North Atlantic Treaty Organization (NATO) allies joined forces to help defend Kosovo, in the former Yugoslavia, from Serbian troops. The NATO action, which the United States and Europeans deemed a human rights effort, was deemed a violation of Yugoslavia's internal affairs by the Chinese. U.S.-China relations really spun out of control, however, when, in May 1999, NATO forces bombed the Chinese embassy in Belgrade. Three Chinese citizens were killed and twenty injured. The Chinese reaction was predictable: disbelief and anger. Beijing, particularly given its high opinion of U.S. technology, found it hard to believe that the bombing had been accidental. The Chinese mass media and populace expressed their fury, some by stoning the U.S. embassy in Beijing. China officially asked that the U.S. "make an open and official apology to the Chinese government, the Chinese people, and relatives of the Chinese victims; carry out a complete and thorough investigation of the NATO missile attack on China's embassy in Yugoslavia; promptly publicize the detailed results of the investigation; and severely punish those responsible for the attack."[44] The United States did investigate and briefed the Chinese government:

> The bombing resulted from three basic failures. First, the technique used to locate the intended target—the headquarters of the Yugoslav Federal Directorate for Supply and Procurement (FDSP)—was severely flawed. Second, none of the military or intelligence databases used to verify target information contained the correct location of the Chinese Embassy. Third, nowhere in the target review process was either of the first two mistakes detected. No one who might have known that the targeted building was not the FDSP headquarters—but was in fact the Chinese Embassy—was ever consulted.[45]

Passions over the bombing were shortly dampened in China, as the government worried about losing control of anti-U.S. sentiment.

The Clinton administration closed with the president defending a policy of engagement with China. In March 2000 he stated:

Voting against permanent trade status won't free a single prisoner (in China) or create a single job in America or reassure a single American ally in Asia. It will simply empower the most rigid anti-democratic elements in the Chinese government. It would leave the Chinese people with less contact with the democratic world and more resistance from their government to outside forces. Our friends and allies would wonder why, after 30 years of pushing China in the right direction, we turned our backs now that they finally appear to be willing to take us up on it.[46]

Clinton-era relations between the United States and China closed on a high note as the Chinese government announced in November 2000 that it would limit arms exports that might be used to develop nuclear capability. The U.S. response was swift: "In consideration of China's commitment to strengthen its missile-related export control system, we have decided to waive economic sanctions required by U.S. law for past assistance by Chinese entities to missile programs in Pakistan and Iran."[47] At the end of the Clinton administration, despite considerable ups and downs over the preceding four years, U.S.-China relations were stabilizing.

George W. Bush

Candidate George W. Bush criticized the Clinton administration for coddling dictators. Rather than engaging China, he said, a second Bush administration would regard Beijing as a "strategic competitor." Many believed that the United States would replace the Soviet Union with China as its great international foe. And, certainly, Chinese-U.S. relations did not begin well for the new president. In April 2001, a Chinese fighter plane collided with a U.S. Navy EP-3 reconnaissance plane over the South China Sea. The EP-3 made an emergency landing on Hainan Island. The Chinese held the twenty-four American crew members and initially used the incident to stir Chinese nationalist sentiment. The U.S. position, according to Secretary of Defense Donald H. Rumsfeld, was as follows:

So the question is, what caused the collision? This is not an unusual practice to fly these reconnaissance flights. The United States has done it hundreds of times. At least six countries fly reconnaissance missions in Asia, including China. There was nothing new or different about the mission on March 31st. What is new is that the Chinese pilots had been maneuvering aggressively against our aircraft in recent months. . . . We were sufficiently concerned about the behavior of the Chinese aircraft, the United States government was, that the concerns were raised in a formal protest, both in Beijing and in Washington, D.C. back in December . . . in the prior administration, where they called upon the People's Republic of China and the PLA to "look into the matter and to prevent its reoccurrence and to ensure that all freedoms and rights under international law for the use of the sea and airspace was not infringed in the future." So the People's Republic of China was well aware, as a result of that demarche.[48]

Eventually, however, Beijing decided that the crisis was detrimental to its foreign policy goals. The American crew members were sent home on April 12. In retaliation, President Bush authorized the sale of defense articles and services to Taiwan, including diesel-powered submarines, antisubmarine aircraft, and destroyers. By June 2001, however, the mood had changed, and Secretary Rumsfeld told journalists that the United States was resuming military contacts with the People's Republic, which had been suspended since the EP-3 incident.

The terrorist attacks of September 11, 2001, changed the equation of U.S.-Chinese relations, perhaps permanently. The George W. Bush administration suddenly became far less interested in China as a strategic competitor and far more interested in China's ability to help thwart the global antiterrorist threat. In February 2002, Bush visited China. His comments, during a meeting with President Jiang Zemin, indicated how once again presidential imperatives trump campaign politics in U.S.-Chinese relations:

> This is the 30th year—30th anniversary of President Nixon's first visit to China, the beginning of 30 years of growth in the U.S.-China relationship. Our ties are mature, respectful and important to both our nations and to the world. . . . I welcome China's cooperation in our war against terror. I encourage China to continue to be a force for peace among its neighbors—on the Korean Peninsula, in Southeast Asia and in South Asia. China as a full member of the WTO will now be a full partner in the global trading system, and will have the right and responsibility to fashion and enforce the rules of open trade. My government hopes that China will strongly oppose the proliferation of missiles and other deadly technologies. President Jiang and I agreed that the United States and China could cooperate more closely to defeat HIV/AIDS. Our talks were candid, and that's very positive. The United States shares interests with China, but we also have some disagreements. We believe that we can discuss our differences with mutual understanding and respect. . . . The position of my government has not changed over the years. We believe in the peaceful settlement of [the Taiwan] issue. We will urge there be no provocation. The United States will continue to support the Taiwan Relations Act. China's future is for the Chinese people to decide. Yet no nation is exempt from the demands of human dignity. All the world's people, including the people of China, should be free to choose how they live, how they worship, and how they work. Dramatic changes have occurred in China in the last 30 years, and I believe equally dramatic changes lie ahead. These will have a profound impact not only on China itself, but on the entire family of nations. And the United States will be a steady partner in China's historic transition toward greater prosperity and greater freedom.[49]

In late 2002 and early 2003, U.S. actions in Iraq dominated world headlines. China's leaders were apprehensive over U.S. willingness to act unilaterally, without the imprimatur of the United Nations. As U.S. forces began Operation Iraqi Freedom in March 2003, China's military leadership in particular became increasingly critical of what they perceived as U.S. aspirations for global hegemony. Their push for Chinese military self-sufficiency accelerated. At the same time, China was able to demonstrate its newfound commitment to the international community by joining many countries in voicing their doubts about events in Iraq. For many years, the People's Republic of China was the outsider in the international system. In 2003, despite or perhaps because of its position as the world's lone superpower, the United States was ostracized. Beijing enjoyed its newfound respectability at the same time that it feared the outcome of the U.S.-led effort to re-create the Middle East.

With George W. Bush's reelection in 2004, China continued to be a contentious subject for his administration. At the same time that Beijing's leaders had become increasingly responsible international citizens and the Chinese-U.S. economies continued to become more interdependent, many groups in the United States viewed China with suspicion and even hostility. Supporters of Taiwan had been joined by groups fearful of Chinese economic growth (including labor groups that traditionally endorse Democratic Party candidates as well as manufacturers in various industries), groups fearful of China's increasing military power, human rights groups, and religious groups to promote a more antagonistic China policy for a second Bush administration. The history of Chinese-U.S. relations since the Shanghai Communiqué would suggest that the second Bush administration will once again favor a balanced approach to the People's Republic of China. Time will tell.

Policy Options

Option 1: Security in Asia

China's leaders and even its intellectuals view the United States with a mixture of dread and desire. Many acknowledge that the Chinese goal of a socialist market economy will be difficult if Chinese-U.S. trade relations are disrupted, but some also fear U.S. hegemony in the post–Cold War era. One classified Chinese analysis states, "The United States may be running out of energy, but it has never abandoned its ambition to rule the world, and its military interventionism is becoming more open."[50] Some even believe that Washington is not averse to disrupting Chinese-U.S. trade relations in the hope that the resulting economic dislocation would bring about political and social dislocation similar to that seen in Eastern Europe and the former Soviet Union. Continued U.S. pressure and even threats on human rights issues, which the Chinese leadership regard as an infringement on their sovereignty, only fuel Chinese fears of the U.S. drive to control and dominate.

Other Chinese security analysts, at least before the September 11, 2001, terrorist attacks, feared that China would justify a continued U.S. military presence in Asia.[51] The increases in Chinese defense spending since 1989, as well as Chinese arms sales, fuel U.S. fears of a Chinese drive for military domination of the area. Concerns over the security of Japan, South Korea, and Southeast Asia are likely to dictate a continued U.S. presence. If Sino-U.S. relations break down over other contentious issues, such as Chinese reluctance to adhere to the Missile Technology Control Regime, China may well be used to provide the rationale by which U.S. officials convince the U.S. public to remain engaged in East Asia.

In the post–Cold War era, the balance of power in East Asia may shift in several directions. The United States will be forced to develop a coherent response to each of the possible scenarios. Winston Lord, former U.S. ambassador to China, told Congress, "We must develop new mechanisms to manage or prevent emerging concerns. We have enormous stakes in the Pacific. We need to integrate our economic, political and security policies. We need fresh approaches and structures of cooperation."[52] One scenario was enunciated by former secretary of state Alexander M. Haig Jr., who argued in October 1993 that Tiananmen should not guide U.S. policy and that the United States cannot impose its human rights standards. Rather, he advocated a balance-of-power approach to U.S. relations with East Asia, whereby the United States pursues good relations with both China and Japan, thereby keeping these two potential superpowers balanced.[53] Many Asian leaders also want the United States to act as a balance between China and Japan, but not at the price of Washington dominating the area.

China, concerned over perceived U.S. attempts to interfere in its domestic affairs (e.g., promoting human rights and political openness), may also ally itself with other nations that are concerned that the United States as the sole superpower may attempt to become the global police force. One U.S. analyst suggests, "Should the relations between Washington and Beijing continue to unravel, China would then become a viable partner for Russia or Japan if either finds itself at odds with U.S. policy in the region. A Sino-Russian or Sino-Japanese alliance thus is possible if the balance-of-power game is steadfastly played in a twenty-first century multipolar world."[54] For now, however, China seeks security arrangements in Asia that preclude any one nation from being too influential. China's goal is to keep the United States, Japan, Russia, and others from dominating the decisionmaking process on East Asian security issues.

The United States, for its part, will have to decide whether to continue its military presence in East and Southeast Asia. Despite a resurgent U.S. isolationism, many still argue that "continued U.S. presence will not stop or even significantly slow the growth of indigenous forces, but it will provide a framework for orderly growth and conservative use of these forces. The sudden decompression resulting from the disappearance of both Soviet and U.S. power from Southeast Asia is not desirable."[55] Yet the United States will also have to recognize the fears of Asian leaders that a formal security structure dominated by the United States would lead to another era of U.S. preponderance in the region. The Chinese leadership, in particular, demands that the United States treat the People's Republic with a respect and dignity befitting the largest regional power in East Asia. If the United States remains militarily engaged in Asia in the twenty-first century, even as the sole remaining superpower, it will have to play by the new rules, which place greater value on local dignity and sovereignty.

Option 2: Economic Relations

The increasing U.S. trade deficit with China, combined with continuing controversies over loss of U.S. jobs, subsidization of the Chinese currency, and copyright infringement, may lead to increased Sino-U.S. tensions and potential future trade disruptions. These might include U.S. sanctions on Chinese products, pressure to revalue the RMB, and efforts to limit sales of advanced technology to China. Although China is now a member of the WTO, controversies over trade remain. If Chinese-U.S. diplomacy is successful, trade issues will be addressed through bilateral diplomacy, with each side compromising somewhat to prevent a breakdown in relations; if diplomatic discussions break down, a trade war may well ensue. Chinese-U.S. trade volume is detailed in Tables 5.3 and 5.4.

Option 3: Greater China

China has never ruled out the use of force to reunite Taiwan with mainland China. Although Chinese leaders in Beijing have always been unwilling to

Table 5.3 China's Trade with the United States, 1997–2003 (in U.S.$ billions)

	1997	1998	1999	2000	2001	2002	2003
U.S. exports	12.8	14.3	13.1	16.3	19.2	22.1	28.4
Percentage change	6.7	10.9	–8.0	24.4	18.3	14.6	28.5
U.S. imports	65.8	75.1	87.8	107.6	109.4	133.5	163.3
Percentage change	21.0	14.1	16.9	22.6	1.6	22.0	22.3
Total	78.6	89.4	100.9	123.9	128.6	155.6	191.7
Percentage change	18.4	13.7	12.9	22.8	3.8	21.0	23.2
U.S. balance	–53.0	–60.8	–74.7	–91.3	–90.2	–111.4	–134.8

Source: U.S.-China Business Council, http://www.uschina.org/statistics/tradetable.html.

Table 5.4   Top U.S. Exports to China, 2003 (in $ millions)

	2002	2003	Percentage Change
Electrical machinery and equipment	3,950.1	4,782.6	21.1
Power generation equipment	4,109.1	4,639.6	12.9
Oil seeds and oleaginous fruits	917.9	2,877.4	213.5
Air- and spacecraft	3,428.8	2,451.2	−28.5
Medical equipment	1,258.6	1,594.0	26.6
Plastics and articles thereof	995.2	1,247.5	25.4
Iron and steel	591.1	1,213.9	105.4
Organic chemicals	619.9	1,105.3	78.3
Cotton	153.4	769.3	401.6
Copper	319.6	652.3	104.1

Source: U.S.-China Business Council, http://www.uschina.org/statistics/tradetable.html, viewed June 2, 2004.

send their military forces across the Taiwan Straits, primarily because of fears of international sanctions, a resurgent China may choose military options, particularly if the Taiwanese independence movement becomes stronger and more outspoken. In addition, if the Beijing succession struggle becomes too disorderly, one or another faction might well seek support by mounting an expedition to unify China.

The implications for both the People's Republic and the United States are obvious. If the People's Republic mounts a military expedition against Taiwan, congressional and public opinion will be aroused. China's leaders could remind Washington of its commitment to a Chinese solution to the Taiwan issue and to a cessation of arms sales to Taiwan. Though commitment of U.S. troops to the actual defense of Taiwan is uncertain, given Washington's reluctance to become involved in ground wars in Asia, U.S. air and naval support activities might be provided to the Taiwanese military. This would end any U.S. rapprochement with China.

What the United States must hope for is the gradual integration of Hong Kong into China, followed by the economic integration of Taiwan into greater China. The economies of China, Hong Kong, and Taiwan are becoming increasingly interwoven. As the three economies become one large interconnected entity, the impetus to maintain good trade relations with Europe and the Americas will increase. At the same time, as China's economy becomes more marketized, its political system will be forced to become more open, which will reduce friction with those nations concerned about human rights violations. The development of the greater Chinese economy is important to the United States for at least four reasons:

- With the increasing ties between southern China and Hong Kong and Taiwan, the Chinese people in Guangdong and Fujian provinces are influenced more by their capitalist neighbors than by Beijing.
- With the southern Chinese, Hong Kong, and Taiwan economies becoming interdependent, the security of the latter two is enhanced.
- The greater Chinese economy provides a platform from which the United States can develop its economic and cultural ties throughout the East Asian region.
- Greater economic growth will lead to the growth of a middle class that will begin to demand change, especially because this middle class will be in contact with the slowly liberalizing societies of Hong Kong and Taiwan.[56]

Greater economic integration would lead to more political cooperation. Closer political ties between the People's Republic and Taiwan would be the next obvious step, perhaps eventually leading to peaceful political unification or at least a Chinese economic and political community.

Option 4: Quiet Diplomacy

Scholars of Chinese-U.S. relations now advocate "quiet diplomacy." Instead of threatening China, they advocate a carrot-and-stick approach. According to Barber Conable, former president of the World Bank:

> We need to develop other instruments to promote our human rights objectives, not only in China, but elsewhere as well. . . . I am inclined to move conflict over human rights into multilateral fora where the accumulated weight of world opinion can have its effect. . . . A package of moves needs to be put together in the next couple of months in which both the PRC and the US seek to meet concerns of the other. A set of confidence inducing, reciprocal, and parallel moves that are clear and understood to both sides should be sufficient.[57]

Isolating China is no longer an option, according to this school of thought; rather, the best way to change a nation is by engaging it.

▨ Discussion Questions

1. To what extent is it in China's interest to comply with U.S. demands for changes in its domestic policies?
2. What is the current status of Chinese-U.S. relations? Are the two nations partners, opponents, or a combination of both? Explain.
3. As an emerging world power, is China entitled to greater respect for its sovereignty and more equal treatment from the United States?

4. If Taiwan seeks to abandon the "one-China" policy, how should China and the United States react?
5. What role do human rights issues play in Chinese-U.S. relations?
6. In what ways can China utilize the assistance of other states to influence Washington to respect its sovereignty and treat it more equally in the international community?
7. How did the September 11, 2001, terrorist attacks on the United States affect Washington's relations with Beijing?
8. How do different interests inside China affect Chinese relations with the United States? How do different interests inside the United States affect U.S. policy toward China?
9. How can Beijing take advantage of different interests of economic interest groups inside the United States to its best advantage?
10. To what extent do Beijing and Washington disagree on the role that China should play in different regions of the world?
11. To what extent do Beijing and Washington disagree on the role that the two states should play in the United Nations?
12. What are the possibilities for overcoming Chinese-U.S. disagreements on issues such as nuclear testing and eliminating nuclear weapons and other weapons of mass destruction, as well as delivery systems for such weapons?
13. Now that the Cold War is over and international terrorism dominates the U.S. agenda, to what extent should the United States cooperate with China in modernizing its military forces during a time period in which Beijing is also working to improve its relationships with the outside world? Explain.
14. In the twenty-first century, to what extent are China and the United States likely to be rivals or partners in the emerging global system? Explain.
15. Why is the United States more likely than any other country to have the greatest impact on China? With the passage of time, is the U.S. impact on China likely to increase, decrease, or remain stable? Why?

▓ Suggested Readings

Bernstein, Robert L., and Richard Dicker. "Human Rights First." *Foreign Policy* no. 94 (Spring 1994): 43–47.

Bert, Wayne. "Chinese Policies and U.S. Interests in Southeast Asia." *Asian Survey* 33, no. 3 (March 1993): 317–332.

Cohen, Warren. *America's Response to China: A History of Sino-American Relations.* 3rd ed. New York: Columbia University Press, 1990.

Copper, John Franklin. *China Diplomacy: The Washington-Taipei-Beijing Triangle.* Boulder, Colo.: Westview, 1992.

Drinan, Robert F., and Teresa Kuo. "The 1991 Battle for Human Rights in China." *Human Rights Quarterly* 14 (February 1992): 21–42.

Dumbaugh, Kerry. *China-U.S. Relations: Issue Brief for Congress.* Washington, D.C.: Library of Congress Congressional Research Service, May 17, 2002. http:// fpc.state.gov/documents/organization/13422.pdf.

Gill, Bates, and Sue Anne Tay. *Partners and Competitors: Coming to Terms with U.S.-China Economic Relationship.* Washington, D.C.: Center for Strategic and International Studies, April 2004. http://www.csis.org/china/0404_partners.pdf.

Harding, Harry. *A Fragile Relationship: The United States and China Since 1972.* Washington, D.C.: Brookings Institution, 1992.

Kristof, Nicholas D. "The Rise of China." *Foreign Affairs* 72, no. 5 (November–December 1993): 59–73.

Lampton, David. M. *Same Bed, Different Dreams: Managing U.S.-China Relations, 1989–2000.* Berkeley: University of California Press, 2001.

Lilley, James R. *China Hands: Nine Decades of Adventure, Espionage, and Diplomacy in Asia.* New York: PublicAffairs/Perseus Books, 2004.

Lilley, James R., and Wendell L. Willkie II, eds. *Beyond MFN: Trade with China and American Interests.* Washington, D.C.: AEI Press, 1994.

Mann, James. *About Face: A History of America's Curious Relationship with China, from Nixon to Clinton.* New York: Knopf, 1998.

Munro, Ross H. "Awakening Dragon: The Real Danger in Asia Is from China." *Policy Review* no. 62 (Fall 1992): 10–16.

Myers, Ramon Hawley, Michel Oksenberg, and David L. Shambaugh, eds. *Making China Policy: Lessons from the Bush and Clinton Administrations.* Lanham, Md.: Rowman and Littlefield, 2002.

Oxnam, Robert B. "Asia/Pacific Challenges." *Foreign Affairs* 72, no. 1 (1993): 57–73.

Ross, Robert S., ed. *After the Cold War: Domestic Factors and U.S.-China Relations.* Studies on Contemporary China. Armonk, N.Y.: M. E. Sharpe, 1998.

———, ed. *China, the United States, and the Soviet Union: Tripolarity and Policy Making in the Cold War.* Armonk, N.Y.: M. E. Sharpe, 1993.

Schaller, Michael. *The United States and China in the Twentieth Century.* New York: Oxford University Press, 1979.

Suettinger, Robert L. *Beyond Tiananmen: The Politics of U.S.-China Relations.* Washington, D.C.: Brookings Institution, 2003.

Sutter, Robert. "Asia in the Balance: America and China's 'Peaceful Rise.'" *Current History* 103, no. 674 (Sept. 2004): 284–289.

———. "Why Does China Matter?" *Washington Quarterly* (Winter 2003–2004): 75–89.

Tan Qingshan. *The Making of U.S. China Policy: From Normalization to the Post–Cold War Era.* Boulder, Colo.: Lynne Rienner, 1992.

Terrill, Ross. *The New Chinese Empire, and What It Means for the United States.* New York: Basic Books, 2003.

Tyler, Patrick. *A Great Wall: Six Presidents and China: An Investigative History.* New York: PublicAffairs/Perseus Books, 1999.

Vogel, Ezra F., ed. *Living with China: U.S./China Relations in the Twenty-First Century.* New York: Norton, 1997.

Notes

1. "The Shanghai Communiqué," in Richard H. Solomon, ed., *The China Factor: Sino-American Relations and the Global Scene* (Englewood Cliffs, N.J.: Prentice-Hall, 1981), pp. 296–300.

2. Warren I. Cohen, *America's Response to China,* 3rd ed. (New York: Columbia University Press, 1990), p. 2.

3. Michael Schaller, *The U.S. and China in the Twentieth Century* (New York: Oxford University Press, 1979), p. 30.

4. Ibid., p. 16.

5. Cohen, *America's Response to China,* p. 42.

6. Thomas G. Paterson, J. Garry Clifford, and Kenneth J. Hagan, *American Foreign Policy: A History Since 1900* (Lexington, Mass.: D. C. Heath, 1988), p. 383.

7. U.S. Department of State, *The China White Paper: United States Relations with China with Special Reference to the Period 1944–1949* (Stanford: Stanford University Press, 1967), pp. xv–xvi.

8. Many U.S. citizens believed that the Communist victory was not inevitable but rather was a result of a "stab in the back" by members of the State Department who supported the Communists. In 1945, Ambassador Hurley's bitter resignation letter charged that the "China Hands" had sabotaged his efforts in China because they favored a Communist victory. Several Foreign Service officers were singled out for being "soft on communism." John Service was arrested as part of the Amerasia case in 1945 and was subjected to loyalty and security hearings in 1946, 1947, and 1949 (as well as 1950 and 1951), which were all resolved in his favor. John Carter Vincent was accused of sabotaging U.S. policy on China in 1947, and only after a spirited defense by Secretary Acheson did the Senate confirm his appointment as career minister. John Paton Davies was also investigated in 1949 and was cleared. Thus began the McCarthy era in the State Department and in the United States.

9. As a result of the Korean War, approximately fifty U.S. citizens were incarcerated in the People's Republic, including eleven members of the U.S. Air Force who were sentenced as spies. Dag Hammarskjold, the UN Secretary-General, traveled to China to lobby for their release in January 1955, but renewed fighting in the Taiwan Straits delayed any further discussions until the issue of direct Sino-U.S. negotiations was raised by the Chinese. To show their goodwill, they released four of the U.S. airmen at the end of May and the eleven accused of spying at the end of July. Nine more were released in September after the ambassadorial-level talks had begun in Geneva. At the same time, the United States agreed to allow any Chinese citizen still in the United States to return to China if he or she so desired. By 1957, only eight U.S. citizens were still being held by the Chinese. After this initial success, however, the prisoner issue stalemated until President Nixon's visit to China in 1972, and so long as even one U.S. citizen was in a Chinese jail, the issue remained a potent rallying factor for the China lobby.

10. The debate between the United States and the People's Republic over the admission of U.S. news reporters to China was the subject of a furious controversy in the late 1950s. Three U.S. newsmen visited China in early 1957, one as a representative of the *Baltimore Afro-American* and two as representatives of *Look* magazine, and many other representatives of the U.S. press criticized the State Department's ban on China travel for reporters. Secretary of State Dulles initially defended the ban, citing the U.S. prisoners, and he stated that "the issuance of passports to a regime which is not recognized is something which is never done." By midyear, to defend himself against charges that the United States was deliberately trying to prevent information on the People's Republic from reaching the U.S. public, Dulles was forced to modify his position. He proposed that a limited number of U.S. reporters be allowed seven-month trial periods in China, but he refused reciprocal privileges to Chinese reporters. There, notwithstanding considerable legal nitpicking by both sides, but particularly by the U.S. government, the matter died.

11. Jacob Beam, *Multiple Exposure: An American Ambassador's Unique Per-spective on East-West Issues* (New York: Norton, 1978), pp. 139–143.

12. Amazingly, even after the Cultural Revolution, some meetings were held in Warsaw. Altogether, twenty-one meetings were held during the Johnson administration, with three in 1966, two in 1967, and one in 1968. Communications between representatives of the United States and the People's Republic were also facilitated: "As the interval between the talks grew longer, the channel between the Embassies in Warsaw was used increasingly to pass messages of interest between the two governments." In addition, starting in September 1966, U.S. officials stationed abroad were allowed to have social contacts with Chinese officials if appropriate.

13. The U.S. Department of Agriculture was particularly interested in a crop exchange, because China was "historically a principal source of some major US crops." *Administrative History of the Department of State, 1945–1973*, Lyndon B. Johnson Library, p. 42.

14. *Administrative History,* pp. 42–43.

15. James Thomson described the efforts to ease travel regulations, once again blaming the secretary of state for delaying initiatives. James Thomson Jr., "On the Making of U.S. China Policy, 1961–69: A Case Study in Bureaucratic Politics," *China Quarterly* 50 (April–June 1972): 220–243.

16. Special State-Defense Long-Range Study on Communist China, S/P 66-71-2a, June 1966, in *Administrative History,* p. 26.

17. There was some talk in Washington of pushing a "two Chinas" policy in the UN more blatantly after the annual General Assembly vote on admission of the People's Republic tied. That talk faltered, apparently because of both bureaucratic reluctance in Washington and the onset of the Cultural Revolution. James Thomson once again blames Dean Rusk. Thomson, "On the Making of U.S. China Policy," p. 240.

18. Cohen, *America's Response to China,* p. 198.

19. Henry A. Kissinger, *Years of Upheaval* (Boston: Little, Brown, 1982), p. 1124.

20. Hong N. Kim and Jack L. Hammersmith, "U.S.-China Relations in the Post-Normalization Era, 1979–1985," *Pacific Affairs* 59, no. 1 (Spring 1986): 72.

21. Taiwan Relations Act, Public Law 96-8, April 19, 1979, 93 Stat. 14.

22. Kim and Hammersmith, "U.S.-China Relations," pp. 77–78.

23. Ibid., p. 73.

24. United States–China Joint Communiqué on United States Arms Sales to Taiwan, August 17, 1982. See Harry Harding, *A Fragile Relationship: The United States and China Since 1972* (Washington, D.C.: Brookings Institution, 1992), pp. 383–385.

25. Tan Qingshan, *The Making of U.S. China Policy: From Normalization to the Post–Cold War Era* (Boulder, Colo.: Lynne Rienner, 1992), p. 101.

26. Harding, *Fragile Relationship,* p. 209.

27. During the Reagan administration, favorable U.S. public opinion of China ranged from a low of 43 percent in 1983 to a high of 71 percent in 1985. By July 1989, only 31 percent of respondents reported a favorable opinion of China. Harding, *Fragile Relationship,* p. 363.

28. From 1984 to 1989, the United States delivered $79 million of military assistance to China. In addition, weapons valued at $195 million were delivered through commercial sales.

29. Donald M. Snow and Eugene Brown, *Puzzle Palaces and Foggy Bottom* (New York: St. Martin's Press, 1994), p. 134.

30. Samuel S. Kim, quoted in Michael Yahuda, "Deng Xiaoping: The Statesman," *China Quarterly* no. 135 (September 1993): 557.

31. China's record was not worse than that of the NATO countries on sales to Iraq. Robert S. Ross, "U.S. Policy Toward China," in Robert J. Art and Seyom Brown, eds. *U.S. Foreign Policy: The Search for a New Role* (New York: Macmillan, 1993), pp. 338–357.

32. Specific measures included the following: formally resuming high-level contacts with the Chinese government; resuming regular exchanges of commercial and scientific commissions; allowing the delivery of specific U.S. military equipment to China agreed on and paid for in the 1980s but held in storage in the United States after the Tiananmen incident; allowing some higher-level military interaction with China; actively considering high-technology sales to China; and reducing export controls on communications and telecommunications equipment. Robert G. Sutter, *CRS Report for Congress: China Policy Decisions at the Start of the 103rd Congress,* January 19, 1993, p. CRS-3.

33. Steven Greenhouse, "State Department Castigates China on Rights Record," *New York Times,* February 2, 1994, p. A9.

34. Executive Order 12850, http://www.archives.gov/federal_register /executive_orders/pdf/12850.pdf.

35. Thomas L. Friedman, "U.S. Pares Imports of Chinese Fabrics," *New York Times,* January 7, 1994, p. D2.

36. Thomas L. Friedman, "Bank Rules Are Eased by China," *New York Times,* January 22, 1994, p. 37.

37. Patrick E. Tyler, "Textile Accord with China Averts Trade Clash," *New York Times,* January 18, 1994, p. D1.

38. Elaine Sciolino, "U.S. Will Allow Computer Sale to Court China," *New York Times,* November 19, 1993, pp. A1, A5.

39. Ibid.

40. Patrick E. Tyler, "U.S. and China Agree to Expand Defense Links," *New York Times,* November 3, 1993, p. A13.

41. John Kohut, "Arms Sellers Accused of Stirring Fears," *South China Morning Post,* March 24, 1993.

42. "Clinton's Call: Avoid Isolating China," *New York Times,* May 27, 1994, p. A8.

43. "Clinton Publicly Reiterates U.S. 'Three No's' Principles on Taiwan," www.china-embassy.org/eng/zmgx/zysj/kldfh/t36241.htm.

44. "Chinese Foreign Minister Lodges Serious Representation and Presents an Official Note to U.S. for the Bombing of the Chinese Embassy by U.S.-led NATO," May 11, 2000, http://www.fmprc.gov.cn/eng/wjb/zzjg/bmdyzs/gjlb/3432/3441/t17312. htm.

45. "Oral Presentation by Under Secretary of State Thomas Pickering on June 17 to the Chinese Government Regarding the Accidental Bombing of the PRC Embassy in Belgrade," July 6, 1999, http://www.usconsulate.org.hk/uscn/state/1999/0706.htm.

46. President Bill Clinton, March 8, 2000, quoted in http://www.wcit.org /topics/china/china_report.pdf, p. 7.

47. "Statement by the Acting Assistant Secretary Richard Boucher," U.S. Department of State, Office of the Spokesman, November 21, 2000, http://www.nti.org/ db/china/mexport.htm.

48. "Secretary Rumsfeld Briefs on EP-3 Collision," U.S. Department of Defense news transcript, April 13, 2001, http://www.defenselink.mil/news/apr2001/t04132001_ t0413ep3.html.

49. "President Bush Meets with Chinese President Jiang Zemin," White House press release, http://www.whitehouse.gov/news/releases/2002/02.

50. Nicholas D. Kristof, "The Rise of China," *Foreign Affairs* 72, no. 5 (November–December 1993): 72–73.

51. Bonnie S. Glaser, "China's Security Perceptions: Interests and Ambitions," *Asian Survey* 33, no. 3 (March 1993): 259–261.

52. John R. Faust, "East Asia's Emerging Security System," *Journal of East Asian Affairs* 8, no. 1 (Winter–Spring 1994): 89.

53. Patrick E. Tyler, "Haig Scorns U.S. for Its Tough China Policy," *New York Times,* October 28, 1993, p. A14.

54. Charles W. Kegley Jr. and Gregory Raymond, *A Multipolar Peace? Great-Power Politics in the Twenty-First Century* (New York: St. Martin's Press, 1994), p. 207.

55. Wayne Bert, "Chinese Policies and U.S. Interests in Southeast Asia," *Asian Survey* 33, no. 3 (March 1993): 332.

56. "Triangular Chinese Economy Quickly Emerging," *United States–China Relations: Notes from the National Committee* (Spring–Summer 1992): 3, 11.

57. "Testimony on U.S.-China Relations from Barber Conable, Submitted to the Subcommittee on Trade, Committee on Ways and Means," February 24, 1994.

China and Its
Asian Neighbors

China's development would be impossible without Asia, and Asia's prosperity without China.
—Hu Jintao during his April 2002 visit to Malaysia[1]

China isn't interested in military expansion; it will seek tribute through trade, like it did before the Western powers came to Asia.
—John Gokongwei, the patriarch of a
Chinese-Fillipino business clan[2]

One of China's major challenges in the twenty-first century will be to develop relations with its East Asian neighbors that will enhance the area's security and economy while maintaining its own agenda as the increasingly dominant power in the region. Forced by the exigencies of the Cold War to follow military policies independent of its neighbors, China is now engaged in what has been called a "charm offensive," particularly in Southeast Asia. Rather than flexing the muscles of its growing military might, China has taken the opportunity to work with its neighbors in Asia and within multilateral organizations to enhance economic interchanges while also addressing a number of dangerous security problems in Asia, including:

- rivalry on the Korean peninsula, with the potent dangers of a nuclear arms race,
- nuclear rivalry between India and Pakistan,
- continuing fears over a future military rivalry between China and Japan,
- political instability in the Philippines,
- rivalries among China, Vietnam, Taiwan, and the Philippines over control of economic resources in the South China Sea,
- potential political instability in Cambodia, Myanmar (Burma), and other South and Southeast Asian nations, and

- the rise of terrorist groups in the Philippines, Indonesia, Malaysia, and other parts of East Asia.

Through spearheading efforts at multilateral cooperation, China could choose to be a key to East Asian stability. If that approach fails, however, China could choose a route that emphasizes its role as the leading military power in the region, particularly if it continues to export military equipment to selected neighbors. China's future security role in Asia is an increasing concern to its Asian neighbors, especially because of the large increases in Chinese military expenditures since the 1980s.[3] Although military expenditures decreased in the world as a whole during the 1990s, they increased in Asia as a region and especially in China. Samuel Huntington, a Harvard expert on military affairs, believes that China's military buildup has important implications at both the regional and global levels:

> Centrally important to the countering of western military capabilities is the sustained expansion of China's military power and its means to create military power. Buoyed by spectacular economic development, China is rapidly increasing its military spending and vigorously moving forward with the modernization of its armed forces. It is purchasing weapons from the former Soviet states; it is developing long-range missiles; in 1992 it tested a one-megaton nuclear device. It is developing power-projection capabilities, acquiring aerial refueling technology, and trying to purchase an aircraft carrier. Its military buildup and assertion of sovereignty over the South China Sea are provoking a multilateral arms race in East Asia.[4]

Three of the world's greatest arms races are now going on in Asia: North and South Korea; China and Taiwan; and India and Pakistan. Currently, there is an even greater military buildup in Asia than in the Middle East, which along with Asia experienced the greatest amount of war and violence during the Cold War era.

Since the end of World War II, the government in Beijing has been involved in military skirmishes along most of its borders, as well as in a major war in Korea. At the turn of the twenty-first century, military tensions continued at high levels to the northeast (the two Koreas), to the east (an arms race between Beijing and Taipei), to the southeast (naval skirmishes between China and Vietnam in the South China Sea, as well as violence in Cambodia and Myanmar), and in South Asia (an arms race and military confrontation over Kashmir between Pakistan and India).

In contrast to continuing military tensions along its borders, China's economic relations with its neighbors have improved dramatically since the implementation of the Open Door policy. Unlike the United States and some of its European allies, China's noncommunist Asian neighbors seem little disturbed by the events of Tiananmen Square. As a result, there has been a rapid increase in Chinese trade and tourism with Japan, Taiwan, and Hong Kong especially, but also increasingly with South Korea and Russia. Through bilateral relations, political, economic, and social transactions continue to grow between China and nearly all of its neighbors.

Multilateral transactions in the late twentieth century took place through China's growing but limited role in the UN system, not at the regional level. An East Asian security community similar to the North Atlantic Treaty Organization (NATO) or an economic community similar to the European Community never developed. A traditional regional distrust of China, combined with Chinese nationalism and isolationism, prevented a security alliance. Similarly, the export-based economies of Japan, South Korea, Taiwan, and Hong Kong did not provide a logical basis for a common economic community.

The Korean War began on June 25, 1950, when North Korean troops moved south of the thirty-eighth parallel. Although some military skirmishes had occurred at the parallel after Korea was divided at the end of World War II, the events in June were perceived as an invasion of the South. President Harry Truman masterminded a UN military operation that was initially successful in driving back the North Koreans. Indeed, U.S. and UN troops were so successful that China felt its security was threatened and sent 1 million volunteers to Korea to fight. After three years of bloody fighting, which ended with troops arrayed along the thirty-eighth parallel as they had been before the war, an armistice was finally signed in July 1953.

In the early twenty-first century, however, much has changed. China has become "cool" in Southeast Asia. Regional economic and security groupings are in various phases of development in both Southeast and Central Asia, and economies ties (particularly and paradoxically between China and Taiwan) have grown exponentially. Yet as in Europe, integration efforts have not progressed to the point where analysis of nation-state relations have been superseded by analysis on a regional level. To analyze China's role in Asia, even in what has been called the "Pacific century," it is still necessary to examine China's relations with Japan, the two Koreas, Southeast Asia, South Asia, and Central Asia on a bilateral basis.

The Question of Two Koreas

To date, the end of the Cold War has been felt most dramatically in the southern part of the Korean peninsula. Surprisingly, China, rather than the United States, was the pivotal actor affecting the changing status of Seoul. First,

President Kim Il Sung, referred to by the people of North Korea as the "Great Leader," established the Communist government after the end of World War II. Kim had been part of the armed Communist opposition to Japanese domination of Korea, and when the Soviets moved into North Korea, they handed the reins of government over to Kim. His regime was one of the most reclusive on earth, having few diplomatic or economic contacts with the outside world. Kim's philosophy of self-reliance, however, was severely tested by the collapse of communism. As Soviet aid moneys were discontinued, North Korea's economy spiraled downward. Production plummeted and widespread shortages of food and other essentials ensued. Kim's son Kim Jong Il, the "Dear Leader," inherited his father's position in 1994, despite a reputation for dissoluteness, which may be accurate or may just be an image promoted by South Korean intelligence agencies.

China supported the admission of the two Koreas to the United Nations in 1991. Second, China extended diplomatic recognition to South Korea in 1992, two years after the Soviet Union had done so.

Both China and South Korea clearly had a tremendous amount to gain by normalizing relations. In playing its China card, South Korea further isolated North Korea, its longtime rival, while reducing its dependency on the United States and Japan. By playing the South Korea card, China created a major new trading partner. Seoul is China's fifth largest foreign investor, with investments of $1 billion and two-way trade that amounted to $44 billion in 2002. This compares with Chinese–North Korea trade of no more than $600 million annually.[5] These economic ties with South Korea have reduced Chinese dependence on trade and investment from other major partners, especially the United States and Japan, giving China greater leverage and bargaining power.

By playing the South Korea card, China also furthered one of its most important foreign policy goals. During the Cold War years, South Korea and Taiwan were united by passionate anticommunism into a strong alliance. Now, as traditional security and economic goals have replaced ideology as a guide to developing foreign policy, South Korea has abandoned Taiwan in favor of rapprochement with China. With Korean-Taiwanese relations reduced to nongovernmental economic arrangements similar to those between Taiwan and its major trading partners, Taiwan has lost one of its very few remaining diplomatic ties.

South Korea has clearly benefited from the end of the Cold War. North Korea is the clear loser. Now that ideological score cards are no longer being kept, Soviet/Russian and Chinese aid to the isolated, neo-Stalinist regime has decreased dramatically, with devastating results. North Korea's economy deteriorated to the point where starvation was so prevalent that Pyongyang actually accepted international food aid.[6] With few other bargaining chips, the North Korean leadership has resorted to rattling its sabers by launching a nuclear weapons development program. A North Korea armed with nuclear weapons is enough to scare every nation in East Asia into working together to develop means to counter this potential security threat. Alternatively, though, a nuclear North Korea could be the catalyst for a nuclear South Korea, Japan, and Taiwan.

Arms Race or Peaceful Coexistence?

Regardless of whether or not the Cold War has come to an end elsewhere, the two Koreas have continued to confront each other with the largest concentration of military forces in Asia. North Korea maintains an active military force of nearly 1 million (5 percent of its population), and South Korea's active force numbers over 700,000. In addition, nearly 40,000 U.S. military personnel are still stationed in South Korea. North Korea's superior numbers are balanced by South Korea's more modern equipment and technology. No longer supported by Russia and increasingly unsure of Chinese support, North Korea is on its own in terms of military might. South Korea has double the population and a far more vibrant economy, so time and international circumstances seem to be working against North Korea. This leaves North Korea's leadership with only the nuclear option to ensure its grip on power.

In March 1993, North Korea announced it would withdraw from the Nuclear Nonproliferation Treaty and bar international inspections on its soil, presumably to be free to develop nuclear weapons without on-site inspections by UN officials. In 1994, the United States and other countries agreed to provide North Korea with alternative energy resources in exchange for Pyongyang's cessation of efforts to develop nuclear power plants. The world was trying to convince the North Koreans to not even consider using the nuclear option as a bargaining chip. The Clinton administration advocated a policy of limited engagement. It agreed to the 1994 "framework" on Korea's nuclear program, and supported South Korea's "Sunshine" policy, announced in 1997 and undertaken to improve ties with the North. Secretary of State Madeleine Albright visited Pyongyang in October 2000, the first time such a high-level U.S. official had visited North Korea. According to Albright, Kim Jong Il responded as follows regarding North Korea's weapons program:

> So it's clear, since we export to get money, if you guarantee compensation, it will be suspended. . . . We also arm our own military as part of our self reliance program. . . . If there is an assurance that South Korea will not develop five-hundred-kilometer-range missiles, we won't either. As for the missiles

already deployed, I don't think we can do much about them. You can't go inside the units and inspect them, but it's possible to stop production. It's been ten years since the collapse of the USSR, the opening of China, and the disappearance of our military alliance with either country. The military wants to update its equipment, but we won't give them new equipment. If there's no confrontation, there's no significance to weapons. Missiles are now insignificant.[7]

The Bush administration, while also stressing a political rather than a military solution to the nuclear program, has a considerably more dubious view of North Korea. President George W. Bush, in his 2002 State of the Union address, famously included Pyongyang in his "Axis of Evil." U.S. curtailment of oil supplies to North Korea after Washington accused Pyongyang of secretly resuming its nuclear program was followed in December 2002 by Pyongyang's announcement that it had in fact done so. In 2002, North Korea revealed that it was pursuing an uranium enrichment program. In 2004, Abdul Qadeer Khan, the "father" of the Pakistani nuclear weapons program, admitted to disclosing nuclear development secrets to North Korea (and other nations) and stated that he saw three nuclear weapons when he visited the country in 1999. Moreover, U.S. intelligence officials now believe that North Korea has an untested intercontinental ballistic missile, against which the Bush administration hopes to deploy a missile defense system.

Given the administration's preoccupation with the Middle East, however, Washington has focused on the Korean issue sporadically. While Washington's long-term goal is undoubtedly regime change, its medium-term goal is denuclearization of the Korean peninsula. To that end, the administration refuses to offer any "carrots" until Pyongyang confirms it has closed down its nuclear weapons program. It has also insisted on multiparty rather than bilateral talks, which both China and North Korea prefer. North Korea has two unpalatable choices: impoverished isolation while working on a nuclear weapons development program or peaceful coexistence probably leading to eventual reunification with the South. It is therefore insisting on a "grand bargain" strategy whereby it will not negotiate on only one issue but seek a series of commitments that will ensure its survival and economic recovery.

China's New Diplomacy on the Korean Peninsula

As a friend of North Korea, one of the world's few remaining communist regimes, China had been unwilling to pressure the North Koreans openly in the past; however, it does periodically send symbolic gestures to the North. Behind closed doors, China is reportedly pressing North Korea to follow the Chinese Open Door model, especially for economic development. The cost of subsidizing North Korea is high. While China fears that a nuclear North Korea could lead to a revival of Japanese militarism, China's worst fear is that North Korea will implode, leaving a security vacuum on the Korean peninsula that will be filled by South Korea, Japan, and the United States. Also, China fears an ever-increasing number of North Korean refugees. In the past, it had periodically repatriated those it locates, but large numbers—perhaps in the hundreds of thousands—still remain in northeast China.

China's response to increased tensions on the Korean peninsula has highlighted Beijing's new aspirations to regional leadership through diplomacy. Although Beijing has grave doubts about the Bush administration's approach to Pyongyang, it agreed to prod North Korea to join multilateral talks proposed by the United States (as opposed to bilateral talks between the United States and North Korea, which both Pyongyang and Beijing preferred). Not only is China at the table, but it is also the host of the multiparty talks. As previous administrations have discovered, however, China's ability to influence North Korea is limited. While Beijing has been roundly praised

> **State of the Union Address Delivered by President George W. Bush, January 2002**
>
> North Korea is a regime arming with missiles and weapons of mass destruction, while starving its citizens. . . . States like these [North Korea, Iran, and Iraq], and their terrorist allies, constitute an axis of evil, arming to threaten the peace of the world. By seeking weapons of mass destruction, these regimes pose a grave and growing danger. They could provide these arms to terrorists, giving them the means to match their hatred. They could attack our allies or attempt to blackmail the United States. In any of these cases, the price of indifference would be catastrophic.

for its mediation efforts during the six-party talks (North Korea, South Korea, China, the United States, Japan, and Russia) in 2003 and 2004, its frustration with both U.S. and North Korean inflexibility became evident. For example, the second round of the talks in February 2004 ended without the planned joint statement, leaving China to issue a statement on its own. The only agreement was to establish a working group for further discussions, which met in June 2004.

The Korean peninsula is still a dangerous place. Washington and Tokyo believe that Pyongyang is a "rogue" regime erratic enough to want to go down in flames if that is the only option left to it. Beijing states it does not know what Pyongyang wants, while trying to influence it to maintain the current uneasy status quo and adopt incremental change. Pyongyang probably will

We stand that the maintenance of peace and stability of the Korean Peninsula is of great significance for the regional and international peace. It is our view that the Peninsula should be free of nuclear weapons, peace and stability be maintained, and the issue be solved through peaceful talks. With the joint efforts of the parties concerned, the nuclear issue of the Korean Peninsula, embarking on the track of the peaceful resolution through dialogue, has witnessed two rounds of six-party talks in Beijing, and the Peninsular situation has been eased after a spell of tension. It is our hope that, in line with the spirit of the mutual respect and consultation on an equal footing, all parties concerned could narrow differences, expand consensus and build mutual trust to look for an early resolution of the nuclear issue through dialogue and achieve lasting peace in the Peninsula. The Chinese side will, as always, play an active role in maintaining peace and stability in the Peninsula (speech by Hua Junduo, Chinese ambassador to India, at the Defense College of India, April 21, 2004).

use its nuclear weapons only as a bargaining chip, at least in the near future; however, the possibility of tensions escalating into open hostilities between the North Korean military and U.S. troops stationed in South Korea and South Korean troops is real. The consequences would be cataclysmic. According to the Perry Report, a new outbreak of hostilities would cause 52,000 U.S. military casualties (killed and wounded) and 490,000 South Korean military casualties in the first nine days of battle.[8] Which approach prevails—regime change or regime evolution—will have a dramatic affect on future security in Northeast Asia.

The Koreans on either side of the thirty-eighth parallel have always stated publicly that reunification is both desirable and inevitable. The question is how. The always suspicious North Korean leaders are unlikely to trust their southern compatriots. Quick reunification is therefore unlikely, especially given the example of Germany, where precipitate reunification led to social and economic distress. Most South Koreans believe that reunification will be a slow process of building mutual trust, expanding trade ties, and defusing the military threat. How long the process will be and how difficult are open to debate. According to former South Korean president Kim Dae-jung, who won the Nobel Peace Prize in 2000 for his "Sunshine" policy:

> To replace the dangerous stand-off with peace and cooperation, I proclaimed my sunshine policy upon becoming President in February 1998, and have consistently promoted its message of reconciliation with the North: first, we

will never accept unification through communization; second, nor would we attempt to achieve unification by absorbing the North; and third, South and North Korea should seek peaceful coexistence and cooperation. Unification, I believe, can wait until such a time when both sides feel comfortable enough in becoming one again, no matter how long it takes.[9]

Future Chinese Relations with the Two Koreas

There are a number of reasons that improved relations between China and South Korea promote China's national interests. First, increased South Korean investment in China reduces China's economic dependence on other outside sources such as Japan. Second, close relations with both Koreas increase Chinese political bargaining with respect to both Japan and Russia, because China and South Korea have a mutual interest in constraining both Japanese and Russian influence in Northeast Asia. Third, because China, Japan, the United States, and Russia all have a common interest in bringing the arms race on the Korean peninsula to an end, close Chinese relations with both Koreas gives Beijing the key role in working with the North and South and others to bring the two sides together.

There are also a number of reasons China wishes to retain good relations with North Korea. To be trustworthy as a mediator, Beijing must retain the respect of the leadership in Pyongyang. Therefore, China's leaders cannot allow North Korea to become isolated and abandoned by threatening to lessen China's traditional security commitments to North Korea. Good relations with North Korea will also enable China to encourage Pyongyang's participation in regional economic projects, including special economic zones in the border areas between Russia, China, and North Korea, which will benefit all three countries. Helping North Korea modernize and develop through using the Chinese model will help stabilize Northeast Asia, reducing the danger of outside intervention in the future. Finally, China's support for North Korea's vital interests enables Beijing to work behind the scenes to head off a dangerous nuclear arms race on the peninsula. China will be a key player in negotiating alternative security arrangements that may enable North Korea to give up its nuclear card, which is its primary bargaining chip, to obtain more favorable terms in settling its differences with Seoul.

With the passage of time, Beijing may gain more advantage from a unified Korea—one that comes gradually rather than through a "shotgun marriage," as was the case with the two Germanys. In the twenty-first century, a unified Korea, because of its own interests and traditional experiences with the Japanese, is likely to align with China on balance-of-power issues in Northeast Asia, both on the question of Japanese influence in the region and on the question of any resurgence of Russian chauvinism. Should a separate Siberian republic emerge in Northeast Asia, China and a unified Korea would have a common interest in working together with their new neighbors to the north to create stability in the region. Japan, on the other hand, may wish to promote the emergence of a non-nuclear and stable North Korea in order to maintain a balance of power on the peninsula. Tokyo has always looked upon the Korean peninsula as its sphere of influence, and it is aware that with further economic development throughout the region, a united Korea might have more in common with the Chinese than the Japanese in the twenty-first century.

▓ Getting Along with Southeast Asia

China's relations with Southeast Asia in the twenty-first century are likely to be dramatically more positive than at any time in the recent past. China's abandonment of revolutionary rhetoric and support of Maoist parties in Southeast Asia has been much appreciated by the leaders of Indonesia, Malaysia, Thailand, Singapore, and the Philippines. The withdrawals of the Soviets from Vietnam and the United States from its Philippine bases dramatically altered the map in Southeast Asia. Before the Cold War ended, the issue of most concern to the members of the Association of Southeast Asian Nations (ASEAN), which comprises six original members—Thailand, Indonesia, Malaysia, Singapore, the Philippines, and Brunei—and four newer members—Cambodia, Laos, Vietnam, and Myanmar (Burma), was the growing Soviet presence in the region and the expansion of Vietnamese influence into Cambodia and Laos. Now, ASEAN's major concerns are China's growing power, both economically and militarily, Japan's relative economic weakness, resolution of intraregional disputes, political fragility in member nations, and the rise of terrorist groups particularly in Indonesia and the Philippines.

China's range of political and economic options in Southeast Asia is wider now than at any time during the Cold War era. However, China's southeastern Asian neighbors have always been wary of their gigantic northern neighbor. If China seeks to broaden its influence in Southeast Asia, it will have to tread carefully. Thus far, China has focused its efforts on cutting its revolutionary ties, signing statements of friendship with ASEAN members, and developing trade ties.

China's ties to the Southeast Asian nations have been varied and complex. Each ASEAN country has a large Chinese minority, which is often the backbone of the nation's commercial and business community. Resentments and prejudices have festered in the past. In Malaysia, ethnic Chinese were officially discriminated against, and Thai Chinese were forced to adopt Thai surnames. Large numbers of Chinese were killed in Indonesia in 1965 during the overthrow of President Sukarno's pro-Beijing government because of lingering fears that the Chinese living in Southeast Asia would have primary loyalty to China rather than the country they lived in. Many overseas Chinese were not even citizens of the countries they and their forebears lived in. Though many Southeast Asians resent what they perceive to be Chinese clannishness, they both fear and admire Chinese business successes. The Chinese in Southeast Asia, in turn, believe that their economic success is due to hard work, and they resent the limitations many Southeast Asian nations have attempted to place on expressions of Chinese culture in the past.

Economic Ties

In 1997, China succeeded in gaining ASEAN's trust at the expense of international financial institutions and particularly of the United States. The Asian financial crisis weakened confidence in Asian regional institutions and in the U.S. commitment to Southeast Asia. China, however, sought to use the crisis to improve its image in the region, which it did by pledging funds to Thailand and not devaluing its own currency to maintain international competitiveness. China's efforts were appreciated by the Malaysian prime minister Mahathir:

> China's performance in the Asian financial crisis has been laudable, and the countries in the region . . . greatly appreciated China's decision not to devalue the [yuan]. China's cooperation and high sense of responsibility has spared the region a much worse consequence. The price China has to pay to help East Asia is high and the Malaysian people truly appreciate China's stand.[10]

China's exports to ASEAN grew from $4.1 billion in 1991 to $17.3 billion in 2000, while its imports from ASEAN grew from $3.8 billion to $22.2 billion over the same period.[11] U.S. foreign direct investment (FDI) in Southeast Asia, however, declined from 75 percent of all FDI in the 1990s to 10 percent in 2000. In 2004, 80 percent of U.S. FDI in East Asia was invested in China.[12] To solidify its economic ties to ASEAN nations, China also signed a framework agreement on comprehensive economic cooperation with ASEAN nations in November 2002. Table 6.1 illustrates the nature of ASEAN's import and export trade with China.

China and the ASEAN countries are in some ways alike. They tend to produce goods for export and are the site of foreign direct investment from outside countries. Given the similarities, many in ASEAN are not sanguine about China's economic growth and the potential growth in its exports as trade barriers come down. The older ASEAN members are nervous that China's trade with the newer ASEAN members is growing at a faster rate than with their countries. Yet ASEAN understands that it must live with the behemoth and try to manage the relationship effectively. Establishment of a free

Table 6.1   ASEAN-Chinese Exports and Imports, 1999

ASEAN Exports to China	Share (%)	ASEAN Imports from China	Share (%)
Computer/machinery	20.3	Electrical equipment	26.6
Electrical equipment	17.9	Computer/machinery	20.0
Lubricant fuels/oil	11.4	Cereals	4.3
Fats and oils	5.4	Lubricants/fuels/oil	3.6
Wood	5.1	Ships/boats	2.5

Source: ASEAN-China Export Group on Economic Cooperation, "Forging Closer ASEAN-China Economic Relations in the 21st Century," October 2001, pp. 9–10.

trade area between ASEAN and China is therefore under discussion. The benefits would include increased intraregional trade and increased economic efficiency as specialization in production based on comparative advantage leads to lower costs and higher income.[13] Whether a free trade association will actually be created depends on the parties overcoming fear of increased competition, displacement of workers, and loss of tariff revenues. Thus China's "charm offensive" in Southeast Asia. To manage its relations with Southeast Asia, China must not appear to be suffocating its southern neighbors.

Southeast Asia was cajoled into accepting China's proposal, despite misgivings over the country's increasing regional dominance, fears that it would come to dominate the regional economy, and concerns over its relationship with Laos, Myanmar, and Vietnam. China has sought to allay these fears through a variety of concessions that will protect developing industries in the newer ASEAN nations while assuring the original members of ASEAN of its commitment to the continued integrity of the entire organization.[14] Japan's coprosperity sphere may become a reality in the twenty-first century. Ironically, however, it is likely to be the Chinese who dominate it rather than the Japanese.

Regional Security in Southeast Asia

China's moves in the political-security spheres will be more difficult. Within the region, there has been little success in creating multilateral structures to compensate for the withdrawal of the Soviet and U.S. military presence. Even ASEAN has failed to move beyond economic cooperation to some type of regional collective security system. This is probably due in part to U.S. opposition (until very recently) to multilateral Asian security ties rather than bilateral security ties with Washington. Similarly, China ignored Mikhail Gorbachev's calls for an Asian collective security system in the late 1980s, and it refused to participate in an Asia Pacific security conference sponsored by Australia, Canada, and Japan. Beijing, too, has favored bilateral security arrangements. China's leaders in the past feared that they would have little influence over multilateral Southeast Asian security arrangements. They believed that their interests were best promoted through security ties with each Southeast Asian nation separately.

China changed its view in the 1990s. In its effort to undermine U.S. influence in Southeast Asia, it signed cooperation agreements with each ASEAN member that committed all parties to regular meetings between political leaders as well as to certain defense cooperation activities.[15] As part of China's effort to improve its relations with ASEAN countries, it joined in a number of multilateral dialogues during the 1990s, including ASEAN Plus Three (ASEAN plus China, Japan, and South Korea) and the ASEAN Regional Security Forum. While China has not resolved its territorial disputes with ASEAN nations, it embarked on a new approach after signing the "Conduct of Parties in the South China Seas" treaty in 2001. Thereafter, China began emphasizing dialogue rather than military might as the means to resolve disputed jurisdictions in the South China Sea.

Territorial Disputes

China's territorial claims in Southeast Asia extend beyond the island of Taiwan to the South China and East China Seas. In February 1992, China passed a territorial waters law claiming control of the Spratly Islands, which are also claimed by every other nation in the area; the Paracel Islands; and the Senkaku Islands, which are currently administered by Japan. Potential oil reserves were the incentive for China's claiming of the Spratly Islands. First, China stunned the world in 1988 when it engaged Vietnam in a military clash over the islands. Then, in 1992, Beijing entered into an agreement with a Denver, Colorado–based oil company to begin joint exploration for oil near one of the Spratlys. Dangerously, Vietnam and other Southeast Asian nations still stake their claims to the Spratlys, which are far closer to their borders than to China's borders; some of the nations have a military presence on one or more of the thirty-three islands.

Although China and the ASEAN members are formally committed to resolving these disputes through political means, the South China Sea is still a disputed and dangerous area. Vietnam, in 2004, sent tourists to one of the Spratlys. Beijing responded that Chinese sovereignty had been violated. Taiwan built a house on stilts, and the United States and the Philippines conducted military exercises in the area. Each of these actions inflamed the situation. While it is unlikely that any of the parties involved will open hostilities, continuing tensions in the South China Sea could easily lead to an incident that would spiral out of control.

China's Role in Cambodia

After the Khmer Rouge took over Cambodia in 1975, they marched the residents of Phnom Penh and other cities into the killing fields. Over 1 million people, one-fifth of the population, were butchered. Most members of society with any education, business experience, or ties with the "bourgeois" classes were eliminated.

Throughout the worst years of Khmer Rouge excesses, China supported Pol Pot and his revolutionary murderers, at least partially through revolutionary affinity. Probably more important, however, was the historical antagonism between China and the Vietnamese. The Soviet-supported Vietnamese government invaded Cambodia in 1978, ostensibly to end the killings but also in no small part because Vietnam had traditionally coveted Cambodia's rich agricultural areas. The Vietnamese established a puppet regime in Phnom Penh led by Hun Sen, but the Khmer Rouge continued to fight in the countryside.

Thailand, another traditional rival of the Vietnamese, entered into an informal alliance with the Chinese to back the Khmer Rouge, who used Thai territory and Khmer Rouge–controlled refugee camps inside Thailand as bases to conduct warfare against Hun Sen's Vietnamese-backed regime in Phnom Penh. Chinese economic and military assistance flowed through Thailand to the Khmer Rouge, and Beijing also ordered a military incursion across China's southwestern border into northern Vietnam in late 1978 and 1979 to try to force Hanoi to stop its military intervention in Cambodia. Vietnamese military forces were successful enough to embarrass the Chinese military. Despite the failure of China's military effort, China remained a major participant in the internal struggles in Indochina. By 1980, Vietnam controlled most of Laos and Cambodia, and the Khmer Rouge occupied sizable rural areas of western and northwestern Cambodia on the Thai border.

Vietnam's increasing power, as well as the Soviet support for Vietnam's expansionism, alarmed many other Asian nations. To check Vietnam, ASEAN joined with the United States to promote a tripartite coalition government involving two noncommunist Cambodian resistance movements and the Khmer Rouge. This so-called coalition government even received the imprimatur of the United Nations, which allowed the coalition to assume Cambodia's seat in the General Assembly. The supporters of this anomalous coalition were more concerned with the expansion of Soviet and Vietnamese influence in Southeast Asia than they were with the moral and ethical implications of allying themselves with the Khmer Rouge.

The end of the Cold War ended Asian fears of Vietnamese expansionism. Vietnam withdrew most of its forces from Cambodia in 1989, and Russia, which is no longer interested in or able to provide aid to its former ally, withdrew its forces from Vietnam. Now Vietnam is seeking normalization of relations with the West—even with China and the United States—and investment funds. Taiwan, with $600 million in investments, and Japan have been leading the way. In 1992, Japan provided $400 million to help rebuild Vietnam's infrastructure. Japanese and other businesspeople are interested in Vietnam's large, educated, and cheap work force.

The end of the Cold War has also allowed more concerted efforts to find a solution to the problems in Cambodia, led by the permanent members of the Security Council, along with Australia, New Zealand, and the ASEAN countries. In October 1991, the Security Council passed a comprehensive political settlement on the Cambodian conflict. A 22,000-strong UN force was sent to Cambodia to supervise the demobilization of all factions and oversee the writing of a new constitution that would lead to election of a new government.

China therefore had a problem in Cambodia. As a member of the Security Council, it was obligated to support UN efforts. Yet China was also afraid of Japanese influence in the region, and the United Nations appointed a Japanese representative to lead the UN effort. This, in turn, led Japan to pledge to send troops to Cambodia to perform nonmilitary duties. The idea of Japanese troops being mobilized anywhere on the Asian mainland was an issue of the greatest sensitivity to China's leaders—so much so that during his visit to Japan in 1992, Party Secretary Jiang Zemin called on the Japanese government to cancel plans for nonmilitary troop deployment in Cambodia.

When the UN-supervised elections were held in May 1993, the Khmer Rouge refused to participate; however, although some political violence continues, Cambodia has been relatively stable politically—certainly compared to its recent history. Chinese relations with Cambodia have also stabilized. Jiang Zemin visited Cambodia in November 2000, and the two countries issued a joint declaration of friendly relations. In November 2002, Zhu Rongji visited Cambodia and announced that China would encourage bilateral cooperation with Cambodia in the fields of politics, economics and trade, culture, education, and tourism, among others. He also announced that China would forgive some Cambodian debts. In 2002, Chinese-Cambodian trade volume reached $270 million, up 15 percent from 2001. China's exports to Cambodia include textiles, steel, electric devices, metals machinery, and building materials, and its imports from Cambodia include rubber, plywood, panels, and furniture. Clearly, China has decided to extend its "charm" campaign to Cambodia. Rather than dwelling on regional rivalries or past allegiances, Beijing is focusing on developing economic ties and on Cambodia's newfound role as a member of ASEAN.

Future Chinese Relations with Southeast Asia

The decline of Soviet and U.S. military influence in Southeast Asia, continuing instability in Cambodia, regional territorial disputes, and growing Chinese military capability are causing concern to all nations with an interest in Southeast Asian security. Over the next decades, Beijing will have to choose from among a number of difficult options. Its decisions will have an enormous effect on the future course of Southeast Asian security.

Beijing could adopt a hard-line policy of threatening to use force, as well as bilateral deals, to assert Chinese control over the island chains in the South China and East China Seas. Such threats would undermine efforts to create regional security arrangements and would work to the detriment of China's good relations with its neighbors. By playing one territorial claimant against another, while offering economic deals to investors from outside the region, Beijing might be able to take advantage of existing disagreements between Southeast Asian states and their inability to create effective regional collective security arrangements.

If Beijing is controlled by conciliators rather than those who favor the use of the military over the next decades, China might signal to its neighbors and the global community that it wishes to avoid bilateral power plays. China might reaffirm the policy it always has adhered to in theory, if not in fact: non-interference in the internal affairs of other states. It could demand similar pledges from its neighbors. In addition, as the sole Asian member of the Security Council, China could become an active partner in guaranteeing the peace and stability of Southeast Asia.

If the influence of those in Beijing who seek peaceful relations with China's neighbors grows, they might seek to reach an accommodation on territorial disputes. In the fall of 1993 China began negotiations with Vietnam in an effort to bring about a peaceful settlement of disputes over islands in the South China Sea. It is hoped that this will lead to a sharing of oil resources. A new policy of seeking joint solutions to regional problems could be the missing link in gradually building an East Asian security community to match the growing economic cooperation in the region. Whereas military confrontation in the South China Sea could lead to regional arms races (especially between China and Japan), as well as to China's isolation from its neighbors, partnership in solving regional disputes could strengthen Asia's role in the emerging global system.

▨ The Balance of Power in South Asia

Throughout the Cold War, South Asia was an important crossroads of confrontation, involving not only the two principal actors in the region, India and Pakistan, but also the two superpowers, the United States and the Soviet Union. The People's Republic of China also became involved in South Asia through its accession of Tibet in 1950 and a number of border skirmishes with India, particularly in the 1960s. India's sheltering of the Dalai Lama after he finally fled Tibet in 1959 led to increasing Chinese mistrust of Prime Minister Nehru's government. Increasing Soviet support for India only heightened

Chinese security sensitivities, and Nehru's aspirations to third world leadership directly conflicted with China's own bid for that title.

Pakistan, adopting the philosophy "The enemy of my enemy is my friend," became China's ally and hence anti-Soviet. The more military equipment the Indians received from the Soviet Union and Eastern Europe, the more U.S. and Chinese military assistance went to Pakistan. By the time of the 1971 war between West and East Pakistan, in which India intervened to ensure the independence of East Pakistan (Bangladesh), the Indo-Pakistani conflict had become a proxy war for the superpowers. The Soviet Union assisted India, whereas the United States "tilted" toward Pakistan as a reward for Pakistani assistance with the Nixon administration's overtures to Beijing.

The Sino-U.S.-Pakistani anti-Soviet alliance found its true cause in Afghanistan in 1979. Not since the end of World War II had the Soviets so blatantly expanded their sphere of influence, although the Russians and the British had been vying for control of the area for nearly two centuries. China and the United States intervened on the side of the anticommunist Afghanis. Predictably, India sided with the Soviet Union and voted against UN condemnations of the invasion. Because many of the anticommunist fighters operated out of camps on the Afghani-Pakistani border, Pakistan became the major supply line for the anticommunist resistance movement in Afghanistan. The civil war heightened tensions in South Asia and, until Gorbachev withdrew his troops in 1989, became the Soviet Union's Vietnam. Withdrawal may have enabled the Soviet Union to escape its quagmire, but it did not fully resolve the situation in Afghanistan. Now the various groups of "freedom fighters" continued to fight among themselves until the Taliban took over.

With the end of the Cold War, tensions in South Asia have actually heightened, and the security alignment has become more complex than ever. India and Pakistan allegedly nearly went to war again in the late 1980s, and there were rumors that both nations were considering the possibility of using nuclear weapons. India exploded a nuclear device in 1974, as did Pakistan in 1998. So long as the Soviet intervention in Afghanistan continued, the United States turned a blind eye to Pakistan's efforts to join the nuclear club. In the late 1980s, however, the Bush administration implemented congressional resolutions that denied foreign aid to any country seeking nuclear capability. The United States also pressured China, presumably unsuccessfully, to cease assisting Pakistan with its nuclear and missile programs. Commercial sales of U.S. military equipment to Pakistan have continued, however, just as Russia has continued to sell arms to India. At the same time, the United States and China have been successfully pursuing better relations with India. The aftermath of the September 11, 2001, terrorist attacks on the United States has further complicated South Asian regional security. India is nervous about fundamentalist-inspired violence from across the Pakistani border, while China is concerned about the increased U.S. presence in Pakistan and Afghanistan, as well as improving U.S.-Indian ties.

Post–Cold War Alignments

Post–Cold War alignments in South Asia have an Alice in Wonderland character—they become more and more curious. Unfortunately, they also become more and more dangerous. Despite the reduced roles of Washington and Moscow, all of the same rivalries and conflicts remain, and new dangers are arising. Nuclear proliferation alarms all, as does the possibility of yet another war between India and Pakistan. Violence directed at India's Islamic minority, border tensions, and tensions over Indian control of Kashmir may flare up yet again. Although Pakistan's military capabilities are far inferior to India's, it could resort to the use of nuclear and chemical weapons to make up for its inferior conventional forces, and India could respond in kind. All in all, the arms buildup on the subcontinent is exceeded only by the arms buildup in the Middle East. Any warfare between India and Pakistan would involve two of the world's largest military forces.

Chinese-Indian Rapprochement

The 1988 visit of Prime Minister Rajiv Gandhi to China signified the normalizing of relations between the two former foes. Despite joint efforts to settle working disputes, old attitudes resurfaced in 1998, when India conducted nuclear tests. Only in 2002, when Zhu Rongji visited India, did relations stabilize again. While no progress has been made on many of the border disputes, India did use China's name for Tibet, the "Tibetan Autonomous Regime," for the first time. Trade between China and India is growing, with Chinese consumer goods entering the Indian market and two-way trade in computer technology increasing. Tensions between China and India continue, with the Chinese nervous about India's increased nuclear capability and with India always concerned about Chinese

India: Forty-five to ninety-five nuclear warheads. The Pentagon projects that New Delhi has a relatively small stockpile of nuclear weapons components that could be assembled and deployed "within a few days to a week."
Pakistan: Thirty to fifty nuclear warheads. The Pentagon believes Islamabad stores its weapons in component form and could assemble weapons "fairly quickly."
Source: Arms Control Association, "Nuclear Weapons: Who Has What at a Glance," April 2004, http://www.armscontrol.org/factsheets/nuclearweaponswhohaswhat.asp.

arms sales to Pakistan and the growth of Chinese military and economic power. Indeed, some Chinese analysts fear that the United States seeks to "contain" China by encircling it with U.S. allies such as India. According to one analyst, "in order to ease pressure from the United States (regarding its nuclear tests), India must challenge China because India and the West have similar strategic aims concerning containing China."[16] For the immediate future, the Chinese desire for a regional balance of power in South Asia will in all likelihood dictate a more evenhanded foreign policy, one that embraces normalization with India while supporting the current Pakistani regime in its antiterrorism efforts.[17]

Future Sino-Pakistani Relations

Beijing has a long-term interest in seeing that Pakistan remains a viable counterforce to Indian domination of the subcontinent and the surrounding regions. So long as domination through force is the order of the day in South Asia, China has a vital interest in supporting a balance of power based on mutual deterrence in the region. In the future, it may be in China's interest to continue providing conventional arms to Pakistan but to cease aiding Pakistan's nuclear program. China's arms sales provide foreign currency to Pakistan's military industrial complex, and China and Pakistan have a common interest in creating a military balance on the subcontinent to prevent Indian domination of the region. Yet no major Chinese arms sales to Pakistan have been reported since 2000.[18]

As China has been developing economic ties with India, its former enemy, it has been counseling Pakistan, its long-standing ally, to enter into discussions with India regarding border disputes and to develop confidence-building measures. Beijing believes that, "if China and India have better relations, India will be able to show more flexibility toward Pakistan."[19] As an alternative to taking an overtly pro-Pakistani stand in South Asia, Beijing currently seems to be emphasizing peaceful economic trade ties with all South Asian countries, thereby strengthening China's reputation as a supporter of peace in the post–Cold War era. From the perspective of the reformist and nonmilitarist interests inside China, it could also be a means of encouraging trade and investment in consumer goods rather than the arms trade coming from military-controlled factories inside China.

China and India as Role Models

China and India are often compared as models of the successes and failure of capitalism versus communism in raising the popular living standard. India has pursued modernization through state capitalism and improvements in agrarian technology. A large, well-educated middle class has developed since World War II, and crop yields have increased markedly. Yet because of the caste system, both the urban and the rural social structures remain unaltered, ensuring that the distribution of wealth remains inequitable. Thus, many rural poor migrate to Calcutta and other large cities to join the low-caste urban population in eking out a miserable existence at odd jobs. To create more efficient and productive industries that will lead to job creation, the Indian government began taking steps in 1992 to privatize its large state industrial sector, create laws more favorable to foreign investment, and even set up special economic zones.

China's model of development has been dramatically different. The Communist Party's first priority was to create a classless society through political controls at all levels of society. Then it utilized a Stalinist model for industrialization that involved collectivization of the peasantry to create a surplus for use in developing heavy industry. The Communist Party claimed that it provided each citizen with a decent diet, but many starved during the politically induced famines during the Great Leap Forward and the Cultural Revolution. Not until agriculture was freed from party control did crop yields rise substantially, and China's state industries have had their own inefficiency problems. After Deng Xiaoping's reforms, China's economy began to grow rapidly but unevenly and inequitably, not unlike India's economy. As both India and China reform their economies, discussion of each as a discrete model of development becomes less persuasive.

As illustrated in Table 6.2, few clear winners emerge in any comparison of Chinese and Indian development statistics. Per capita annual income in China is higher than in India. Human rights are generally considered to be more honored in democratic India than China. Yet many minorities in India, including the large Muslim minority—and especially women—are often treated ruthlessly by government authorities.[20] China bests India in the areas of primary education and infant mortality rate. But the discrepancies may decrease as China abandons its basic health care system, one of the most prized outcomes of the Communist revolution. In the post–Cold War world, doctrinaire models of development are giving way to messy experimentation with elements of socialism and capitalism. Neither China nor India can present any clear model to the other developing countries of the world.

China and India as Regional Powers

China and India will continue their traditional rivalry, which is not unusual for two regional powers with contiguous borders. China is unlikely to abandon its support for Pakistan, both because Pakistan is a counterweight to India on the subcontinent and because a friendly Pakistan might be able to influence moderates in the new Central Asian Islamic republics on China's borders. Further, in the post–Cold War era, Sino-Indian economic rivalry will become an issue.

Table 6.2   Chinese and Indian Development Indicators, 1998–2002

	1998		2001		2002	
	China	India	China	India	China	India
Population, total (billions)	1.2	0.9	1.3	1.0	1.3	1.0
Population growth (annual percentage)	1.0	1.7	0.7	1.6	0.7	1.6
Gross national income per capita, Atlas method (current U.S.$)	740	420	900	460	960	470
National poverty rate (percentage of population)	4.6	—	—	—	—	—
Life expectancy (years)	—	—	—	—	70.7	63.4
Fertility rate (births per woman)	—	—	—	—	1.9	2.9
Infant mortality rate (per 1,000 live births)	—	—	—	—	30	65
Literacy, total (percentage of population age fifteen and above)	83.8	55.7	—	61.3	—	—
Literacy, female (percentage of population age fifteen and above)	76.1	43.5	—	—	—	—

Source: World Development Indicators Database, August 2003, www.worldbank.org/data/.

Despite increases in Sino-Indian trade,[21] the two nations compete with each other for foreign investment and development aid from the World Bank. China and India also compete for export markets in Southeast Asia, and India's attempts to improve relations with Vietnam must certainly concern China.

Either as competitors or potential partners, relations between China and India will have a tremendous effect on the stability of southern Asia as well as on the leadership alignments within the third world in the emerging global system. If the past is a key to the future, China might pursue both approaches simultaneously. Beijing wishes to improve both political and economic relations with India on a bilateral basis. Yet multilateral arms control negotiations seeking to end the nuclear and conventional arms race in South Asia would undoubtedly at some point raise India's demand for China to dismantle its nuclear capability as a condition for New Delhi's agreement to abandon the nuclear military option. Until now, China's political and military leaders have refused to consider such an option other than as part of a total world package to eliminate all nuclear arms.

Policy Options

Option 1: Emphasis on Bilateral Relations

In dealing with its neighbors, China's easiest choice would be to continue most of its current policies with Japan, the two Koreas, Southeast Asia, South Asia, and Central Asia. Based on past behavior, this has meant reliance on bilateral rather than multilateral transactions with all its neighbors. From Beijing's perspective, the advantages were clear. Because multilateral fora may create alignments more favorable to other regional actors than to China, in terms of both political-security and economic issues, it was to the advantage of Beijing to deal with each neighbor separately. China's leaders seem to feel this approach may pay even greater dividends in the future, as China's development increases its bargaining power on both security and economic issues.

Beijing will have to work diligently to try to convince its neighbors that bilateral rather than multilateral arrangements are in everyone's best interest. This may become increasingly difficult if other Asian countries see China's rising military expenditures as a growing threat to their security. In the economic sphere, however, many of China's neighbors may agree with Beijing that rather than belonging to regional economic groupings dominated by Japan, the dominant Asian economic actor, it is better to work out individual arrangements to protect each Asian country's interests. Indeed, in recent years, there have been an increasing number of bilateral treaties in East and Southeast Asia, spearheaded by Singapore, which has a Chinese majority. In the twenty-first century, if China's economy continues to grow at its present rate and if Japan has internal economic troubles, perhaps Beijing may feel more confident of its ability to protect its interests in any regional economic groupings.

Option 2: Support for Regionalism

If regional organizations emerge regardless of Beijing's wishes, then China will no doubt join them, if only for the purpose of protecting its interests (i.e., to limit damage should others support policies that seem unfavorable to Beijing). This is the policy China seems to be adopting in the early twenty-first century, as it extends its "charm offensive" to its Asian neighbors and as it becomes increasingly active in Asian multilateral organizations.

Option 3: Settlement of Regional Disputes in Northeast Asia

It is logical for China to work with its neighbors to settle Asiatic disputes that might upset the current balance of power in Asia, which currently seems favorable to Beijing. Especially in Northeast Asia, a settlement of differences would benefit China, because it would minimize the danger of a remilitarized

Japan or of disturbing developments in Russian Siberia. It is in China's interest to defuse the nuclear arms race on the Korean peninsula. Beijing is currently attempting to do this by working quietly behind the scenes as a mediator between the two Koreas, while at the same time publicly reaffirming its security commitments to North Korea and Pyongyang's policy positions in its negotiations with Seoul.

From the point of view of all the actors in the region, with perhaps the exception of the current leaders in North Korea, the ideal security arrangement would be the emergence of a low-key, informal security community similar to the one that exists between Canada and the United States. For 150 years, these two countries, without any formal regional security structures, have been able to settle all their political and economic conflicts through peaceful negotiations without the threat of force. Logically, it is in China's interest to encourage the emergence of such an informal regional security system, which is most likely to come about through functional economic integration. An informal zone of peace would reduce the danger of future coercive actions by two of China's greatest protagonists in modern history: the Russians and the Japanese.

Option 4: Exercise Influence in Southeast Asia

The situation in Southeast Asia, from the Chinese perspective, seems to be very different from that in Northeast Asia. Now that Russia and the United States have either left or reduced their presence, China may emerge as the dominant military force in the region, especially in the South China Sea. China's current buildup of air and naval power gives Beijing the ability to defeat any other regional actors that might wish to contest its control of the Paracel and Spratly island chains. But in building up their military, China's leaders must be careful not to stimulate a buildup of arms or a renewal of alliances with countries outside the region. This could be difficult to avoid, however, because the vast majority of China's people take pride in the fact that the post–Cold War era is the first time in modern history that their country has the possibility of restoring some former parts of the Middle Kingdom to Chinese control—mostly in Southeast Asia.

Option 5: Create Peace in Southeast Asia

If it wishes to avoid remilitarization of Southeast Asia, which in turn may stimulate a Japanese military buildup, Beijing may find it necessary to pursue an approach that it has so far been reluctant to undertake: promoting a settlement of regional disputes, especially in the South China Sea, so that no one power or alliance could dominate the area. But achieving an informal security community similar to the one that exists in North America could be very difficult. China would clearly have to change its policy of viewing the South

China Sea as its exclusive zone. In the past, Beijing has not shown any willingness to share oil and fishing rights in the South China Sea with others, including Vietnam, Malaysia, Singapore, Brunei, the Philippines, and Taiwan. Beijing would also have to give up the possibility of building a Chinese naval base in Myanmar, because this could become a destabilizing factor in both Southeast and South Asia.

Option 6: Promote a Peaceful Balance-of-Power System in South Asia

Since the Communists came to power in 1949, security along China's borders with South Asian countries has seemingly been enhanced by instabilities within the region. If India and Pakistan concentrate their military efforts against each other, the balance of power in the region would help China protect its interests in Tibet against any outside influence. Yet China's principal interests and key goals in South Asia are regional stability and a balance of power. To that end, China has been implementing some degree of rapprochement with India.

According to Zhang Guihong, a Chinese analyst:

> China should develop constructive relations with India while improving traditional friendly relations with Pakistan. Considering India's increasing influence in regional affairs, China should pay more attention to New Delhi by taking more active steps to establish individual relations with Indian leaders and to promote negotiation of the border dispute. That said, it is also reasonable to invest more on Pakistan's economic reconstruction and social transformation. A healthy Pakistan is in China's interests. On the non-proliferation issue, it is in China's interest to ask India and Pakistan to sign the NPT and CTBT. In the meantime, China should help Pakistan to improve the safe management of its nuclear arsenal and work with the US and the international community to prevent any possibility of nuclear conflict in South Asia. China should invite both India and Pakistan to join the Shanghai Cooperation Organization, which would provide an institutional framework to engender cooperation. It would also be helpful from the perspective of countering US military influence in South and Central Asia.[22]

▓ Discussion Questions

1. In pursuit of nationalist pride and a leadership role in Asia, will China's modernization and buildup of its military capabilities strengthen or undermine its role in Asia in the early twenty-first century?

2. Can China's future security in Asia be better enhanced by unilateral and bilateral relations with its neighbors or by cooperation in the creation of multilateral security arrangements in East Asia, Southeast Asia, South Asia, and Central Asia?

3. Would China be more secure in the future with the continued existence of North Korea and South Korea as separate states or with a reunified Korea?

4. What can China do to become an equal to Japan as an economic power in the early twenty-first century?

5. Would it be to China's advantage to support a common economic market in Asia similar to the European Community or the North American Free Trade Agreement?

6. Should China continue its policy of occupying parts of the Spratly and Paracel island chains in light of conflicting claims by its neighbors? Would it be more to China's advantage to enter into arrangements with its neighbors to jointly exploit the economic resources located in these island chains than seek to exploit them through unilateral actions?

7. Should China seek a partnership with Japan in determining Asia's future development, or should it try to join with other Asian states to contain Japan's dominant economic and potential political role in Asia?

8. Is it in China's interest to seek an end to the conventional and nuclear arms race between India and Pakistan?

9. What policies should Beijing's leaders pursue with Turkey, Iran, and Pakistan in order to promote Chinese interests in Central Asia?

10. What are the implications for China of the changing U.S. strategy toward South Asia? How does the transforming U.S.-Indian-Pakistani triangle concern China? And what about the U.S.-Indian-Chinese, U.S.-Pakistani-Chinese, and Chinese-Indian-Pakistani triangles, which also merit China's attention?[23]

Suggested Readings

Albright, Madeleine. *Madam Secretary: A Memoir.* New York: Hyperion Books, 2003.

ASEAN-China Export Group on Economic Cooperation. *Forging Closer ASEAN-China Economic Relations in the 21st Century.* October 2001. http://www.aseansec.org/asean_chi.pdf.

Ba, Alice D. "China and ASEAN: Renavigating Relations for a 21st Century Asia." *Asian Survey* 43, no. 4 (July–August 2003): 622–647.

Bennett, Michael. "The People's Republic of China and the Use of International Law in the Spratly Islands Dispute." *Stanford Journal of International Law* 28 (Spring 1992): 425–450.

Brown, Frederick, ed. *Rebuilding Cambodia.* Washington, D.C.: Johns Hopkins Foreign Policy Institute, 1992.

Choo, Yong Sik. "Handling North Korea." *Strategy and Issues* 23, no. 1 (Winter–Spring 2003): 43–51.

Clark, Cal, and Steve Chan, eds. *The Evolving Pacific Basin in the Global Political Economy: Domestic and International Linkages.* Boulder, Colo.: Lynne Rienner, 1992.

Dittmer, Lowell. "East Asia in the 'New Era' in World Politics." *World Politics* 5 (October 2002): 38–65.

Faust, John R. "The Emerging Security System in East Asia." *Journal of East Asian Affairs* 8, no. 1 (Winter–Spring 1994): 56–89.

Foot, Rosemary. "Chinese-Indian Relations and the Process of Building Confidence: Implications for the Asia-Pacific." *Pacific Review* 9, no. 1 (1996): 58–76.

Frankel, Francine R., and Harry Harding, eds. *The India-China Relationship: What the United States Needs to Know.* New York: Columbia University Press, 2004.

Garver, John. *Protracted Contest: Sino-Indian Rivalry in the Twentieth Century.* Seattle: University of Washington Press, 2002.

Heo, Uk, and Shale Horowitz. *Conflict in Asia: Korea, China-Taiwan, and India-Pakistan.* New York: Praeger, 2003.

Kim, Samuel S., ed. *The International Relations of Northeast Asia.* Lanham, Md.: Rowman & Littlefield Publishers, 2004.

Malik, J. Mohan. "South Asia in China's Foreign Relations." *Pacifica Review* 13, no. 1 (February 2001): 73–90.

Mitra, Pramit. "A Thaw in India-China Relations." *South Asia Monitor* no. 62 (September 1, 2003).

Norbu, Dawa. "Tibet in Sino-Indian Relations: The Centrality of Marginality." *Asian Survey* 37, no. 11 (November 1997): 1078–1095.

O'Hanlon, Michael, and Mike Mochizuki. "Toward a Grand Bargain with North Korea." *Washington Quarterly* 26, no. 4 (Autumn 2003): 7–18.

Pollock, Jonathan D. "The United States and Asia in 2003." *Asian Survey* 44, no. 1 (January–February 2004): 1–13.

Scobell, Andrew. "China and North Korea: The Limits of Influence." *Current History* (September 2003): 274–278.

Sommers, Justin, rapporteur. "The India-China Relationship: What the United States Needs to Know." Asia Society/Woodrow Wilson Center for International Scholars Conference Report. November 30, 2001.

▓ Notes

1. Quoted in Alice D. Ba, "China and ASEAN: Renavigating Relations for a 21st Century Asia," *Asian Survey* 43, no. 4 (July–August 2003): *Asian Survey* 43, no. 4 (July–August 2003): 647.

2. Quoted in James Hookway, "Now It's Hip to Be Chinese," *Wall Street Journal,* March 16, 2004, p. A18.

3. Samuel S. Kim, "China as a Regional Power," *Current History* (September 1992): 248.

4. Samuel P. Huntington, "The Clash of Civilizations?" *Foreign Affairs* 72, no. 3 (Summer 1993): 47.

5. Andrew Scobell, "China and North Korea: The Limits of Influence," *Current History* (September 2003): 276.

6. From April 2003 through January 2004, the United States provided about 100,000 tons of food to North Korea. The United Nations has distributed 2 million metric tons of food aid, valued at $500 million, since 1995. Christopher Marquis, "Modest U.S. Aid for North Korea," *New York Times,* April 27, 2004, p. A6.

7. Madeleine Albright, *Madam Secretary: A Memoir* (New York: Hyperion Books, 2003), p. 463.

8. Yong Shik Choo, "Handling North Korea: Strategy and Issues," *SAIS Review* 23, no. 1 (Spring 2003): 47.

9. Nobel lecture given by Kim Dae-jung, Nobel Peace Prize laureate, Oslo, December 10, 2000, http://www.nobel.no/eng_lect_2000k.html.

10. Ba, "China and ASEAN," p. 637.

11. ASEAN-China Export Group on Economic Cooperation, *Forging Closer ASEAN-China Economic Relations in the 21st Century,* October 2001, p. 7.

12. Caryle A. Thayer, "Southeast Asia's Marred Miracle," *Current History* 103, no. 672 (April 2004): 178.

13. ASEAN-China Export Group, *Forging Closer,* pp. 30–31.

14. Ba, "China and ASEAN," pp. 639–640.

15. Thayer, "Southeast Asia's Marred Miracle," p. 181.

16. J. Mohan Malik, "South Asia in China's Foreign Relations," *Pacifica Review* 13, no. 1 (February 2001): 80.

17. "A Thaw in India-China Relations," *South Asia Monitor,* September 1, 2003.

18. Ibid.

19. Jay Solomon, Charles Hutzler, and Zahid Hussain, "China Steps Up Diplomatic Role," *Wall Street Journal,* December 8, 2003. p. A13.

20. M. Ali, "Kashmir Keeps South Asia Hostage While Visitors to U.S. Seek Solution," *Washington Report on Middle East Affairs* (October 1992): 43–44.

21. The latest Chinese statistics put the bilateral trade between the two neighbors for January to April 2003 at $2.313 billion, an increase of 70.8 percent over the same period for 2002. Although Indian exports to China between January and April 2003 increased by a whopping 100.5 per cent, compared to the same period in 2002, Bejing's exports to New Delhi rose by 42.1 percent. The trade balance for the first three months of 2003 is in India's favour to the extent of $354 million. (http://economictimes.india times.com//articleshow/msid-37123,prtpage-1.cms?) *The Economic Times Online,* "China, India to Cooperate in WTO Talks: Jiabao," June 23, 2003.

22. Zhang Guihong, "U.S. Security Policy Towards South Asia After September 11 and Its Implications for China: A Chinese Perspective," *Strategic Analysis: A Monthly Journal of the IDSA* 27, no. 2 (April–June 2003).

23. Ibid.

China and
Japan

In modern times, Japanese militarism caused us to suffer huge damage. . . .
But Japanese people were also victims. . . . Japanese people are not responsible. . . . With history as a mirror, we want to move towards the future. I
hope history will never repeat itself.

—*Zhu Rongji, Chinese premier,*
1998–2003, speaking in Japan[1]

At the beginning of the twenty-first century, the geopolitical structure in Asia
and the world looks very different from that of a decade earlier. China and
Japan loom ever larger as Asia's dominant powers. How they perceive and interact with each other, as partners or rivals, may well determine whether the
next 100 years will be an Asian century of prosperity and global leadership or
one of tragedy and suffering. The Chinese and Japanese experience during the
past century, in which both have suffered in world wars and regional conflicts,
should be incentive enough for them to avoid such tragedies in the future.

But if this is to happen, Beijing and Tokyo will have to make difficult decisions at home and in their relations with each other. The economic miracles
in both China and Japan, as well as their potential military capability, mean
that their future relations will vitally affect not only their very existence, but
also the well-being of the rest of Asia and the world as a whole. Even before
the collapse of the Soviet Union, Japan had become the world's second largest
economy, with three-fifths the production of the United States but only half
the population. The World Bank estimated that if China continued its
1992–1993 rate of 11–12 percent increases in annual production, mainland
China alone would exceed Japanese production in the year 2010 and rival that
of the United States or the European Union.[2]

But many critics are questioning the ability of both China and Japan to
continue their economic miracle, because of problems both at home and in
their market relations abroad. In Japan, major political parties have been discredited by charges of corruption involving high-level politicians. Liberal

Democratic Party leaders, as well as those of other Japanese parties, have been exposed by the mass media for taking bribes from corporate interests for favors. In addition to political scandals, Japan's economy has suffered from a long recession. With weak coalition governments mostly treading water, tough decisions in both domestic and foreign policy as well as on economic issues are not being made.

Decisionmakers in Beijing and other capitals wonder when and if Japan's decisionmakers will take steps to play a regional and global political-security role commensurate with Japan's powerful economic role, both as Asia's dominant economic power and as a world trader and investor, second only to the United States. Beijing likes the fact that Japan has maintained only a self-defense force since World War II. China has also been a primary beneficiary of Japan's powerful economy. In the future, however, both China and Japan will have to make difficult decisions about how far to open up their economies to foreign competition. How to avoid a Sino-Japanese arms race, which could undermine the economic and military security of both countries, will also be critical. Yet observers believe that Japan's identity crisis about its future role is only temporary. Japan, they believe, is destined to emerge as a strong economic power, dedicated increasingly to the liberal open-borders paradigm, and to being a world leader in dealing with political-security issues.[3]

Japan: Partner or Rival?

China and Japan are the two major powers in East Asia. The United States and Russia, the two other great powers that have exerted a dominant influence in Asia over the past century, are reducing their Asian commitments. Sino-Japanese relations will therefore become the key to stability and peace in the Far East over the next decade. The forces for a partnership are strong: Japan is China's most important trading partner and both nations are still wary of their Russian neighbor. But the forces for rivalry are equally strong: a historical animosity that was heightened during World War II. How these two nations manage these forces for rivalry and partnership over the next decade will shape the future of international relations in East Asia and perhaps the entire globe.

Military Rivalry

Any contest for military superiority between China and Japan would seemingly favor China, given its population, its location on the Asian land mass, the fact that it has the largest standing army in Asia, and its possession of nuclear weapons. Yet Japan, with only a self-defense force, has the fourth largest military budget in the world, ranking after the United States, Russia, and China. As a result, Japan's military technology and its budget allocations allow it to maintain a military force that revives fears of World War II imperialism among Japan's neighbors. Japan's comparative ranking is listed in Table 7.1.

At the end of World War II, after the collapse of Japanese efforts to create an Asian coprosperity sphere, the nation's military position during the Cold War was solely defensive. The 1947 postwar constitution, written by U.S. general Douglas MacArthur, states, in Article 9, that Japan will never again have any offensive military capability. As a consequence, Japan's self-defense force has been limited to 250,000 soldiers. With memories of the U.S. firebombing of Tokyo and of the nuclear explosions in Hiroshima and Nagasaki still vivid, a majority of the Japanese people and all the major political parties have endorsed the antiwar provision in the constitution.

During the Cold War, a time of great instability in East Asia, Japan accepted this provision at least in part because it was protected by U.S. ground troops and by the U.S. nuclear umbrella. There are currently about 50,000 U.S. military personnel in Japan, and the United States has the ability to assist rapid mobilization of Japan's military potential, including the possibility of deploying nuclear and thermonuclear warheads and delivery systems. Chinese leaders will all ask how China can avoid such a Japanese scenario while at the same time increasing the prestige and capability of its own military services, to which it feels rightfully entitled.

Economic Interdependence

In the early part of the twentieth century, when Chinese intellectuals were seeking models of nation building that would allow China to drive out the European powers, they looked to the Japanese model. Sun Yat-sen, the "father"

Table 7.1   Top Five Major Military Spenders in 2003

		Ranking in Market Exchange Rate		Ranking in Purchasing Power Parity	
Rank	Country	Level ($ billions)	World Share (%)	Country	Level ($ billions)
1	United States	417.4	47	United States	417.4
2	Japan	46.9	5	China	151.0[a]
3	United Kingdom	37.1	4	India	64.0
4	France	35.0	4	Russia	63.2[a]
5	China	32.8[a]	4	France	38.4

Source: Information from Stockholm International Peace Research Institute, http://www.sipri.org/contents/milap/milex/mex_major_spenders.pdf, viewed November 29, 2004.

Note: Levels are in U.S.$ billions at constant (2000) prices and exchange rates.

a. Estimate by SIPRI.

of modern China, studied in Japan, as did many other Chinese revolutionaries. All were searching for ways to lead China to "wealth and power," the motto of their movement.

Japanese military power inspired the respect of all Asians through its defeat of the Russian empire in 1905. A country that had its initial contacts with the Netherlands, Portugal, and then the United States (via Commodore Perry in 1853) inflicted a humiliating defeat on one of Europe's mightiest land powers within a few short decades. Quick modernization and industrialization were the basis of this military victory. With the Meiji Restoration in 1868, Japanese society was reorganized and opened to Western science, technology, and capitalist economic structures. The *zaibatsu,* huge industrial conglomerates such as Mitsubishi, were established; government administration was modernized; and popular education was emphasized. All this was achieved with very little actual foreign penetration of Japanese society and the Japanese economy. After World War II, fearful of disrupting what was left of the Japanese economy, General MacArthur limited his economic initiatives to land reform in the countryside. The *zaibatsu* were allowed to survive and, as many U.S. car owners can attest, to prosper.

Japanese models of development were discounted by the Communist Chinese, who initially looked to the Soviet Union for guidelines to quick industrialization. Just as Stalin had brutally collectivized the Soviet farmers, so Mao collectivized the Chinese peasants. Just as Stalin promoted heavy industry above all else, so did Mao. In his mercurial way, Mao experimented with models of economic development, but within the socialist mode of production. Japan's statist capitalism was contemplated neither by Mao nor by those within the ruling hierarchy who still looked to Moscow, despite the fact that Japan's gross national product overtook that of the Soviet Union in the 1980s.

Zhou Enlai's announcement that China would pursue the Four Modernizations changed the Chinese attitude toward the Japanese economic model. Zhou and his successor, Deng Xiaoping, observed that the Japanese model (as noted in Chapter 3) inspired the economic miracles in the Four Little Tigers (Taiwan, South Korea, Hong Kong, and Singapore). The combination of centralized, authoritarian political power with land reform, emphasis on industrial investment leading to quick growth, and promotion of exports was attractive to the Chinese leadership.

To implement the Four Modernizations, China needed capital investment. Although concerned about becoming too dependent on a single country, China has nonetheless allowed a high level of Japanese investment. Yet Japan's growing economic dominance in East Asia, with the growing dependence of not only China but also most of Southeast Asia on Japanese investment and trade, is a major worry for China's leaders. Japan is China's largest source of technology and capital goods, whereas China is a major source of raw materials for Japanese industry. Japan is the major market for Asian, Australian, and potentially Siberian raw materials. Japanese high-technology products already dominate most Asian markets, either through imports, joint ventures, or Japanese subsidiaries. Further agreements among Asian countries to lower trade barriers might further promote Japanese domination, in effect creating the Japanese coprosperity sphere through peace rather than war. Like many other Asian countries, China has an unfavorable balance of trade with Japan because China sells low-priced raw materials and labor-intensive industrial goods while purchasing expensive high-technology and finished products from Japan.

Future Sino-Japanese Relations

In view of the continuing military buildup in Asia, at a time when the Asian rimland has become the world's most rapidly developing economic region, Sino-Japanese relations perhaps provide the key to both Asian economic progress and regional security. Up to the present, all Sino-Japanese interactions have been in nonsecurity fields: trade, technology, investment, academic exchanges, tourism, and diplomacy. China is concerned about Japan's growing domination of trade and investment throughout Asia, but it nonetheless needs more investment, a higher level of technology, and more trade with Japan. Basically, Japan and China are natural trading partners, with China providing a wide range of natural resources, including coal, oil, timber, and agricultural products.

These economic relationships are extremely beneficial to both countries, but there are also problems. As China continues to develop economically, both countries see each other as rivals throughout the Asian rimland. Japan may play the Southeast and South Asian cards by seeking cheap raw materials, markets for its products, and labor-intensive investments in these Asian regions as an alternative to further dependence on China. In addition, Japan's more advanced technology is not exported to China, because Japan seeks to maintain its technological advantages over its chief Asian rival in the twenty-first century. Japan is also concerned about China's modernization of its military forces, through both arms purchases and development of military technology inside China, which Japan avoids helping, a policy also followed by Japan's Western allies.

Currently, neither China nor Japan poses major security problems to the other. The problem is in the future. If military arms races continue to grow in Asia, it is highly unlikely that Japan will accept a situation in which China uses its growing economic strength to develop a dominant military capability in Asia. China is also concerned about Japan's growing political and security role in Asia—for example, through its leadership in UN peacekeeping in Cambodia, including the sending of Japanese troops to a Southeast Asian country for the first time since World War II.

▨ Trade and Investment

Growing complexity in Asian trade and investment patterns increasingly tie China to Japan, and both to the rest of Asia. According to the Japanese Ministry of Foreign Affairs, the total value of China-Japan trade in 2002 increased 15 percent from 2001: "China surpassed the United States as the largest exporter to Japan, and Japan is China's largest trade partner. In the first half of fiscal year (FY) 2002, investment to China was 113.2 billion yen (approximately US$900 million) on a contractual basis, indicating a growth of 23.2 percent over the same period a year ago."[4] Chinese-Japanese commodity trade statistics are listed in Tables 7.2 and 7.3.

But the United States remains the largest market for both Chinese and Japanese exports. Asia's two emerging economic giants also have the world's largest trade surpluses with the United States. In 2002, Japan had a $70 billion trade surplus with the United States, while China's surplus with the United States was $103 billion. For many years, Japan's trade surplus with the United States made Tokyo a favorite whipping boy in Washington. Now, Beijing has become the target of U.S. criticism.

The complexity and importance of economic interdependence among China, Japan, the United States, and the rest of Asia is also revealed by investment patterns. As noted in earlier chapters, mainland China receives over 75 percent of its investment from Hong Kong, Taiwan, and overseas Chinese. But Japan and the United States are also key investors. Japan is especially important for infrastructure development, including power, transport, and communications, whereas the United States is now the major source of Chinese passenger airliners. Japan is the largest investor in Southeast Asia, and overseas Chinese in the ASEAN countries work very closely with the Japanese. At the same time, Southeast Asian overseas Chinese are a major source of investment in mainland China.

Growing economic interdependence in Asia is tied to interdependence with other regions, especially the United States. This suggests the need for China and Japan, as Asia's two economic dynamos, to adjust economic relations not only with each other, on the basis of mutual self-interest, but also with the rest of Asia as well as the United States and the West. Asia has become the largest trading partner of the United States, larger than either Western Europe or Latin America. But both Japan and China will have to work out more equitable trade relations with the United States, as will most other U.S. trading partners in Asia, to prevent future trade wars.

▨ Possibilities for Sino-Japanese Partnership

Indecision about Japan's political and security role at the regional and global levels has not prevented Tokyo from playing a key role in opening up China

Table 7.2   Japanese Imports from China by Commodity, 1994–2000 (in million yen)

	1994	1995	1996	1997	1998	1999	2000
Total imports	2,811,395	3,380,882	4,399,676	5,061,673	5,061,673	4,875,385	5,941,358
Foodstuffs	482,214	440,805	547,438	609,509	599,098	598,224	633,120
Raw materials of textile	34,842	18,414	—	—	—	—	—
Metal ores	4,782	6,450	5,309	10,662	1,268,419	—	—
Other raw materials	92,744	103,192	154,606	168,250	171,574	143,480	161,658
Mineral fuels	196,671	196,765	261,352	292,526	201,175	153,803	232,628
Chemical products	96,143	124,270	151,930	177,946	220,751	152,316	176,132
Machinery and equipment	287,088	485,743	795,669	1,058,728	1,136,053	1,175,947	1,553,423
Others	1,616,912	2,005,243	2,483,372	2,744,051	1,247,064	2,651,614	3,184,398

Source: Web Japan, http://web-japan.org/stat/stats/08TRA38.html, viewed June 2. 2004.
Note: Not all totals add up, due to rounding.

Table 7.3 Japanese Exports to China by Commodity, 1994–2001 (in million yen)

	1994	1995	1996	1997	1998	1999	2000	2001
Total exports	1,913,705	2,061,960	2,382,363	2,630,721	2,620,905	2,657,428	3,274,448	3,763,723
Foodstuffs	5,453	8,848	13,045	13,331	12,260	11,388	15,039	19,911
Textile and textile articles	183,420	221,043	283,680	307,106	279,847	292,212	318,947	346,045
Chemical products	139,080	192,079	222,414	267,112	301,471	341,798	429,941	476,112
Mineral products	25,330	24,558	39,749	41,132	47,013	43,669	65,395	69,700
Metals and metallic products	277,971	292,729	258,412	295,134	301,126	290,378	351,845	405,921
Machinery and equipment	1,131,601	1,152,472	1,354,048	1,427,263	1,435,981	1,423,550	1,797,894	2,066,577
Others	150,851	170,232	211,015	279,642	243,208	254,432	295,386	379,457

Source: Web Japan, http://web-japan.org/stat/stats/08TRA38.html, viewed June 2, 2004.
Note: Not all totals add up, due to rounding.

to the outside world. Japan also helped China finesse the problem of how to normalize diplomatic relations with other nations while these nations continued their trade and nondiplomatic ties to Taiwan. In 1971, eight years before formal Sino-U.S. diplomatic relations were established, Tokyo simultaneously established diplomatic relations with Beijing, broke diplomatic relations with Taipei, and established a nongovernmental office on the island of Taiwan to conduct economic and other nondiplomatic functions. This ingenious arrangement not only benefited China, Taiwan, and Japan, but also served as a precedent for the United States and other countries when they switched their diplomatic relations from Taipei to Beijing.

Japan has also played a key role in opening up China to trade and investment. Tokyo successfully supported renewal of China's membership in the World Bank and the International Monetary Fund (IMF). While the United States convinced the World Bank to cut off further lending to China after the Tiananmen Square incident, Japan played a leading role in persuading the other Group of Seven nations to support renewal of World Bank lending to China. According to the World Bank, China received $1.3 billion in loans in 2003, the fourth largest recipient of World Bank loans after Argentina, Turkey, and Brazil. Japan also supported China's participation as an observer at the 1987–1993 Uruguay Round negotiations, sponsored by the General Agreement on Tariffs and Trade (GATT), to further reduce international trade barriers and upgrade GATT into the World Trade Organization (WTO). Japan also supported China's admission to the WTO. Tokyo has taken the position that internal Chinese human rights policies should not be a criterion for integrating China into the global economic system and that conditionalities should not be placed on China's international trade relations. Japan's development aid to China from 1980–2001 is summarized in Table 7.4.

What has Japan received in return? Opportunities beckon. For example, Japanese retail chains have expanded sales in China following the relaxation of restrictions.[5] One Japanese retail chain, Yaohan, says that it can employ twenty-eight Chinese workers for the same cost as one Japanese.[6] China is also a major source of raw materials, including oil, coal, and agricultural products, as well as a growing source of cheap consumer goods, which are popular in Japan.

China's ties to overseas Chinese are also important to Sino-Japanese relations. Overseas Chinese, as noted earlier, provide much of the business class in Southeast Asian countries. Through informal relationships that help Japan's multinationals, which are the major source of investment in Southeast Asia, they have worked very closely with Japanese investors and traders. The triangular partnership that has developed, based on informal business ties among overseas Chinese, mainland China, and Japan, further promotes economic integration and interdependence among Japan, Southeast Asia, and greater China, as well as with the rest of the world.

Table 7.4 Japan's Official Development Assistance to China, 1980–2001 (in hundred million yen)

Fiscal Year	Loan Aid	Grant Aid	Technical Cooperation	Total
1980	660.00	6.80	5.64	672.44
1981	1,000.00	23.70	10.17	1,033.87
1982	650.00	65.80	19.78	735.58
1983	690.00	78.31	30.45	798.76
1984	715.00	54.93	26.77	796.70
1985	751.00	58.96	39.48	849.44
1986	806.00	69.68	48.10	923.78
1987	850.00	70.29	61.92	982.21
1988	1,615.21	79.58	61.49	1,756.28
1989	971.79	56.98	40.51	1,069.28
1990	1,225.24	66.06	70.49	1,361.79
1991	1,296.07	66.52	68.55	1,431.14
1992	1,373.28	82.37	75.27	1,530.92
1993	1,387.43	98.23	76.51	1,562.17
1994	1,403.42	77.99	79.57	1,560.98
1995	1,414.29	4.81	73.74	1,492.84
1996	1,705.11	20.67	98.90	1,824.68
1997	2,029.06	68.86	103.82	2,201.74
1998	2,065.83	76.05	98.30	2,240.18
1999	1,926.37	59.10	73.30	2,058.77
2000	2,143.99	47.80	81.96	2,273.75
2001	1,613.66	63.33	77.77	1,754.76
Total	28,292.75	1,296.82	1,322.49	30,912.06

Source: Japanese Ministry of Foreign Affairs, *Overview of Japan-China Relations (Diplomatic Bluebook 2003: Regional Diplomacy),* http://www.mofa.go.jp/policy/other/bluebook/2003/chap2-a.pdf.
Note: Not all totals add up, due to rounding.

A key advocate of growing Asian economic and political cooperation was Singapore's senior statesman and former prime minister Lee Kuan Yew. Lee spoke for most Asians when he said that they share a common heritage, take pride in Asia's growing modernization and development, and share common values such as Confucianism (family values and a desire for order) and a desire to work hard. Lee, who is himself Chinese, believes that Asians share many desirable traits, some of which he thinks are declining in the West, including the desire to strive to improve oneself through education and hard work. Most of all, Lee believes that the Chinese, Japanese, South Koreans, and Southeast Asians share a common desire to work together as partners to make the twenty-first century an Asian century.[7]

To achieve this, Lee rejected Malaysia's proposal for a closed Asian trading system in favor of one in which barriers not only between Asian countries but also between Asian countries and the rest of the world are gradually eliminated. China and Japan agreed with Lee and with the United States on the need to avoid closed trading systems in Asia, in North America, or between Asia and North America; however, China and Japan opposed formal bilateral structures for eliminating trade barriers between Asia and North America because they feared U.S. domination of such structures.

Japan and China instead prefer to work through the global trading system. Both countries resent U.S. bilateral economic threats aimed at changing Chinese and Japanese policies on access to internal markets. The greatly strengthened World Trade Organization should handle some complaints between trading partners that were previously handled through bilateral negotiations. In the future, disagreements between China and the United States over the relationship between trade and human rights and between Japan and the United States (with threats to impose specific penalties on Japan as a means of opening up Japanese markets) will theoretically be resolved through the WTO. Thus, both China and Japan stand to gain from China's reentry into the world trade regime.

Cooperation on Security Issues

Sino-Japanese security relations are more difficult. Both countries have reaped security benefits from the new Asian geopolitical structure emerging after the Cold War. To continue to reap these benefits, China and Japan, as East Asia's two major powers, will have to work out ways to avoid rivalry between themselves. If they do not, arms races are likely to occur not only between China and Japan, but also in other Asian countries, to the detriment of all.

Economic well-being and the prevention of Asian instability and disorder are the prime reasons China and Japan should cooperate on security matters. But the history of Sino-Japanese relations during the first half of the twentieth century makes it difficult for Chinese and Japanese leaders to cooperate other than through informal talks, which indeed have occurred between Tokyo and Beijing. They can cooperate on security issues such as defusing the North Korean nuclear threat. Yet unless they can gain confidence in each other's security roles, Beijing and Tokyo could potentially become bitter rivals and even military enemies in a new type of cold (or hot) war based solely on geopolitical and nationalistic considerations rather than on disagreement over political ideologies. China and Japan, with their future military potential, hold the key to Asia's future security and well-being in the twenty-first century.

Since the end of the Cold War, with the reduced influence of outside powers in the region, Japan's greatest initiative to promote regional stability and security came in 1992–1993, when Japanese prime minister Miyazawa enunciated what became known as the Miyazawa Doctrine, a Japanese initiative to create a regional forum to discuss Asian security issues, modeled on the Conference on Security and Cooperation in Europe (CSCE). Throughout the Cold War era, Japan had followed the Yoshida Doctrine, named after Prime Minister Yoshida's policies of the 1950s, which mandated that Japan concentrate on economic development at home and increased trade and investment with Asia and the rest of the world. Japan pursued economic development while relying on the U.S. security umbrella to protect itself militarily, thus avoiding any Japanese military buildup other than a self-defense force of 250,000 personnel who were responsible only for the defense of the main islands. The Japanese people, as well as most political leaders, accepted Article 9 of the Japanese constitution, which outlaws the right to make war except for strictly defensive purposes.

Under the Miyazawa Doctrine, Japan sought to continue its military alliance with the United States while at the same time undertaking initiatives of its own to play a more normal regional and global security role. Participating in UN peacekeeping operations, gaining a permanent seat on the UN Security Council, and promoting an Asian regional forum to discuss growing Asian security issues in the post–Cold War era are possible initiatives. Under the first Bush administration, Washington hesitated to support a multilateral forum to discuss Asian security issues, even though Tokyo insisted on including the United States, Canada, and the European Community (now the European Union). But the Clinton administration supported the Japanese initiative, which was presented to the Association of Southeast Asian Nations (ASEAN) at its June 1993 meeting and thereafter to ASEAN's dialogue partners (South Korea, Australia, New Zealand, Canada, the United States, and the European Union). ASEAN and the dialogue partners also agreed to include Russia, China, and Vietnam as observers to the ASEAN Regional Security Forum.

Japan has always insisted that any regional security structure must include China. However, the inclusion of China, Russia, and Vietnam along with other Asian actors is only a beginning. For an East Asian security organization to be successful, its members must be willing to work within its structures. The North Atlantic Treaty Organization (NATO) and the European Community achieved this goal primarily because of the perception of an outside threat. This sort of threat does not currently exist to unite the leaders of all the East Asian nations; instead, the smaller nations in the area are increasingly nervous over the growing economic and military might of both China and Japan.

Sino-Japanese Rivalry: Structural
Realism and the Balance of Power

China may get a lot more pushy, while Japan becomes somewhat less so. More realistic is that an age is dawning for the smaller Asian countries, an age in which they face not one but two giant neighbors impinging heavily, each increasingly interested in politics inside and outside the region, and each increasingly capable of making a host of new demands.[8]

Just as a triangular relationship of economic interdependence has emerged among China, Japan, and the rest of Asia, a structural power system is emerging in Asia in which the little states of East and Southeast Asia find themselves fearful of Asia's two major powers. Japan and other Asian countries share a fear of China as an emerging military power that may try to exert pressure on its neighbors to the east and south. Their fear is fueled by the fact that China, already one of the world's greatest military powers, has steadily increased its military budget.

China's continuing military buildup, especially its expansion and modernization of its air naval units and its deep-sea naval capability, is a matter of growing concern to Japan's political leaders. China has made specific territorial claims that pose difficult choices for Tokyo. How should it respond, either politically or through additional measures, to China's authorization of deals for oil exploration in the East China Sea? These waters are closer to the Senkaku Islands than to mainland China. The Senkaku Islands, which are halfway between Taiwan and Okinawa (the latter of which is part of Japan's home islands), were claimed by Japan in 1890. It was not until more than a century later, in its February 1992 proclamation, that China claimed these islands, along with the Paracel and Spratly island chains in the South China Sea, as Chinese territory.

All of this is occurring while Russo-Japanese tensions continue over Japan's request for the return of the four Kurile islands seized by the Russians from the Japanese at the end of World War II. Tensions on the Korean peninsula over North Korea's presumed development of nuclear arms also continue to heighten. At a time when other countries such as Russia, France, Germany, and Great Britain are cutting back their military budgets, China's military expansion and its territorial claims are alarming to its neighbors, including the Japanese.

In response to these developments, a great debate is raging in Japan over its future security policies. But a consensus seems to be emerging, supporting the Miyazawa Doctrine, as follows: (1) maintain military ties with the United States, keeping a residual (even if reduced) U.S. military presence; (2) incrementally build up air and naval capability; (3) keep the self-defense force at its current level (250,000—less than one-tenth the size of China's People's Liberation Army); and (4) reserve for the future the decision of whether to go nuclear.[9] Japan and the United States also announced their continued commitment to the U.S.-Japan alliance (1996) and issued new guidelines on defense cooperation (1997).

North Korea also plays a major role in the Chinese-Japanese defense relationship. In 2003, after North Korea fired missiles into the Sea of Japan and then announced that it intended to conduct nuclear tests, Tokyo's leaders began planning their own missile defense shield, rather than continuing to rely solely on U.S. protection. While seemingly still within the bounds of "self-defense," the Chinese government fears that missile defense is the first step in Japan's rearmament. Asia and the world fear that China might feel threatened and respond in kind, by increasing its offensive military capabilities vis-à-vis Japan. A Chinese-Japanese arms race, which could destabilize the region, would be the worst possible scenario, especially with the North Korean wild card thrown into the mix.

There is also a consensus developing among Japan's policy elites over their country's role in the United Nations. If Japan sends military personnel outside the home islands, peacekeeping operations will be the instrument for now. In the summer of 1992, after great debate in the Japanese Diet (parliament), the government was authorized to send up to 2,000 military personnel to serve as UN peacekeepers, but only in a nonmilitary capacity. Following the passage of the resolution, 600 Japanese noncombatants (engineers and service personnel) were sent to Cambodia to serve with the UN Transitional Authority (for details on this operation, see Chapter 6), which was under the direction of Yasushi Akashi, a Japanese. Later, a token noncombatant unit of fifty Japanese self-defense force personnel was sent to Mozambique to serve with the UN peacekeeping operation there, the first time that Japanese soldiers had ever been sent to the African continent.

Japanese citizens have served in other capacities in the UN system—for example, as head of the UN's World Health Organization (WHO) and as the UN High Commissioner for Refugees (UNHCR). Because of his success in directing the UN operation in Cambodia, Akashi was later appointed by the United Nations to head its peacekeeping operation in Bosnia, an even more difficult task. The one UN leadership role that has eluded Japan, even though the country has been a major financial contributor to UN security operations, is a permanent seat on the Security Council. (Japan contributes approximately 20 percent of the UN budget, the United States 25 percent, and China 1 percent.) This would require a formal amendment of the UN Charter, which would require a supporting vote of both China and Russia—potential security threats to Japan in the post–Cold War era.

▓ Chinese Perceptions of Japan's Security Role

Beijing does not wish to see Japan emerge as a major regional or global military actor. According to Gerald Segal, "China will expect Japan to accept a subordinate role."[10] Beijing would like to discourage Japan's military buildup and any increase in its regional and global security role for a number of reasons: memories of Japanese imperialism, China's own desire to be the major military power in Asia, and China's current inability to match Japan's dominant economic role in Asia. According to Segal, "When Japan's self-defense forces participated in the United Nations Transitional Authority in Cambodia, Beijing objected strongly because China hopes to keep Japan in "an abnormal state so it would not challenge China."[11]

Japan's first substantial participation in a UN peacekeeping operation was in 1989, when twenty-seven electoral observers were dispatched to the UN Transition Assistance Group in Namibia. Then in 1992, the enactment of the International Peace Cooperation Law enabled Japan to send not only its civilian personnel but also its self-defense force personnel to UN peacekeeping operations. Based on that law, Japan participated in peacekeeping operations in Angola, Cambodia, Mozambique, El Salvador, and East Timor, and since 1996 has been dispatching a self-defense force contingent to the UN Disengagement Observer Force, which is deployed on the Golan Heights. Japan's self-defense force personnel were also sent to assist Rwandan refugees and East Timorese displaced persons as part of international humanitarian relief operations. In addition, Japan cooperated in international election monitoring activities in Bosnia and Herzegovina, which were conducted by the Organization for Security and Cooperation in Europe in 1998 and 2000. To date, Japan has also made contributions in kind. For example, Japan provided refugee relief materials such as tents and blankets to the UNHCR as aid for Kosovar refugees and East Timorese displaced persons in 1999. In the same year, Japan also provided the UN Mission in East Timor with radios for public information purposes in support of the direct ballot in August 1999.[12]

Japan's contribution to the Iraq effort has been equally controversial. In 1991, under pressure from the coalition fighting against Iraq (following a heated debate in the Japanese Diet), Japan contributed $13 billion to the costs of the operation. Then, after the fighting was over, Japan sent four mine sweepers to help clean up the shipping lanes in the Gulf. In 2003, after much difficult deliberation and debate, Japan decided to send several hundred Japanese troops to support the U.S.-led stabilization effort. This commitment of self-defense force personnel to Iraq marked the first time since World War II that Japanese troops had served in a combat area.

Should Japan decide to markedly increase its support for peacekeeping operations, this would pose a problem for Beijing. Nevertheless, the other permanent members of the Security Council, given the current constraints on their military budgets, will push Japan for greater contributions, economically and perhaps militarily, to any future peacekeeping operation.

Asia's Future Balance-of-Power System

Asia's balance-of-power system in the twenty-first century may take many forms based on the different geopolitical and economic variables. In all likelihood, Japan will react to events beyond its four main islands rather than initiating new power structures. Japan benefits from the present system, in which relative stability exists with no immediate threats to Japan's security. At the

Figure 7.1   Military Expenditures in East Asia, 1994–2003

Source: Information from the Stockholm International Peace Research Institute (SIPRI), http://web.sipri.org/contents/milap/milex/mex_graph_asia_e.html.

same time, Japan, as Asia's economic dynamo, prime investor, and trader, has been able to emphasize its regional and global economic primacy while remaining essentially a free-rider on security issues. As noted earlier, a continued U.S. presence in Japan, as well as in South Korea, enables Japan to use its resources and scientific research to promote its economic primacy. Japan's people are overwhelmingly dedicated to maintaining a low military profile, including avoidance of the nuclear option if possible. Other than among the far right, there is little hankering for restoration of Japan's past military grandeur as Asia's hegemon during the first half of the twentieth century.

China as Hegemon

The situation may take a very different turn in mainland China. Tokyo's concern over China's continuing military buildup, even though China's neighbors pose no major threat to mainland China's security, has already been noted. Some possible reasons Beijing may wish to be the dominant Asian military power in the twenty-first century were given in earlier chapters. Before looking at Japan's probable reactions, it is important to review future Chinese policy choices:

- Should Beijing's central authority be threatened, including the power base of China's ruling Communist elite, the leaders in Beijing may appeal to nationalist revisionism and pride in China's ancient grandeur as the Middle Kingdom.
- Should the next generation of leaders seek to demonstrate China's new prowess as Asia's regional hegemon to head off further decentraliza-

tion of power to China's regions, the continuing Chinese military buildup will be perceived as threatening by the surrounding nations.
- Should China continue to grow economically at its present rate, and should other states including Japan continue their current rates of investment in China, this may lead to further dependence on the Chinese market. Beijing may then believe that others will have no choice but to kowtow to China's views on how disputes should be settled with its neighbors.
- Should China gain both economic and military regional supremacy in the twenty-first century, Beijing may wish to use its new strength to further expand its territorial claims (on both land and sea) based on ancient Chinese maps of the Middle Kingdom.
- Should Taiwan at some point declare itself an independent state, Beijing may seek to coerce it into submission by confiscating Taiwanese investments on the mainland. Or Beijing might seek to use its increasing military capability to coerce the independent-minded Taiwanese into submission.
- Should instability develop inside Russian Siberia, Beijing may wish to use its growing economic and military strength to increase its influence inside the region, which at one time was either part of the ancient Middle Kingdom or under its sphere of influence.
- Should China gain military supremacy, it may be tempted to expand its claims to territorial waters and their resources in the East China and South China Seas at the expense of its neighbors.

How would Japan react to any combination of the above scenarios? Such events would surely serve as a wake-up call to the Japanese.

Nuclear Options

Because pacifist and antinuclear sentiments are likely to remain very strong in Japan, it is highly unlikely that Japan will enter into a conventional or nuclear arms race with China. More likely is a scenario in which Tokyo will seek to create a limited second-strike capability to deter nuclear and conventional attacks from abroad. To date, Tokyo has relied on the U.S. nuclear umbrella, as have the NATO countries and South Korea. In the face of a massive nuclear threat from abroad, however, Tokyo may fear that Washington, not wanting to risk its own destruction to save the Japanese, would renege on promises to come to its aid. A continually declining U.S. military presence in Asia in the twenty-first century might further convince the Japanese that U.S. security guarantees will have to be supplemented with a second-strike nuclear capability.

Japan will not be able to match China tit for tat in conventional and nuclear forces for the foreseeable future. Rather than trying to match China in each weapon category, Japan's best option is to provide for a strong defense, but one that would not threaten the Chinese mainland through an equal or superior capability. The Japanese are well aware of their geopolitical situation, one in which four one-megaton thermonuclear bombs could obliterate Japan's four main islands. To counter the threat posed by an expanded Chinese nuclear military capability in the twenty-first century, Tokyo may seek a deep-ocean second-strike option. In this scenario, all of Japan's nuclear capability would be on submarines, and Japan would have the ability to cause grave damage to the Chinese mainland, thereby deterring attack. Japan would not, however, have the capability of destroying China's existence through a first strike—the ability to win by destroying the opponent's nuclear capabilities through a surprise attack.

Balance of Power

Should China seek to be the Asian hegemon in the twenty-first century, Japan is likely to become its chief opponent. There is little likelihood that Japan will seek to match China's ground forces, or even contemplate a major use of ground forces, either in mainland China or in other parts of Asia. Not only does Japan's past militarism continue to stir up fears in China and the rest of Asia, but the realities associated with the attempt to occupy and control other countries by force argue against such a response. Napoleon, Hitler, Mussolini, Stalin, and Tojo come to mind, as do more recent U.S. efforts to control Vietnam and Russian efforts to control Afghanistan through military force. All ultimately ended in failure.

Instead, Japan would join together with other nations to oppose future Chinese hegemony in the region. Other powers, such as the United States and Russia, might play a backup role, but Japan would be the logical leader of future coalitions reacting to Chinese threats of coercion or actual initiation of military conflict. This would echo the classical balance-of-power era in Europe, when Great Britain used its naval power to play the role of balancer. Japan, too, may seek to use its extensive air power to take on the role of balancer.

Conflict Inside China

Another scenario that could also stimulate Japan to play a greater political-security role in Asia would be the development of tensions inside China that might lead to the decentralization of power or even internal regional conflict. Such possibilities were noted in earlier chapters. Tokyo's reactions to such developments might include the following scenarios:

- Because the PLA is increasingly a government within a government, with 80 percent of its economic facilities producing civilian goods that provide much of its income, in a future internal crisis between Beijing and different regions, the military could conceivably back regional rather than central forces. This could cause problems for Japan because China's nuclear forces, as well as its ground, air, and naval units, might be divided into opposing factions, some backing the leadership in Beijing and others backing powerful regional provinces.

- Should mainland China actually break apart into different regions, logically Japan would at least tacitly support those groups advocating liberal economic and political values. A divided China is a weak China, which (unless the devolution of power leads to chaos) the Japanese might prefer. Japan's primary security interest is to maintain a stable order in Asia that is conducive to trade and investment. Should open conflict break out on the mainland—most likely through Beijing's efforts to reassert its central control—Japan is unlikely to become involved militarily. Japanese leaders are more likely to seek the role of mediator while avoiding direct intervention.

The Pull of the Past in the Twenty-First Century

In 1995, the Japanese prime minister issued an "apology" for his country's actions during World War II. For China, official remorse for Japan's past imperial history was long overdue and appreciated, and paved the way for Jiang Zemin's visit to Japan in 1998, the first time that a Chinese head of state had ever visited the country. Yet for many Chinese the Japanese apology was not convincing.

Territorial disputes between China and Japan continue to ignite, even in the twenty-first century. The Senkaku/Diaoyu Islands were traditionally considered part of the island chain congruent to Taiwan. After the Japanese defeat in World War II, however, the islands were nominally left under Japanese authority. The Chinese have long disputed Japanese control, and they were especially inflamed by increasingly strong Japanese statements on the issue in the late 1990s. In March 2004, Chinese activists landed on the Senkaku/Diaoyu Islands, claiming them for the People's Republic. Japan's response was measured. It did not detain the Chinese but sent them home and ignored inflammatory rhetoric from Beijing. According to Deng Xiaoping, "the question of Diaoyu Island . . . could be set aside for the moment; probably the next generation would be cleverer than we and would find a practical solution."[13] Deng's prediction has yet to be fulfilled.

Chinese-Japanese relations are repeatedly strained by incidents that bring back memories of World War II. Events in 2003 illustrate the continuing power of the past. For example, Chinese constructions workers were injured and one died when they discovered some leftover Japanese mustard gas. The Chinese government demanded a response. According to Defense Minister Cao Gangchuan, "The chemical weapons left by the invading Japanese armies still

During a certain period in the not too distant past, Japan, following a mistaken national policy, advanced along the road to war, only to ensnare the Japanese people in a fateful crisis, and, through its colonial rule and aggression, caused tremendous damage and suffering to the people of many countries, particularly to those of Asian nations. In the hope that no such mistake be made in the future, I regard, in a spirit of humility, these irrefutable facts of history, and express here once again my feelings of deep remorse and state my heartfelt apology. Allow me also to express my feelings of profound mourning for all victims, both at home and abroad, of that history (Japanese prime minister Tomiichi Murayama on the fiftieth anniversary of the end of World War II).

remain a threat to the safety of the Chinese people and China's environment. . . . The Japanese government must pay a high level of importance to this and adopt effective measures to quickly resolve the issue."[14] Japan responded by offering to compensate the victims. Also in 2003, China accused Japanese tourists of engaging in a sexual orgy on the anniversary of the Japanese occupation of Manchuria, and Chinese students in Xian engaged in several days of anti-Japanese violence. Old memories die hard, especially when the Chinese government is willing to exploit them for its own uses. According to a Chinese scholar, "The Japanese try to hide the truth, but it is hard for the Chinese people to forget. The Japanese invasion is passed down to the younger generation inside families. There are so many individual cases; every family lost an uncle, a cousin, a daughter. With so many relatives killed by Japanese it is hard to forget. I will tell my son, and he is telling my grandson."[15]

China and Japan at the Crossroads

It is likely that China and Japan will be partners rather than rivals in the twenty-first century. Both are likely to see the increasing advantages of complex interdependence and of Chinese and Japanese partnership at the regional and global levels. China and Japan, as well as other Asian countries, also share feelings similar to those of Singapore senior statesman Lee Kuan Yew. They are likely to reject a future Asia with extreme forms of individualism in favor of an orderly civil society with strong community values. Similar societal values and strong economic ties may be the ties that bind.

It has already been noted how Japan is likely to act in its relations with China, as well as other Asian countries. As for China, its leaders will have a wide variety of domestic and foreign policy choices. If they increasingly adopt the liberal paradigm and seek regional stability through negotiation and compromise with their neighbors, they are likely to find Tokyo a strong friend and partner rather than rival. Should China seek to play the role of hegemon, however, it will surely find Japan uniting with other Asians to try to persuade Beijing to abandon such a role.

Rivalries over economic and political ideologies are giving way to alternative scenarios as the Cold War recedes into the past. Renewed nationalistic conflict vies with the growing appeal of complex interdependence, in which all benefit from seeking solutions based on mutual self-interest, as the dominant force in the world. To prevent future conflict, Japan will have to take further steps to avoid using its economic power to gain benefits at the expense of its neighbors, and China will have to decide whether to impose a more liberal paradigm in economic as well as political-security concerns.

Policy Options

Beijing's decisionmakers face both opportunities and dangers that should lead them to consider seriously the following policies toward Japan:

Option 1: Make Japanese Trade and Investment Conditional on Better Terms

- In return for further trade and investment concessions, Japan should agree to more coproduction agreements that would provide China more advanced technology, especially dual-use technology such as advanced computers.
- Further Chinese concessions should be contingent on Japan opening up its markets further to Chinese consumer goods and other products.

Option 2: Balance Concessions to Japan and Other States

- As China's domestic market and production grow, Beijing should balance the influence of Japan or any other country by making similar concessions and demands with other states, taking advantage of China's improved bargaining position.
- Bilateral negotiations with other states, including Japan, may be preferable to general concessions through WTO or regional economic regimes.

Option 3: Seek Further Japanese Aid Without Conditionalities

- Unlike the United States, Japan provided China assistance without questioning domestic human rights policies after Tiananmen Square. Because decisionmakers in Tokyo have a greater understanding and willingness to avoid attaching conditionalities on trade, investment, and aid, Beijing can use Tokyo as a mediator in supporting Chinese interests in global regimes such as the IMF, the World Bank Group, and GATT/WTO. Japan strongly supported Chinese readmission to GATT and to its successor, the WTO.

Option 4: Work Informally with Tokyo to Solve Asian Security Problems

- Both Beijing and Tokyo have problems with formal regional security structures. But as Asia's key powers, they share a common interest in defusing regional security threats, assuming that neither Beijing nor Tokyo wishes to use force or the threat of force to promote its own regional influence.
- If Beijing wishes Japan to limit its own military buildup, it must work informally with Tokyo's decisionmakers in deciding the legitimate military capabilities of each country, as well as the capabilities of other regional actors. Beijing cannot expect Tokyo to avoid indefinitely the nuclear military option if it continues to build up its own nuclear capability while others in East Asia have no nuclear forces.
- In the immediate future, Beijing needs to work closely with Tokyo to defuse the danger of nuclear and conventional conflict on the Korean peninsula, as well as in South Asia.
- Beijing and Tokyo can work quietly behind the scenes to avoid not only arms races and potential conflicts between themselves (for example, over the Senkaku Islands), but also potential conflicts throughout the region, thereby strengthening nonmilitary solutions to regional tensions.

Option 5: Seek Understanding with Tokyo on Global Security

- Beijing can work with Tokyo to reform the UN Security Council structure to provide a better balance between the roles of the rich Western countries and developing countries. Seating Japan, from Beijing's perspective, would require not only greater agreement on the respective security roles of the two countries but also cooperation in increasing the security role of the non-Western world (with permanent seats for non-Western countries in addition to China and Japan).
- Both Japan and China are undergoing major debates about their own future global security roles, including support for and participation in UN peacekeeping operations in Asia and other regions, so both states need to come to a better understanding of each other's UN security roles to ensure they will not be a source of tension in the twenty-first century.

Discussion Questions

1. In what ways has China patterned its economic development on the Japanese model?
2. How have Sino-Japanese economic relations benefited each country?
3. In what ways do China and Japan share similar or different views on economic relations at the regional and global levels?
4. What is the relationship between mainland Chinese, overseas Chinese, and Japanese business interests?
5. What are the reasons China and Japan are likely to be economic partners in the twenty-first century? Economic rivals?
6. In what ways are political-security decisions in Beijing likely to affect Japanese political-security decisions in the future, including the question of Japan's nuclear option?
7. Regardless of what happens, why are the capabilities and purposes of Chinese and Japanese military forces likely to be different in important ways in the twenty-first century?
8. In what ways do Chinese and Japanese decisionmakers share similar or different views on regional and global security structures, including their perceptions of the UN Security Council and its activities?
9. What circumstances might lead to Sino-Japanese rivalry on security issues in the future?
10. In what ways does Asian preeminence and well-being in the twenty-first century depend on how China and Japan perceive and interact with each other and the rest of Asia?
11. In what ways do decisionmakers in Beijing and Tokyo share similar or different views of their relationships with Washington?

Suggested Readings

Armacost, Michael. *Friends or Rivals? An Inside Account of U.S.-Japan Relations.* New York: Columbia University Press, 1996.
Chalmers, Johnson, *Japan: Who Governs? The Rise of the Developmental State.* New York: Norton, 1996.
Drifte, Reinhard. *Japan's Security Relations with China Since 1989: From Balancing to Bandwagoning?* New York: Routledge/Curzon, 2003.
Hamani, Andrew K. "Japan and the Military Balance of Power in Northeast Asia." *Journal of East Asian Affairs* 8, no. 2 (Summer–Fall 1994): 363–395.
Iriye, Akira. *China and Japan in the Global Setting.* Cambridge: Harvard University Press, 1992.
Soderberg, Marie, ed. *Chinese-Japanese Relations in the 21st Century: Complementarity and Conflict.* New York: Routledge, 2002.

▨ Notes

1. October 13, 2000, http://www.seaiba.com/sinoasian/chinajapan.htm.

2. See Gerald Segal, "China's Changing Shape," *Foreign Affairs* 73, no. 3 (May–June 1994). Segal notes that the World Bank has a reputation for conservative estimates. The size of China's current economy is also hidden by official currency exchange rates. As a result of undervaluation, the World Bank and the International Monetary Fund believe that real purchasing power is three times as high as China's official gross national product per capita would indicate.

3. See Merrill Goozner, "Don't Be Blinded by Bright Talk of a Japan on the Wane," *Chicago Tribune*, July 3, 1994, sec. 7, pp. 17, 20.

4. Japanese Ministry of Foreign Affairs, *Overview of Japan-China Relations (Diplomatic Bluebook 2003: Regional Diplomacy)*, http://www.mofa.go.jp/policy/other/bluebook/2003/chap2-a.pdf.

5. Jennifer Cody, "Big Japanese Retailers Rush to Set Up Operations in Asia's Developing Markets," *Wall Street Journal*, July 8, 1994, p. A4.

6. Ibid.

7. See Fareed Zakaria, "A Conversation with Lee Kuan Yew," *Foreign Affairs* 73, no. 2 (March–April 1994): 109–126.

8. Charles F. Doran, "Security and Political Economy in U.S.-Asian Relations," *Journal of East Asian Affairs* 8, no. 2 (Summer–Fall 1994): 240.

9. See David Arase, "Japan's Evolving Security Policy After the Cold War," *Journal of East Asian Affairs* 8, no. 2 (Summer–Fall 1994): 413–415; Selig S. Harrison, "A Yen for the Bomb?" *Washington Post*, October 31, 1993, p. C1; and "Official Says Japan Will Need Nuclear Arms If North Korea Threatens," *Los Angeles Times*, July 29, 1993, p. A4.

10. Quoted in Andrew K. Hamani, "Japan and the Military Balance of Power in Northeast Asia," *Journal of East Asian Affairs* 8, no. 2 (Summer–Fall 1994): 374.

11. Ibid.

12. Japanese Ministry of Foreign Affairs, *UN Peacekeeping Operations*, http://www.mofa.go.jp/policy/un/pamph2000/pko.html, viewed June 2, 2004.

13. Charles K. Smith "Senkaku/Diaoyu Island Dispute Threatens Amiability of Sino-Japanese Relations," *Power and Interest News Report*, May 3, 2004, http://www.pinr.com/report.php?ac=view_report&report_id=165&language_id=1.

14. "Chinese, Japanese Defense Ministers Discuss War, Chemical Weapons," *Space War*, http://www.spacewar.com, viewed May 18, 2004.

15. Robert Marquand, "Japan's War Past Sparks Chinese Rage," *Christian Science Monitor*, November 14, 2003, http://www.csmonitor.com.

China in the Global Regime

The present-day world is at a vital turning point. The old structure has come to an end while a new one has yet to take shape. The world is moving in a direction of multipolarization. World peace, national stability, economic development are the aspirations shared by the people everywhere.

—*Li Peng, speaking before the summit meeting at the UN Security Council, January 11, 1992*

In August 1991 the world order, as it had existed since 1945, collapsed. The bipolar world, in which two superpowers maintained a balance of power and kept their client states in check, dissolved, leaving uncertainty and, in some parts of the world, chaos. Today, no new world order has emerged. The international system is still unsettled, which is inherently dangerous. Each of the world's largest powers, including the members of the UN Security Council, is trying to redefine its role in the emerging world regime.

Peaceful Coexistence

China's philosophy of the proper relationship among states in the international system is summarized in its "Five Principles of Peaceful Coexistence":

1. Each country should have the right to choose its own political, economic, and social system in line with its own circumstances.
2. All nations of the world, especially the big powers, should strictly abide by the principle of not interfering in other nations' affairs.
3. All nations should respect and treat others equally, cherish mutually beneficial cooperation, exist in harmony, and seek common ground while resolving differences.
4. International conflicts should be resolved fairly through peaceful means, not through the use or threat of force.
5. Each country, no matter how big or small, strong or weak, should have the equal right to participate in consultations to settle world affairs.[1]

The Westphalian System

The norms of the Westphalian system include the following: each state is sovereign in its own territory; each state is equal in its relations with other states; there is no higher authority above each state; sovereignty within states resides in the ruling elites; the people are subjects of their government, which derives legitimacy through good government; international security is based on a system of balance of power in which states pursue their self-interest but do not interfere in the internal affairs of other states; international transactions are conducted by governments, not individuals or groups within states; and a citizen of one state traveling in another state is subject to the latter's jurisdiction.

China's principles of interstate conduct are in accord with the basic norms that have guided Europe and therefore the international system for the past 350 years. The Treaty of Westphalia, signed in 1648, established the accepted principles of state sovereignty and equality of nations. Throughout the Cold War period, China and other third world countries struggled to maintain the norms of the Westphalian system in order to allow freedom of action in a world dominated by the two superpowers. Ironically, the end of the Cold War both strengthened and weakened elements of the Westphalian system.

The collapse of the Soviet Union should theoretically have freed the less powerful nations of the world from their previous role as pawns in the Cold War battle. Each nation's freedom of action within its borders and in the international system should have been enhanced. Yet many nations, China included, fear that they will be the losers in the post–Cold War era.

In the UN Security Council, Russia has joined the Western voting bloc on several crucial occasions, such as the 1991 vote to authorize a war against Iraq, leaving China as the only self-professed advocate of the third world. One nation alone cannot uphold the interests of the third world, and because the poor nations of the world are of less importance to the security interests of the United States and Russia, economic aid is likely to disappear as well. The new order leaves the third world with less power and influence than ever.

Interdependence

Even before the collapse of the Soviet Union, the Westphalian system was being eroded by increasing global interdependence. China itself, since the implementation of its open economic policy, has become tied to the international trade and financial system. Overseas Chinese interact freely with all levels of Chinese society, and their enormous financial investment in China gives them tremendous influence. Thus China's once proudly self-reliant economy is now influenced by world-trade trends and the financial interests of Chinese living outside the jurisdiction of the Beijing government.

In an era of mass communication and mass movement of people across boundaries, Chinese interest groups and individual citizens increasingly interact with their counterparts in other countries independently from the Chinese government. Tourism, educational exchanges of students and faculty members, and electronic communications also limit the powers of the Beijing government. For example, during the Tiananmen Square incident, Chinese students used fax machines to inform the outside world about what was happening, even after the transmissions sent by foreign reporters were cut off by the national news agency. Now, the Internet, even in a censored form, disseminates a wide variety of information throughout China. Though party authorities are concerned about the "spiritual pollution" brought in from outside China's borders, they can no longer completely control the flow of information. No government is truly autonomous, even within its own borders, in this era of increasing global interdependence.

The Global Commons

Increasing global interdependence underscores the commonality of global resources. Traditionally, each nation has controlled the resources present within its borders and used these resources for its own benefit, even though the future consequences of such use might affect the well-being of a far wider population. Immediate benefit to one nation or one group outweighs future costs, which are charged to the global community. For example, seventeenth-century English farmers all grazed their cattle on the village commons. Even though they realized that overgrazing would be the ruin of them all, the farmers still sought the immediate benefit of increasing their own herds. Such behavior has come to be known as the "tragedy of the commons."

Protection of the environment and a fair division of the global commons are both such complex issues that the current international system has only recently begun to grapple with them. Each and every attempt to develop an equitable division of the global commons and to assign responsibility for cleanup of past environmental misdeeds has been fraught with controversy, often between the major Western powers and the nations of the third world. The many controversies associated with the Law of the Sea (which regulates economic rights to sea regions), the 1992 global environmental conference in Rio de Janeiro, and other proposed international environmental regimes, illustrate the problems only too well.

A just resolution of global commons issues may require establishment of global institutions with supranational authority. This, in turn, would require that each nation abandon some of its sovereignty to the international system, in contradistinction to the Westphalian system of rule. Voluntary global regimes based on mutual self-interest rather than national self-interest will have to be accepted by all nations of the world.

In an era of transition, all nations will have to adapt their national policies to meet the demands of the emerging global regimes. China, too, will have to adapt to the new world environment. No one approach, whether it be state sovereignty, interdependence, or voluntary global regimes, will be sufficient. Rather, China's leaders will have to balance the demands of those who favor greater Chinese independence from the international system with those leaders who believe that in the future no nation can afford to remain aloof from global institutions or economic and political transactions.

China, the United Nations, and Collective Security in the New Era

After being denied entry into the United Nations for twenty-two years, the General Assembly voted to designate the People's Republic of China as the official holder of its China seat in 1971. The Republic of China (Taiwan) then withdrew from the UN Security Council. At the same time that the vote was taking place in the General Assembly, President Richard Nixon's national security adviser, Henry Kissinger, was visiting Beijing. No better symbolism of the distance China had traveled could be imagined. Once condemned by the General Assembly in absentia for "aggression" in Korea, the People's Republic had become one of the five most important actors responsible for world order.

The Western world feared the presence of a Communist China on the Security Council. Yet China behaved conservatively once on the Security Council, often abstaining rather than vetoing controversial votes. According to former secretary of state Madeleine Albright:

> China has a strong dislike for any UN action that it regards, from the glass house, as interference in the internal affairs of others. During one council meeting . . . I saw the Chinese charge exercising his muscles by squeezing a hard rubber ball. I sent him a note asking, "what's with the little ball?" He replied that he was building up his strength because that day he was actually going to raise his arm and vote yes.[2]

Ironically, China became a strong advocate for the third world by virtue of its membership in the United Nations, but it also became a major player in the international system, which many in the third world abhorred because of its inequality.

When the Soviet permanent seat on the Security Council was given to Russia, Beijing's leaders found themselves facing new opportunities and new dangers in the United Nations. Russia began to join the United States, Britain, and France in promoting UN security initiatives. China was now the sole permanent member that professed to view Security Council actions from a third world perspective.

In the emerging global system, traditional sovereignty issues are giving way to new challenges to international security and the global commons. The end of the Cold War has lessened fears of a major world war. Instead, new and dangerous problems are developing: regional wars, instability within nations, growing violations of human rights caused by a return to extreme forms of nationalism, a surge in racial and ethnic hatreds, and threats of economic warfare as states struggle over whether to pursue mercantilistic economic policies or open up their economies to global competition based on comparative advantage. For Chinese decisionmakers, policy choices are especially difficult. In the confusion of the post–Cold War world, Security Council initiatives have often been sponsored by the United States and its allies, and these initiatives seem to have enhanced the global role of the West. During the Cold War battle for allies, China and the third world were able to influence the two superpowers by awarding allegiance. With the United States the only remaining superpower, the contest for allies has weakened. However, at a time when many third world nations are faced with increasing economic and political problems at home, the United Nations is in many ways less responsive to their needs than in the past. Moreover, the role of the United States in today's United Nations is deeply troubling to China. Always sensitive to the infringement of its or others' sovereignty, China's leaders were alarmed by the George W. Bush administration's manipulation of the United Nations during its preparation for war against Iraq in 2003 and the failure of the United Nations to prevent U.S. action.

> ### Changing the UN Security Council
>
> Several proposals for a restructured Security Council have been offered, including the following: a revolving European seat to be shared sequentially by France, Germany, and the United Kingdom; permanent seats for both Germany and Japan; and permanent Security Council seats for Brazil, Nigeria, Egypt, Japan, and Germany, although only the original five would have veto power.

Changing the UN Structure

Calls for change in the structure of the UN Security Council have increased since the collapse of the Soviet Union. The permanent members of the Security Council, those with veto power, are the victors of World War II. In the twenty-first century, this structure seems anachronistic. China's official position on UN reform is as follows:

> China supports the effort to reform the UN with the aim to a stronger and more effective organization and catching up with the pace of times. During the process of reform, the legitimate rights and interests of the developing countries should be taken care of, and the UN's role in promoting economic and social development should be strengthened. . . . China is in favor of appropriate and necessary reform of the Security Council to enhance its authority, further improve its working method and transparency in decision making and promote its efficiency. The reform should follow the principle of equitable geographical distribution while giving priority to increasing representation of developing countries.[3]

China, along with the other 163 members of the United Nations that together contribute less than 20 percent of the organization's budget, would no doubt vigorously oppose any measures to change the "one member, one vote" provision in the UN Charter to reflect more accurately a member's contributions to the operating budget. China's uncertain role on the Security Council is reflected in its contribution to the UN budget. Whereas the other four permanent members contribute nearly half the UN's regular budget, China contributes less than 1 percent. Most states of both the first world and the third world would oppose any amendments to make representation proportional to population, because China and India would gain the most seats in the General Assembly. And virtually all members of the United Nations are strongly opposed to any Charter changes that would maintain or enhance Western dominance of the organization.

China's position on reforming the Charter is complicated by its membership on the Security Council. Though China seeks leadership of the third world, it does not relish the prospect of sharing permanent membership in the Security Council with other third world nations, especially with India, one of its two greatest potential rivals for dominance in Asia in the twenty-first century. A permanent Security Council seat for Japan also makes Chinese leaders uneasy. Yet the demands for restructuring the Security Council to reflect the post–Cold War era will undoubtedly increase. Paradoxically, China, which has long been an advocate of greater power for the third world in the United Nations, will lose more than any other permanent member if third world membership is increased in the Security Council. Although China could veto any proposed change to the structure of the Security Council that it does not approve of, in reality China's options are limited.

UN Peacemaking and Peacekeeping

There are numerous details concerning the range of actions the United Nations can take to promote peacemaking and peacekeeping:

- Article 41 of the UN Charter provides authority to impose political and economic sanctions such as breaking off diplomatic relations or limiting exports or imports (binding actions by the Security Council).
- Article 42 provides authority to take military action to prevent or resist aggression (binding actions taken by the Security Council).
- Under the Uniting for Peace resolution, which was passed in 1950, the General Assembly can recommend sanctions of a political, military, or economic nature. These recommendations are nonbinding on UN members. Under this precedent, the General Assembly could recommend any other actions listed below on a voluntary basis, including both peacemaking and peacekeeping operations.
- The Security Council can create military forces to take limited military actions to restore or maintain order.
- The Security Council can create multilateral forces to observe or conduct elections.
- The Security Council can create multilateral forces or deputize national forces to disarm combatants in order to restore order.
- The Security Council can provide government services such as administration, finance, communications, and health care in order to restore effective government where services have broken down. Sites of such operations have included the Belgian Congo from 1960 to 1964 and Cambodia beginning in 1992.
- The United Nations can create multilateral forces to observe armistice agreements and report any violations of such agreements. This has usually been done by the Security Council, but it also has been done by the General Assembly, which created the United Emergency Force in the Middle East in 1956.
- A number of practices have developed in deploying peacekeeping operations, including the following: at least one of the countries that is a party to the peace agreement must be willing to allow the UN forces to be deployed on its soil; the lightly armed UN observers are instructed to use force only in self-defense; and the membership of the peacekeeping force must be acceptable to all the parties to the peacekeeping agreement.
- Peacemaking and peacekeeping operations are financed through a combination of sources including the following: assessments through the General Assembly budget, voluntary contributions by individual states, and partial or total financial support for forces being deployed by the troop suppliers.

Beijing's role in Security Council activities is complicated by the changing nature of the post–Cold War era and the growing demand for global solutions to regional and local instabilities. There is no new world order. Instead, as instabilities emerge in the post–Cold War era, the United Nations reacts on an ad hoc basis.

During the Cold War years, UN security activities were largely limited to peacekeeping operations that were acceptable to the two opposing superpowers. Both the United States and the Soviet Union readily used their veto powers to stop any actions detrimental to their interests. Thus, by the time peacekeeping forces were deployed, the danger of the situation was generally defused to the point where UN observers were acceptable to both the combatants and the superpowers.

In contrast to the many peacekeeping operations since 1956, the United Nations has undertaken collective security actions only two times since its establishment. The first time was in Korea in 1950, when the Security Council voted to send a UN force to defend South Korea. Authorization was forthcoming only because the Soviet Union was boycotting the Security Council to protest the continued presence of Taiwan, rather than Beijing, in the China seat. Not until the end of the Cold War was another collective security operation possible. Much to the surprise of Iraq, Security Council Resolution 678 in 1990 authorized the use of force to restore the sovereignty of Kuwait. In order to gain economic assistance from the West, the Russians abandoned their Iraqi allies and voted for the resolution.

China's leaders wish to play an active global role along with other major world actors, but China has largely avoided intervening in affairs other than those along its recognized boundaries. The UN's condemnation of Chinese actions during the Korean War further reinforced Beijing's suspicions of global actions initiated by the West in the Security Council. Since its accession to the Security Council, the People's Republic has generally avoided involvement in peacekeeping operations. In 1990 and 1991, Chinese leaders therefore viewed Western-sponsored anti-Iraqi resolutions with grave misgivings. Though condemning the invasion of Kuwait, Beijing favored limited sanctions against Iraq rather than the use of force. When it became clear that Resolution 678 would pass unless the Chinese vetoed it, Beijing's leaders chose to abstain. In return for this favor, the United States worked to end the moratorium on further World Bank loans to China that had been in place since the Tiananmen incident.

China has also faced other difficult voting decisions in the post–Cold War Security Council. For example, China abstained rather than support a resolution authorizing sanctions against Libya that sought to bring alleged Libyan terrorists to trial in the United States or France. China has traditionally affirmed its support of the Arab world, but it was not willing to veto the resolution and alienate the West. Beijing has also supported limited Security Council resolutions related to humanitarian relief operations in the former Yugoslavia, while abstaining on economic sanctions against Belgrade. Because many Islamic countries were in favor of the strongest possible anti-

Serbian sanctions, China's position on the Yugoslavian issue lost it some of the Arab goodwill it had been accorded for its position on Libya. Concerning Somalia, Beijing's leaders finally supported the U.S.-sponsored Security Council resolution authorizing a U.S.-led coalition force to restore order and ensure that food supplies reached the hungry. Beijing always prefers actions under the UN flag over other military actions, and therefore it was not willing to veto the U.S.-led Somalian force.

The reasons for China's inconsistent voting pattern on the post–Cold War Security Council are clear. Beijing, unable to take the initiative, has had to decide whether to support Western initiatives that go beyond traditional peacekeeping operations, or abstain. If China vetoes resolutions supported by the other four permanent members of the Security Council and their allies, it runs the risk of isolating itself from all major groupings within the United Nations. A Chinese veto might also lead the Security Council to invoke the Uniting for Peace resolution, which allows a deadlocked Security Council to call the General Assembly into session to vote on the issue at hand. Although General Assembly resolutions are only recommendations and are nonbinding, it is hardly conceivable that Beijing would be willing to isolate itself from most of the world by forcing the United Nations to act through the General Assembly after a Chinese veto in the Security Council.

In the late 1990s Beijing finally began to take part in selected UN peacekeeping efforts. No longer willing to cede these efforts to other UN powers, Chinese citizens began to participate. China first participated in UN peacekeeping operations in 1990. In March 2004, China contributed 648 military observers, civilian police, and troops to UN peacekeeping operations.[4] To date, it has participated in the UN peacekeeping operations listed in Table 8.1.[5] The principle guiding Chinese participation seems to be that those operations clearly defined as peacekeeping are acceptable, while any operations that might give rise to questions of infringement on sovereignty are not acceptable.

The Future United Nations

In January 1992, leaders of the major world states held a summit at the United Nations to make recommendations on ways to promote international stability and peace. Li Peng, China's premier, was a major participant. He and the representatives of other permanent members of the Security Council sponsored a proposal asking the UN Secretary-General to develop a plan for more effective utilization of the UN system for the maintenance of peace and the prevention of war. The Secretary-General's final report, however, called for the creation of a permanent UN peacekeeping force of 50,000 for immediate use in crises. Because this proposal requires a joint UN high command, the United States and probably other powers are unlikely to accept it. Although global

Table 8.1   Chinese Participation in UN Peacekeeping Operations

Service Region	Abbreviation	Date	Number of Observers
UN Truce Supervision Organization	UNTSO	From April 1990	66
UN Iraq-Kuwait Observation Mission	UNIKOM	From April 1991	161
UN Mission for the Referendum in Western Sahara	MINURSO	From September 1991	214
UN Transitional Authority in Cambodia	UNTAC	December 1991 to September 1993	97
UN Operation in Mozambique	ONUMOZ	June 1993 to December 1994	20
UN Observer Mission in Liberia	UNOMIL	November 1993 to September 1997	33
UN Special Mission	UNSMA	May 1998 to January 2000	2
UN Observer Mission in Sierra Leone	UNOMSIL	From August 1998	24
UN Transitional Authority in East Timor	UNTAET	From January 2000	178[a]
UN Mission in Ethiopia and Eritrea	UNMEE	From October 200	15
UN Mission in Bosnia and Herzegovina	UNMIBH	From January 2001	20[a]
UN Mission in the Congo (Kinshasa)	MONUC	From April 2001	20

Source: Permanent Mission of the People's Republic of China to the UN, white paper on China's defense issued December 9, 2002, http://un.fmprc.gov.cn/eng/39095.html.
Note: a. Number of civilian policemen.

UN military operations multiplied to over 50,000 personnel in 2004, voluntary participation is likely to continue on an ad hoc basis. Beijing is likely to remain a free rider, choosing with great care which peacekeeping operations it will participate in.

In the future, events outside China are likely to be the primary determinants of China's UN policy. Although interdependence may grow, China and the other nations in the international system continue to react to global problems on an ad hoc basis. What has distinguished Beijing's leaders from those in the West has been a continuing hesitancy to join regional or global regimes that reduce sovereignty or internal control over each state's destiny. In the past, Beijing was more reactive than proactive with respect to global and regional events, whether political, economic, environmental, or humanitarian. National self-interest, the dominant value of the international system since the Treaty of

Westphalia in 1648, remained the key to understanding China's actions in the UN and other international fora. However, in the 1990s, deciding what constituted the national self-interest for China and other world actors became more uncertain than during the Cold War years, when the East-West rivalry provided a compass for determining regional and global power balances. In the early twenty-first century, China has decided to adopt the stance "if you cannot fight them, join them." Beijing is balancing more active participation in a wide variety of international organizations with its traditional prickliness regarding sovereignty and national interest. So far, it has been able to balance the two nicely. If forced to chose between the two, as with any major power, sovereignty and national interest are likely to prevail.

Arms Control or Arms Races? Chinese Alternatives

The end of the Cold War greatly reduced the danger of world war and has resulted in extensive military restructuring in both the United States and the former Soviet Union. Both to lessen tensions and as a result of lessened tensions, Mikhail Gorbachev and George H. W. Bush agreed to reduce troop deployments in Europe, to destroy intermediate-range nuclear weapons, and to drastically cut back on the number of strategic nuclear weapons. Although the collapse of the Soviet Union has complicated implementation of these accords, the new republics have stated their commitment to the terms of the agreements in words, if not always in action.

China's military and security position has been fundamentally altered by the events of 1991 as well. After years of vigilant anti-Soviet defenses on its borders, China is now no longer threatened by a major military power on its northern or western borders, although the new republics may develop small arms races of their own. This, combined with the phased withdrawal of U.S. troops from Asia, poses both opportunities and risks for Beijing. For

China's Nuclear Policies

With the end of the Cold War, China had a public relations problem. Before the Soviet Union and the United States agreed to cut their nuclear stockpiles drastically, Beijing claimed it would reduce its nuclear arsenal if Moscow and Washington agreed to destroy half of their nuclear arsenals. After the Start III agreements, China changed its position, arguing that Russian and U.S. nuclear capabilities were still so large that further reductions were necessary before Beijing could consider entering into serious negotiations to reduce its own stockpile.

the first time since the Western imperialists first visited China, China's leaders find themselves in a position to influence events beyond their borders rather than be pressured by superior external military forces.

China is now expanding its own military capabilities and increasing its military budget. Its reasons are internal as well as external. Ever since the Communist Party began its Long March to power, the military has played an important role. Mao's people's army was a peasant army—overstaffed, underequipped, and poorly trained. Yet it performed well in Korea, and reliable troops were used to clamp down on the worst excesses of the Cultural Revolution. In 1989, the military again played a crucial political role when it crushed the protesters at Tiananmen Square.

Military budgets, however, have not always been commensurate with the military's political role. Deng Xiaoping drastically reduced the number of troops from 4 million to 3 million, both to reduce personnel costs and to reform the military into an educated professional force. Only after the military displayed its loyalty at Tiananmen Square did military budget allocations start to rise dramatically. Despite the reduced external threat, the regular Chinese military budget has increased in real terms by over 10 percent every year since 1989. Moreover, large purchases of Russian military equipment have allegedly been paid for from a secret fund controlled by the Central Military Commission.[6]

The years of low military budgets have had unintended side effects, both within China and within the international system. During the early years of Deng's reforms, those remaining in the military did not receive pay increases. Morale plummeted because of a loss of purchasing power. To supplement limited government funding, many military units sought outside funding sources. In cities such as Guangzhou, military units operated nightclubs, tourist hotels, and other enterprises—even shooting galleries. More dangerous, many Chinese military units began to sell weapons on the international market, especially in the Middle East and Asia. Competitively priced conventional weapons, as well as dual-use nuclear technology and short- and medium-range missiles, were marketed to eager nations stymied by Western arms embargoes. Using *guanxi* (personal gifts and rewards)—often the military export corporations are staffed by the children of senior Chinese leaders—the military often completed these transactions without the knowledge of the Ministry of Foreign Affairs.[7]

Though domestic stability is a major reason for increasing military resources, there are other reasons as well. Beijing has always reserved the ultimate right to use force if a peaceful solution to reunification with Taiwan is not achieved. Despite greatly improved relations between China and Taiwan, particularly trade relations, U.S. and other arms sales to Taiwan have very much upset Beijing. In September 1992, President Bush announced a $6 billion deal to sell 150 F-16 fighter planes to Taiwan, which Beijing denounced as a clear violation of the 1982 Sino-U.S. communiqué in which the United

States agreed not to upgrade its military sales to Taiwan. This was followed by a multibillion-dollar deal in which France agreed to sell sixty Mirage fighter jets and 1,000 short- and medium-range missiles to Taiwan. China responded by purchasing Russian military hardware. More recently, the second Bush administration planned to sell an early-warning radar systems, valued at $1.78 billion, to Taiwan. Beijing's response was predictable. A Chinese foreign ministry spokesman said, "Especially under the current complicated and sensitive situation across the Taiwan Strait, we ask the United States to be faithful to what it says and abide by its promises and not send the wrong signal to Taiwan's independence (seekers)."[8]

The message is clear: Beijing's leaders intend to maintain a military position strong enough to convince Taiwanese leaders that a declaration of independence from China is not feasible. Just as important is China's sense of honor and pride. Beijing believes that as an emerging world power it is entitled to play a larger regional and global role. China believes all states are entitled to up-to-date military forces. Beijing argues that its military buildup is not only justified but also poses no danger to the world balance of power.

Regional Arms Sales: A Chinese Perspective

Although China may develop a more formidable military force, Western observers in the recent past were most concerned by China's emerging role as a major arms merchant in the Middle East, West Asia, and South Asia. Prior to the collapse of the Soviet Union, China played a relatively minor role in the Middle East, but Beijing's arms merchants became an important factor in regional balance-of-power structures in the 1990s. China's diplomatic activities have also greatly increased. In 1991, Beijing established diplomatic relations with a number of key Arab states, such as Saudi Arabia. Playing both sides, China also established diplomatic relations with Israel in 1992.

China justifies its arms sales to the Middle East by pointing out the enormous amount of military equipment sold to the region by the United States, the former Soviet Union, and the nations of Western and Eastern Europe. In light of the large sales by these states since Operation Desert Storm, Beijing believes it also has the right to sell arms to the Middle East. China's arms industries, like those in Russia and the West, need hard cash, and China therefore believes that the United States and its allies are unjustified in trying to prevent China from selling arms and military technology to Iran, Syria, Sudan, and other states in the Middle East. From Beijing's perspective, Western and especially U.S. leaders speak with two voices: what is acceptable for Israel, including a probable nuclear stockpile, is not acceptable for the Arab states.

The statistics bear out this viewpoint. According to the Stockholm International Peace Research Institute:

The five-year moving average level of global arms transfers fell in the period 1997–2001. This is explained mainly by a reduction in deliveries by the USA, which was the largest supplier in 1997–2001 despite a 65% reduction in its arms deliveries since 1998. Russia was the second largest supplier during this period. A 24% increase in arms transfers from 2000 to 2001 made Russia the largest supplier in 2001. China was by far the largest arms recipient in 2001 after an increase of 44% from 2000. Imports by India increased by 50%, making it the third largest recipient in 2001. The other major recipients in the period 1997–2001 were Saudi Arabia, Taiwan and Turkey.[9]

Nuclear Weapons and Delivery Systems

In actuality, China behaves no differently than other actors in the international system with respect to arms sales and transfers of dual-use technology. It is now widely acknowledged that U.S. businesses sold Iraq (prior to its invasion of Kuwait) a wide variety of components that Saddam Hussein used in his atomic bomb and missile-building projects. Similarly, critics claim that "Beijing is turning these dictatorships in the Middle East and Asia into missile producing and missile-transferring states themselves—North Korea for instance."[10]

At the same time, after considerable negotiations with the United States, China finally ratified the Nuclear Nonproliferation Treaty of 1968 in March 1992. It is now formally obligated not to help other countries acquire nuclear capability. Although China reached agreements with Iran and Algeria in the early 1990s to assist with the development of nuclear power plants under the supervision of the UN International Atomic Energy Agency, it has provided Pakistan with dual-use technology for more than twenty years.

Similarly, Beijing supported the 1987 Missile Technology Control Regime after the Bush administration offered the incentives of sales of U.S. supercomputer technology to China and U.S. use of Chinese satellites for space launches. The Missile Technology Control Regime, an effort by the United States and its allies to prevent further escalation of the arms race in the Middle East and South Asia, seeks to prevent the exports of advanced missiles into these regions. By 1992, however, U.S. intelligence reports indicated that Beijing was violating the spirit, if not the letter, of the law by selling missiles to Iran and Pakistan. Further reports of missile sales to Pakistan in December 1992 created a high-level debate in the Bush administration just as it was about to leave office. The commerce and state departments wanted to go ahead with the sale of high-speed computers, but they were opposed by the Pentagon and the Arms Control and Disarmament Agency, which were concerned about both China's failure to keep its promises and the potential use of the high-speed computers to upgrade Chinese military capabilities.[11]

Export Controls

As Beijing increasingly became a part of international arms control regimes during the 1990s, it became more sensitive to U.S. and other reactions to its missile exports. In November 2000, the People's Republic "promised the Clinton Administration that it would stop making missile sales to unstable Middle East and South Asian regimes and would institute an export control regime, and the United States promised to lift existing sanctions against certain technology exports."[12] While relations with China improved after the terrorist attacks of September 11, 2001, arms export issues periodically arise between the two countries. Despite Beijing's increasingly stringent regulations controlling arms exports, the United States believes that the Chinese, or Chinese companies with military ties, are still exporting to Iran and Pakistan, among other nations. The United States has therefore periodically sanctioned particular companies. For example, in July 2003 the George W. Bush administration imposed economic sanctions on five Chinese firms suspected of shipping missile technology to Iran. Given Washington's need to cultivate Beijing in the war on terrorism, at the same time that the United States is working with Pakistan on antiterrorist activities, the sanctions have been limited.

As with so many of its positions on international issues, China's official position on export controls has changed over the years, from skepticism to support. The old position was that "non-proliferation should not hamper the normal and legitimate technological co-operations among nations, or be used as an excuse for discrimination and even willful sanctions against developing countries. A small number of discriminatory and exclusive export control groups should be reformed or dismantled, if necessary, to be replaced by international arrangements reached on a fairer, more transparent and more representative basis."[13] In 2003, a Chinese white paper on nonproliferation policy stated, "China will continue to take an active part in international non-proliferation endeavors, and exert great efforts to maintain and strengthen the existing non-proliferation international law system within the UN framework. It will constantly increase consultations and exchanges with the multinational non-proliferation mechanisms . . . and continue to take an active part in international discussions related to non-proliferation."[14]

International Finance: The International Monetary Fund and the World Bank

China's role in global economic regimes stands in marked contrast to its somewhat secretive and isolated role on security and arms issues. Prior to 1978, most of Beijing's economic and security relationships were bilateral, but with Deng Xiaoping's opening to the outside world, China changed its view on global economic institutions in what amounted to a revolutionary transformation. After Mao came to power in 1949, China supported the revolutionary overthrow of capitalist systems and viewed international economic regimes such as the World Bank and the International Monetary Fund (IMF) as stooges of the Western capitalists. When the Soviets became the primary threat to Chinese security and Beijing started working with Washington in the early 1970s to contain Moscow, the Chinese position shifted to reformation rather than transformation of the global economic system.

After reclaiming its UN seat in 1971, the People's Republic also gained observer status in the Third World Committee of 77 and strongly supported its demands for a new international economic order. Since 1978, Beijing has again changed its approach and indicated a desire to join existing global capitalist institutions such as the International Bank for Reconstruction and Development (IBRD) and its affiliated agencies: the International Development Association (IDA), which makes soft loans to less developed countries; the International Finance Corporation (IFC), which helps underwrite investments in the private sector; and the IMF, which facilitates the international exchange of currencies and makes short-term loans based on conditionality (i.e., compliance to the IMF's recommended economic practices).

What was the reasoning behind this radical change in Beijing's thinking? Apparently Deng Xiaoping and his supporters had come to the conclusion that these capitalist multilateral regimes were an important source of not only capital but also technical assistance, technical training, and information on how to develop and modernize China. Beijing decided that if these international economic regimes helped China finance infrastructure projects such as energy, education, power, communications, and transport, this would give foreign governments and private investors greater confidence in investing inside China.[15] China was further integrated into the global economic system when its request was approved by the UN Development Programme (UNDP) in 1978 to change its status from an aid donor to an aid recipient, enabling it to receive funding for a wide range of technical assistance for which it previously had not been eligible.

Since reclaiming its UN seat in 1971, Beijing has developed close working relationships with the various special UN agencies for projects such as those carried out by the World Health Organization (WHO), the Food and Agricultural Organization (FAO), and the UN Educational, Scientific, and Cultural Organization (UNESCO). Because of limited UNDP funding, which comes mostly from voluntary donations from Western UN members, this aid has been much less important to China than funding received from the World Bank Group and the International Monetary Fund, which China joined in 1980.

Beijing has also extended its multilateral ties to the regional level. For example, its application for admission to the Asian Development Bank (ADB) was accepted in May 1986. However, membership in this organization posed a serious problem because Taiwan was a charter member of the ADB and also a major source of ADB funding for development projects throughout Asia.[16] Other ADB members, while supporting Beijing's admission, wished to keep Taiwan in the organization. In the past, when the issue of dual membership with Taiwan arose, Beijing had refused to participate in any organization of which Taiwan was also a member, but in the case of ADB it accepted an arrangement in which Taiwan would continue its membership under the name "Taipei, China." This provision conformed to the principle of "one China, two systems." Separate membership by Beijing and Taipei in the ADB, where the two regimes have gradually learned to get along with each other, may be a precedent that will help bring further reconciliation between the two governments. Taiwan is also a participant in the World Bank Group as "Taiwan, China." When China was finally admitted to the World Trade Organization (WTO), Taiwan was also admitted as "Chinese Taipei." Because Taiwan is one of the world's major economic success stories in achieving economic modernization and development, as well as an important factor in world trade and investment, the membership of both Beijing and Taipei in these organizations further strengthens them and helps spur international economic integration and development, not only in Asia but also in other regions of the world.

China and the International Monetary Fund

Beijing's admission to the IMF in 1980 brought immediate benefits that have been very important to the success of China's Open Door policy and internal development (see Table 8.2). After paying its financial obligations to the IMF, Beijing was able to draw sizable allotments of hard currency, interest-free, to

Table 8.2   China's Transactions with the International Monetary Fund, 1984–1992 (in Special Drawing Rights)

	Total Disbursements	Total Repayments	Total Charges/ Interest Paid
1984	0	0	1,547,633
1985	0	0	1,547,634
1986	597,725,000	30,952,668	1,508,201
1987	0	61,905,336	37,833,954
1988	0	61,905,336	37,511,116
1989	0	61,905,336	52,342,638
1990	0	360,767,836	48,243,068
1991	0	329,815,170	17,427,183
1992	0	0	241,157

Source: International Monetary Fund, http://www.imf.org/external/np/tre/tad/extrans1 .cfm?memberkey1=180&enddate=2004%2d03%2d31&finposition_flag=yes, viewed May 5, 2004.

help shore up its balance-of-payments deficits. Because China's record of repayment to the International Monetary Fund has been excellent, it has been able to obtain short-term drawings from the IMF at reasonable rates while at the same time avoiding stringent IMF conditionalities for borrowing additional money. In its relations with the IMF, China stands in stark contrast to many third world countries, which because of their difficulties in repaying IMF loans have had to accept IMF-proposed economic reforms as a condition of obtaining further financing.

China and the World Bank

China's admission to the World Bank came at the same time as its admission to the IMF, and it has benefited not only from large IBRD loans at reasonable rates, but also from extensive World Bank studies of the Chinese economy done in cooperation with Chinese planning agencies. The World Bank has instituted macro and sectoral studies of China's economy on a continual basis since 1980. The Bank's 2001–2005 goals for China are as follows:

1. Growth of 7 percent per year which will help achieve a doubling of total output by 2010 (implying an ambitious 7.4 percent target for 2006–2010).
2. Sustainable development, with increased productivity in agriculture and industrial state-owned enterprises. Job creation by promoting labor-intensive activities, including services; developing collective, private, and individual businesses to create 40 million new urban jobs; and safeguarding the natural resource base.
3. Economic restructuring, rural reform, and opening to the world, to be achieved through better macroeconomic management, fiscal reform, and financial stability; establishment of modern corporate structures; establishment of competitive and globally integrated markets; acceleration of agricultural diversification and rural reforms to raise incomes; improvement of science and technology inputs into production; and strengthening of cooperation with other countries.
4. Coordination of economic and social development, to be achieved by paying greater attention to quality-of-life issues, including investing in human capital (e.g., antipoverty measures, better education), protecting natural capital (e.g., through enhanced ecological conservation and environmental protection), improving social protection (e.g., through strengthening the social security system), promoting the rule of law, and broadening democratic participation (e.g., through political reform and strengthening legislative oversight).
5. Development of economically and socially lagging western and central provinces, to be achieved by fostering economic development zones

through investments in strategic physical infrastructure for transport, water resource management, energy, and mining, accelerating other development objectives cited above, and introducing advanced technologies to upgrade local industries and increase competitiveness.[17]

China continues to follow its Open Door policy and utilizes the World Bank and International Monetary Fund to obtain loans and valuable assistance in transforming its economy; indeed, China has become one of the largest recipients of IMF and World Bank funding. China also succeeded in obtaining 50 percent of its World Bank lending through the IBRD's soft loan window—the International Development Association, which does not charge interest for needed projects in countries with very low living standards. Other third world countries complained, however, that China was much better off than they were, and in the late 1980s IDA loans to China were reduced to 40 percent of World Bank funding (see Table 8.3).

After the Tiananmen Square incident, Washington did convince the World Bank to suspend further aid to Beijing. In 1990, however, the Japanese prime minister took the initiative in persuading the Group of Seven (the

Table 8.3   World Bank Lending to China, 1981–2003 (in U.S.$ millions)

1981	200.0
1982	330.0
1983	538.5
1984	869.5
1985	1,166.9
1986	1,237.0
1987	1,471.6
1988	1,718.0
1989	1,297.0
1990	1,202.9
1991	6,293.9
1992	4,036.6
1993	6,479.3
1994	9,770.7
1995	9,157.8
1996	6,401.7
1997	8,013.0
1998	7,098.9
1999	5,364.6
2000	5,203.3
2001	1,472.6
2002	3,533.9
2003	2,475.9

Source: http://www.worldbank.org.

United States, the United Kingdom, France, Germany, Italy, Canada, and Japan) to support new World Bank lending to China. Later in 1990, Beijing was able to bring further pressure on the United States to support IBRD loans for China by making such support a condition of China's abstaining rather than vetoing the Security Council resolution authorizing the use of force to remove Iraq from Kuwait. From the Chinese point of view, tying bank loans to events inside China is an illegal interference in China's internal affairs. Therefore, Beijing believed that it was entitled to use leverage against the United States on other issues as a means of stopping these illegal actions. China was successful in changing U.S. policy and restoring its World Bank funding.

U.S.-led efforts to use the World Bank to penalize Beijing after the Tiananmen Square events in 1989 were only a temporary setback for China. Both before and after Tiananmen, Beijing was moving further toward privatization of the economy with the assistance of the International Finance Corporation (IFC). The IFC lends seed money to private ventures in third world countries for the purpose of promoting private investment. In China, these are often joint ventures between Chinese businesses and multinational corporations with headquarters in Hong Kong, Taiwan, South Korea, Singapore, Japan, the United States, and Western Europe. For example, in 2002 the IFC funded a joint venture international banking and finance institute in Shanghai to provide world-class training to Chinese financial institutions, primarily commercial banks. The objective of establishing Shanghai International Banking and Finance Institute is to help meet the strong and rapidly growing needs in China for acquiring international best practices in banking and finance.[18] IFC ventures often serve as a precedent for further financing of private investment in China—multinational corporations are more inclined to risk venture capital when part of the funding comes from one of the World Bank lending windows.

IBRD and IMF aid to China has been instrumental in helping the People's Republic achieve annual growth rates averaging 8–9 percent in gross national product (GNP). And World Bank lending continues to grow. Ironically, while China, a communist country, continues to receive IBRD and IMF aid, former communist countries in Eastern Europe and the former parts of the Soviet Union, such as Russia and the Ukraine, have had difficulty in obtaining World Bank lending, because economic conditions inside their countries fail to meet World Bank standards.

International Trade: Open or Closed Systems?

One of the most remarkable developments in recent international trade has been the explosive increase of Chinese exports over the past two decades. Chinese trade has continued to increase very rapidly, and exports continue to increase even more rapidly than China's annual 8–9 percent increase in GNP. Hong Kong is China's largest trade partner, serving as a transshipment point for Chinese exports to other destinations. Japan is second, closely followed by the United States.

China's rapid foreign trade expansion has been one of its major sources of revenue and capital. In the 1980s, China's special export zones, where overseas investors invested with few restrictions and also brought in raw materials and sent out exports with few regulations or duties, became China's greatest economic success story. Chinese exports have also come from agricultural commodities. In the 1980s the People's Republic became the world's second largest corn producer and exporter, with 14 percent of the global market. In 1993, China was also the world's largest rice producer, with an estimated 185 million metric tons, as well as the world's largest wheat producer, with 101 million metric tons. Remarkably, China's overall grain production doubled during Deng's rule. China became an importer of wheat in the 1990s and a major customer of the United States and other wheat exporters.[19] At various times during the 1990s, China imported as much as 17 percent of the world's traded wheat, 25 percent of its fertilizer, and 28 percent of its soybean oil, while exporting as much as 10 percent of the world's traded corn; however, the agricultural share of China's trade fell from about 33 percent in 1980 to about 7 percent in 1999—reflecting export-led industrial growth.[20] (See Figure 8.1.)

According to the U.S. Department of Agriculture,

> For a country with nearly 1.3 billion consumers and limited natural resources, China's level of food imports is surprisingly low. China is nearly self-sufficient in food and is a major net exporter of many food products, including manufactured food and beverages, animal products, vegetables, fish and seafood, tea, and fruits. China's agricultural exports go primarily to neighboring Asian countries, including Japan and South Korea, which are also among the top markets for U.S. agricultural products. Overall, China is a net importer of bulk commodities, primarily wheat. In some years, China has been a major importer of corn and cotton, and in other years, it has been a major exporter of those commodities. . . . During the 1990s, China emerged as a major market for imports of oilseeds, vegetable oils, and oil meal.[21]

Bilateral and Regional Trade Agreements

With the exception of China's adherence to the Multifiber Agreement in January 1984, most of China's trade agreements have been bilateral. Probably the granting of most-favored-nation status by the United States in 1980 was the single most important Chinese trade agreement since the beginning of Deng Xiaoping's Open Door policy. In a single stroke, average duties on Chinese

Figure 8.1   China's Agricultural Exports and Imports, 1992–2000

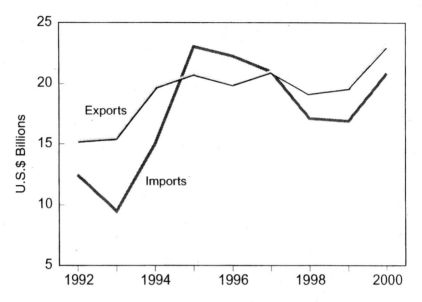

Source: ERS analysis of China customs statistics reported in Hsin-Hui Hsu and Fred Gale, *China: Agriculture in Transition*, USDA/ERS Agriculture and Trade Report no. WRS-01-2, November 2001, app. tabs. 5–6: www.ers.usda.gov/publications/aib775/aib775k.pdf.
Note: Data not adjusted for inflation.

exports to the United States fell from about 50 to 8 percent on a number of products, including toys and textiles. Since then, through bilateral negotiations, the United States and China have also signed a number of agreements protecting each others' trading rights, including copyrights, banning of prison-made exports, and the elimination of a number of nontariff trade barriers. In the past, China has had a wide range of restrictions on imports, and Beijing has preferred to make large purchases such as civilian jet airliners and wheat on a quid pro quo basis. For example, in 1993, Boeing Aircraft Corporation received an order for forty-three airliners from the Chinese government, which was 7 percent of Boeing's total production at a time when Western airlines were cutting back on orders because of competition and recession. Because of the size of its market, China, unlike most third world countries, is able to exercise considerable leverage in its bilateral trade negotiations.

Yet, as Table 8.4 illustrates, China is the world's most attractive country for foreign direct investment. But future Chinese trade leverage has been limited because of the emergence of regional trading blocs in the 1990s. The European Community, having eliminated all its internal trade barriers by 1993, places numerous restrictions on a wide range of imports, especially agricultural

Table 8.4   The Most Attractive Countries for Foreign Direct Investment

1	China
2	India
3	United States
4	Thailand
5/6	Poland/Czech Republic
7/8	Mexico/Malaysia
9/10/11	United Kingdom/Singapore/South Korea

Source: UNCTAD-DITE, Global Investments Prospects Assessment (GIPA) 2004, http://www.unctad.org/templates/webflyer.asp?intitemid=3005&lang=1.

products. At the same time, the European Community subsidizes certain exports such as wheat. The North American Free Trade Agreement (NAFTA), between the United States, Canada, and Mexico (signed in 1992 and ratified in 1993), makes North America the world's largest free trade zone. Mexico, with its cheap labor, will compete for investments and trade that might otherwise go to China and other Asian Pacific Rim countries. Significantly, because of NAFTA, China is considering building manufacturing plants in Mexico.

Although the Pacific Rim is the world's fastest-growing economic region and is already a larger market for U.S. products than is the European Community, in the past there were almost no regional economic trade agreements in Asia, with the exception of limited arrangements among the Association of Southeast Asian Nations (ASEAN). Asian states have been dependent on either bilateral agreements or the World Trade Organization for international trade. In the 1990s China became a key actor in these bilateral arrangements, which now involve extensive bilateral agreements between China, Japan, Hong Kong, South Korea, Thailand, Taiwan, Indonesia, and even Vietnam, despite its border war with China in 1979. China has a common interest with other Asian countries in avoiding an Asian trade bloc dominated by Japan. In addition, because of its comparative cost advantage in the production of an ever wider variety of manufactured products, China opposes the emergence of trading blocs, whether in Asia, North America, or Europe. Nevertheless, in response to international trends, in the early twenty-first century China has taken the lead in a proposed ASEAN free trade association.

China and the World Trade Organization

In contrast to its refusal to support regional economic trade agreements, after the 1980s Beijing sought to reactivate its membership in the WTO (formerly the General Agreement on Tariffs and Trade [GATT]), which is designed to provide a multilateral forum through which states can negotiate reduction of

tariff or nontariff trade barriers. The members of GATT invited China to become an active member of the organization when it reclaimed its UN seat in
1971, but China at first refused. When Deng Xiaoping came to power, however, he viewed GATT and other global economic regimes as a means of gaining access to world finance and markets. In 1982, two years after joining the
IMF and IBRD, China was given observer status in GATT, and in 1986 China
sought to reactivate its full membership. China's rejoining GATT/WTO was a
logical step in its efforts to participate fully in the global market economy, but
reentry was predicated on reforming Chinese trading practices that failed to
meet trade and membership rules. Indeed, China endured a series of difficult
talks with the United States before it was finally allowed to accede to the
WTO in December 2001. (Hong Kong became a member in 1995 and "Chinese Taipei" in 2002.) China's membership in the WTO ties it to the international system in ways that directly violate its previous defense of sovereignty
at all costs. Tariffs will be reduced, exports will be allowed into China without controls, and business transactions will be held to an international level of
transparency. China no longer will be an independent actor with total control
over all its economic inflows and outflows.

Dealing with the Environment

Environment and development are two major concerns of the international
community. Through its arduous efforts of many years, especially those
made since the industrial revolution, mankind has made brilliant achieve-
ments in transforming nature and developing economy. Yet neglect of environment in the course of industrialization, particularly the irrational exploitation and utilization of natural resources, has caused global
environmental pollution and ecological degradation, posing a real threat to
the survival and development of mankind. It is therefore an urgent and formidable task for all countries around the world to protect the ecological environment and maintain a sustainable development.[22]

The tension between development and environment is of overwhelming concern to all nations of the world, but particularly to the third world. The nations
of the third world believe that their primary task is development and the elimination of poverty. Within these parameters, the third world must take steps to
protect their environment; yet many in the third world believe that the primary
responsibility for environmental remediation should be taken by the industrialized world, which in the course of development has caused most of the
world's environmental damage.

Even the definition of environmental damage in the industrialized world
differs from that in the third world and China. Many in the West devote their
attention to climatic change, ozone depletion, and biodiversity, and worry
about the global environmental effects of each Chinese family owning its own

car and its own refrigerator. The Chinese, however, define environmental problems in terms of pollution and ecological degradation in developing countries, such as soil erosion, desertification, diminished vegetation, droughts, floods,[23] and the problems of overpopulation.

China's record of dealing with its own environmental problems has been mixed. The problems are many. Any visitor to China can testify to the pervasive air pollution. Equipment to control air pollution is rarely installed at industrial facilities. Water treatment is minimal if it occurs at all, and wastewater from domestic and industrial sources often flows directly into the nearest river without any treatment. In some highly industrial areas, health officials suspect that local residents are suffering from pollution-related illnesses. Thus China has the same air and water pollution problems as most third world countries undergoing the process of industrialization.

China also has degraded its environment. Population growth during the past two centuries has resulted in deforestation, which is readily apparent to even the uninformed eye. The results can be dramatic. Rainfall is not absorbed but instead rushes down parched gullies into defenseless villages and towns. Lands become less fertile, and agricultural yields decrease. Increasing use of chemical fertilizers, paradoxically a by-product of increasing wealth, results in contaminated rainwater runoff. A vicious cycle of ever-decreasing yields and greater pollution results.

Officially, the Chinese government advocates strict pollution control measures. At home, the government advocates a combination of planning measures at all levels, interministry coordination, and legal measures to control pollution. It created the State Environmental Protection Administration in 1998, a ministry-level organization, as a successor to the National Environmental Protection Agency (NEPA). Government experts interact regularly with foreign researchers to study the causes and cures for local pollution problems. At the international level, China regularly participates in environmental programs and conferences. Even the World Bank commends China on its environmental regulatory regime:

China's repertoire of environmental laws, regulations, and standards is quite comprehensive and has been continuously updated and expanded to improve effectiveness and cover emerging issues. Among comparable developing nations, China is unquestionably in the front rank, but it cannot become complacent. The demands it faces are unprecedented and it cannot settle for being among the best in its class. It needs to measure its performance against the best OECD [Organization for Economic Cooperation and Development] countries in the world. By this standard, it still has a long way to go. It has to work harder on legal and administrative measures, on getting the fundamentals of development policy right, and on human resources development. Most importantly, it has to move the concept of environmentally sustainable development onto the front page of all policy documents.[24]

The reality, however, may be quite different. Claims that the government is paying attention to environmental problems have not always been borne out by field research. Four of the world's ten most polluted cities are in China. Coal dust emissions in northern China are five times WHO standards. Drinking water for 60 percent of the Chinese people does not meet WHO standards, and acid rain is a severe problem. According to Pan Yue, deputy director of China's State Environmental Protection Administration, as quoted in the *New York Times*, "acid rain falls over two-thirds of China's land mass. Of 340 major Chinese cities surveyed last year, 60 percent had serious air pollution problems. In China's seven major waterways, pollution is so severe that vast stretches are not suitable for fish." Pan states, "The pressures China is now facing simply can't be sustained, the population and resource pressures. . . . They cannot be ignored. . . . The serious problem we're facing is not lack of people," Pan said. "More important is, we need the laws and power to enforce environmental protection. This requires systemic reform."[25] Proper environmental management requires cooperative planning and monitoring by the government, a relatively uncorrupted legal system, environmental experts, and concerned citizens. With the diffusion of power in China, the central government has lost much of its ability to enforce environmental protection measures.

Population and the Environment

Even with one of the most comprehensive family planning systems in the world, 15 million people are added to China's population each year, almost one-fifth of the world's population increase. The Chinese people form one-quarter of the world's population, yet only 11 percent of China's land is arable, and up to 10 percent of cultivable land has been lost to erosion and urbanization. With 70–80 percent of the Chinese population still living in rural areas, population density has risen to over 1,100 people per square kilometer in the densely populated provinces.

Population pressures have led to more intensive farming, which has been extended into marginal land. This, in turn, has contributed to forest degradation and soil erosion. Water supply for both rural and urban populations is also becoming increasingly scarce, as one-third of the wells in Beijing have gone dry.

Although Mao and the Communist leadership initially encouraged population growth, by the mid-1950s family planning and contraception were being encouraged. During the early years of the Cultural Revolution, all attempts at family planning were abandoned to the rigors of ideological purity—the Red Guard made love as well as war.

But by 1971, development of the Four Modernizations policy led China's leaders to launch a massive program that encouraged birth control and delayed marriage. The controversial one-child-per-family program, which used both coercive and monetary incentives to convince Chinese families that having only one daughter would not anger the ancestors, was initiated in 1979. Currently, over $1 billion is spent annually on family planning in both rural and urban areas. Almost all of the funding comes from domestic sources, although technical assistance, valued at less than $10 million per year, has been provided from international agencies such as the UN Population Fund. UN assistance has been limited by the refusal of the Reagan and both Bush administrations to provide funding because of concerns that the Chinese government promotes abortion as a means of birth control. Some disturbing aspects of the campaign to slow birthrates were the dramatic drops in live births per 1,000 people and in women's fertility (from 22.4 live births per 1,000 people and 2.5 per woman in 1988 to 18.2 per 1,000 people and 1.9 per woman in 1992). In 2004, according to the United Nations, the birth rate per thousand was 14.3, and the total fertility rate per woman was 1.8.[26] Furthermore, after the government began vigorously limiting birthrates in 1989, there were 113.8 reported boy births for every 100 reported girl births.[27] This seems to indicate that female infanticide is occurring because of the age-old Chinese desire to have sons rather than daughters.

China's Population

What should be done about China's inexorably increasing population? Experts offer a number of suggestions, including the following:

1. More help should come from the international community, since China's population problem is also a world problem.
2. Additional funding is needed, from both domestic and international sources.
3. Investments are needed to achieve greater educational and employment opportunities for women.
4. State-assisted pensions are needed for all.
5. New types of high-quality contraceptives are needed.
6. Foreign technical assistance is needed to develop clinical service and counseling networks.

China's population growth rate did decrease during the early 1980s, but it began to climb again in the late 1980s before decreasing again in the early 1990s. When asked how this sudden shift from increasing to drastically decreasing fertility rates could occur, the head of China's State Family Planning Commission said, "Above all because party and Government officials at all levels paid greater attention to family planning and adopted more effective measures." These more effective measures included increased use of contraception and sterilization, as well as some methods reportedly used by local officials, such as forced abortions, much to the embarrassment of the central government.[28]

Paradoxically, as the Chinese standard of living has increased, the desire for more children has become stronger, despite the dangers of overpopulation. Many rural families can afford to pay whatever fines and bribes are necessary to have more children, with the result that the average rural family now has three children. These children are needed to provide security to the elder generation in their old age, since another side effect of privatization has been the abandonment of the social safety net that communism promised. In urban areas, the one-child policy has been more successful because government control is more established and because more people still work for state enterprises that provide social benefits for old age and unemployment.

China's one-child policy had many unintended consequences. While the birthrate has stabilized (see Table 8.5), it will do so at some economic and social cost. The "little emperors," spoiled children of one-child families, will eventually have to support their aging parents while trying to make their way in society. Poorer Chinese men are already finding a dearth of possible brides, which has led in some cases to kidnapping and makes demographers nervous. This situation may destabilize society. Some even speculate that a large group of unattached men may lead to a larger military, with a greater possibility for hostilities to erupt. Female children, usually second daughters, are sometimes aborted and sometimes left for adoption. The one-child policy was an understandable response to the intractable problem of China's population growth. In the early twenty-first century, however, that policy is becoming less viable, since successful implementation requires a draconian regime that does not exist in China anymore. Moreover, the government is conscious to some degree of public sentiment, and this sentiment, especially in rural areas, favors

Table 8.5   China's Population, 1950–2050

	1950	2000	2015	2025	2050
Total population (medium variant in thousands)	554,760	1,275,215	1,402,321	1,445,100	1,395,182
Total fertility (average number of children per woman)	1.80	1.83	1.85	1.85	1.85
Annual population growth rate (percentage)	0.90	0.73	0.54	0.22	−0.37

Source: UN Population Information Network, *World Population Prospects: The 2002 Revision,* http://www.un.org/esa/population/publications/wpp2002/wpp2002annextables.pdf.

more than one child. Beijing has therefore decided to change its one-child policy. According to Zhao Baige, a director-general at the State Family Planning Commission, "A one-size-fits-all family-planning policy doesn't work. . . . China is a large place with diverse citizens and diverse needs."[29]

Energy, Resources, and the Environment

China's 8–9 percent annual growth rate in GNP and 1.5 percent growth rate in population place a tremendous strain on all its resources, especially energy, water, and soil. As the economy expands, so do resource depletion and pollution. For example, China's people use coal and charcoal for 90 percent of their heating and cooking and for 50 percent of their electricity generation. Mainly because of this coal usage, China is the world's third largest producer of carbon dioxide, after the former Soviet Union and the United States.

Government subsidies have also had a deleterious effect on the nation's water supply. In Beijing, water is subsidized, costing only 2.5 cents a cubic meter. Yet since the 1970s, there has been an acute water shortage in northern China, as well as a drop in the water table. Chinese authorities estimated that northern China would need 78.9 billion cubic meters of water per year by the year 2000 but that the supply would be only 74 billion cubic meters. To meet the ever-increasing water needs, the Chinese government is now developing complex plans to divert water from central China to northern China through a series of channels.[30] The prohibitive expense of subsidizing water usage and rerouting water supply halfway across the nation is apparently less onerous than risking the wrath of China's city dwellers, who will be faced with higher water bills. In dealing with these problems, China's leaders are faced with difficult choices when weighing economic development against environmental and resource problems. The World Bank has suggested approaches to increase energy efficiency and reduce pollution, including eliminating governmental subsidies on coal. Eliminating the subsidies would simultaneously ease the national deficit, increase the efficiency of coal usage, and reduce carbon dioxide emissions by 10 percent.[31] Ending coal subsidies would save the government $15 billion a year, but coal mining is one of China's major industries, employing 3 million people. The government has tried to close some of the least-productive state-owned mines,[32] but judging each coal mine on a profit-and-loss basis raises uncomfortable questions about unemployment.

To solve its energy and resource problems, China is increasingly turning to multinational development agencies and to foreign investment. For example, China is using World Bank funds to build one of the largest dams in the world at the Three Gorges on the Yangtze River. Long debated as to its feasibility, the completed dam is expected to provide one-sixth of China's electricity. The environmental costs will be great, however, including relocation of over 1 million people who live in areas that have been flooded. Until recently, however, the World Bank has ignored the environmental costs of the projects it funds.

In the early twenty-first century, China has taken some steps to improve its environment, but each step forward seems to result in a step backward. Environmental rules and regulations have been improved, but enforcement is a problem. Emissions from state-owned enterprises have actually decreased, but enforcing environmental rules on private and quasi-private companies has proven difficult. Control of smokestack emissions has been a concern, but the number of private automobiles has grown exponentially in China. The unprecedented demand for raw materials has led to deforestation, pollution from mining, and other detrimental effects. Combining rapid economic growth and sustainable environmental growth is never easy—the contentious energy policy review conducted by Vice President Dick Cheney shows that even the United States is not immune to this controversy—and China will have a difficult time controlling growth while also providing the Chinese people with clean air, clean water, and clean land.

Policy Options

In the twenty-first century, China is seeking to actively participate in the international discussion over important issues such as the role of the United Nations in promoting international security; arms sales; emerging global financial and trade regimes; and the growing linkage between the problem of global environmental damage and the policies of individual countries. Yet although China is becoming more important as a major actor on all of these issues, most of the initiatives still come from the first world, which clearly plays the dominant role in emerging global regimes in the post–Cold War era.

Option 1: Damage Limitation

On questions of UN structural change, Beijing is likely to follow a policy of damage limitation, supporting the least-unfavorable options initiated by other states for changing the role and structure of the Security Council, the General Assembly, and the Secretariat. These bodies seem unable to deal effectively and efficiently with post–Cold War responsibilities, but proposed changes, including amendments to the UN Charter, could adversely affect Chinese interests and influence, especially in the Security Council:

- In the Security Council, Beijing may tactfully resist any proposal to eliminate the veto power of the five permanent members. Although this 1945 Charter provision seems an anachronism in the changing post–Cold War military and economic balance-of-power structure,

China cherishes its privileged position as the only third world power in the Security Council. So long as the other permanent members resist the elimination of the veto or the addition of other permanent seats, Beijing may be content to go along with the United States, the United Kingdom, France, and Russia.

- If change seems inevitable, especially because of growing demands by third world members for a greater voice in the Security Council, Beijing may support changes strengthening third world representation, both through the addition of permanent seats for countries such as Brazil, Nigeria, Egypt, and India, and through the expansion of the Security Council to include more members of the General Assembly. Most of these selections would be third world countries, the predominant bloc in the General Assembly.

- In response to pressures by the West to give permanent Security Council seats to Germany and Japan, China may bargain for a number of concessions. For example, China's leaders may simultaneously demand the admission of third world powers such as Brazil, Nigeria, Egypt, and India, but without the veto power of the five current members. China also agrees that Japan and Germany are prime candidates for permanent Security Council seats, but would insist that they also have no veto power. China's leaders may also try to strike a deal with the new applicants for permanent seats, especially Japan and Germany, to gain long-term economic concessions from these states as a condition of supporting their applications.

- On the question of representation on the basis of financial contributions, China will lead third world members in resisting changes to the current system, which allows one vote for each member despite their contribution to the UN budget. China would prefer representation based on population, but any such change would be resisted not only by the West but also by most third world countries. Budget reform has been and continues to be a critical issue facing the United Nations.

- On the question of administrative reform of the UN Secretariat and the specialized agencies, China is unlikely to support Western demands for budget and staff cuts, as well as for depoliticization of UN agencies. Generally, Beijing has adopted the third world position on issues of administrative reform.

Option 2: Limited Support of UN Security Operations

Expanding ad hoc peacemaking and peacekeeping operations also poses difficult choices for Beijing's decisionmakers. On the one hand, China's leaders wish to participate and be consulted on any new UN security operations. Yet China has only tentatively increased its participation in these operations and it continues to be hesitant about committing funds or personnel to operations it believes will be controlled by the Western powers:

- China is highly unlikely to take the initiative in proposing new UN peacemaking and peacekeeping missions, but it is unlikely to veto missions supported by the other four permanent members of the Security Council.

Option 3: China's Arms Sales

In a world in which China has no military allies, Beijing views the problem of weapons of mass destruction from a perspective that is not well understood in the West. Chinese leaders believe that arms races in places like the Middle East and South Asia are the result of local conflicts of interests that have traditionally been solved by military force. From the Chinese perspective, the United States, Russia, and their allies are primarily responsible for regional arms races. By taking sides, these countries have not exerted sufficient pressure to bring about an end to conflicts in these regions. In comparison, China's diplomatic role is minimal, and the total value of its arms sales is far below that of the United States, Russia, and a number of other countries. Similarly, China maintains that it has abided by the provisions of the Nuclear Nonproliferation Treaty and the inspection requirements of the International Atomic Energy Agency:

- Because China has always been a secondary nuclear power, and because other states sell greater amounts of military technology in conflict-prone regions, greater efforts must by made by the United States, European powers, and former communist states to limit their arms sales and respect the legitimate interests of all states in these regions. The major initiatives in seeking peace based on mutual self-interest must come from these states.
- Beijing is making a contribution to peace in these regions by taking into account the legitimate security interests of states in the Middle East and South Asia that are being ignored by Western powers. Arms assistance, which does not violate the Nuclear Nonproliferation Treaty or specific agreements that Beijing has accepted, provides needed balance in these regions. The security interests of China are also promoted by giving Beijing the means to play an active role in political negotiations to bring about peace in these regions.
- Until greater efforts are made by the countries within these regions to end their conflicts, accompanied by greater efforts of the major arms sellers to support the legitimate interests of all parties to these disputes by reducing their own huge arms sales, a military version of the tragedy of the commons will continue. China will, in these circum-

stances, reserve the right to sell arms to those who want them as a means of promoting its legitimate self-interests.

- Beijing's leaders will continue to insist that countries such as the United States have no right to link questions of arms sales and military security to terms of trade relations and trade agreements.
- On the question of regional nuclear arms races, China has become directly involved in the negotiations between North and South Korea and between Pakistan and India. Beijing wishes to see relations improve between North and South Korea, but its long-standing commitments to North Korea prohibit any direct pressure on the Communist regime. There is no doubt, however, that Beijing would like to see increased stability in Northeast Asia and avoid any pretext for Japan to develop nuclear weapons because of a nuclear arms race on the Korean peninsula. As for South Asia, so long as India and Pakistan fail to resolve the danger of a regional nuclear arms race, Beijing is likely to give low-key support to the Pakistani position.
- Beijing is likely to continue its demand for total elimination of all nuclear weapons. Such elimination is highly unlikely, however, given the danger of nuclear weapons proliferation throughout the world. Even with the U.S. and Russian agreement to reduce nuclear weapons to 3,500 warheads each in 2002, these two countries will still have ten times China's current nuclear arsenal. Moreover, all nations speak about destroying nuclear weapons, but few seriously contemplate a complete elimination.

Option 4: Participating in Global Financial and Trade Regimes

Although there are risks, especially from the perspective of the conservative wing of Chinese leadership, Beijing clearly has opted for further integration into the global economic system, in which the global regimes, whether international finance, investment, or trade, are clearly controlled by the Western world:

- The International Monetary Fund and the World Bank Group will be viewed in the future, as in the past, as a valuable source of technical assistance and advice, as well as a major source of international funding. If China continues to develop in the future as it has during the past fifteen years, its leadership will be in a position to use the country's excellent record in paying off loans to gain new financing on very favorable terms.
- Although China will have to open its market further and eliminate many domestic restrictions on imports, its leaders are convinced that

the country will gain much more than it will lose through its accession to the WTO. China's domestic enterprises, whether public or private, will have to become more efficient to compete with overseas enterprises that will have greater access to Chinese markets. But China seems convinced that as its own economy develops, comparative advantage will be in its favor in both domestic and overseas markets.

- As a member of these global regimes, China is in a position either to exclude Taiwan from participation or to orchestrate future arrangements for the participation of Hong Kong and Taiwan as associate members or observers (rather than as independent members) of the World Bank, the IMF, or the WTO. Beijing seems convinced that as Taiwan increases its investment and trade with the mainland, China's leverage with Taiwan, both bilaterally and at the multilateral level, will increase.

Option 5: Limiting Population

Although there is no clear response to the conundrum of environment versus development, virtually all development experts and environmentalists throughout the world agree that population control is crucial to sustainable development. Population control not only reduces pressures on the environment, but also stimulates development, raises living standards, and helps to promote political stability. China's leaders would agree with all of these points. Their problem is not whether to promote family planning, but how vigorously and in what ways. In making policy choices, there may be a number of costs in vigorously pushing for smaller families:

- With the substantial increase in living standards since the economic reforms of 1978, people feel they can afford to have more children, especially in rural areas. They blame party leaders and officials for unpopular restrictions on having children. How can the party enforce strict birth control policies without alienating its rural constituency?
- The Chinese government already spends over $1 billion per year on family planning clinics and contraceptives. Given the seeming inability of the government to reduce rural family size below three children, might government resources be better spent for other purposes such as transportation, electric power, communication, and port facilities?

With China's high GNP growth rate and rising living standards, China's leaders may feel that it is not necessary to increase family planning efforts. Demographic research shows that as living standards rise, people will naturally have smaller families. This is already happening in Asian societies that have relatively high living standards, such as Taiwan, South Korea, Hong Kong, and Singapore. In Japan, birthrates are currently below replacement levels.

Before abandoning the one-child campaign, however, China's leaders will have to consider the following:

- Even with current family planning efforts, the 15 million additional mouths to feed each year threaten to undermine stability, the environment, full employment, the provision of adequate social services, and the overall quality of life. China simply cannot wait for the demographic transition to lower birthrates resulting from higher living standards and less desire for children.
- Whereas negative threats and penalties are unpopular, a number of positive sanctions may improve the image of the party, the government bureaucracy, and the legitimacy of the leadership. For example, local government and production units, especially in rural areas, should be encouraged to provide more social services, such as education (especially for women), retirement benefits, information about how family planning benefits society, and inexpensive and more modern means of contraception combined with less reliance on sterilization and abortion. Substantially increased funding from international sources is unlikely, but China's leaders may be able to benefit from greater use of foreign expertise and technology.

Option 6: Promoting Sustainable Development

On issues such as energy, water quality and supply, deforestation and the timber industry, agriculture, and the mineral industry, Beijing may have a number of choices available for serious consideration:

- Simply by ending subsidies on fossil fuels, it may simultaneously be possible to create greater energy efficiency, reduce atmospheric pollution, and make renewable energy sources more competitive with coal and oil.
- While continuing reforestation efforts, China may also utilize currency gained from exports to either purchase timber or invest in overseas timber operations.
- While taking advantage of biotechnology and other techniques to increase agricultural production, China may purchase more agricultural products, such as wheat and feed grains, from overseas.
- China may carefully consider the cost and benefits of marketplace devices to reduce ground, water, and atmospheric pollution. With the assistance of both domestic and international environmentalists and economists, the current and future costs of pollution can be weighed against tax benefits or penalties that will motivate both public and private producers to become more efficient and utilize pollution controls.

Perhaps China has an advantage over democratic societies in introducing marketplace incentives, because these measures may be
adopted with less public controversy and organized opposition than in
Western societies. Extensive information programs can be helpful in
gaining support for these environmental incentives.

Discussion Questions

1. Should China change its policy of minimal participation in UN peacemaking and peacekeeping operations? Should it follow the example of
   India and provide troops and personnel for these operations in different
   regions of the world?
2. What stand should China take on the question of expanding the number
   of permanent members of the Security Council or doing away with the
   veto power of the permanent members?
3. Beyond supporting international treaties on nuclear proliferation and bi-
   ological and chemical weapons, should China support or oppose additional actions to eliminate weapons of mass destruction?
4. What policy should China follow on the question of arms sales to regions
   such as the Middle East and South Asia?
5. Although China is already a member of the International Monetary Fund,
   should it also agree to make its currency fully convertible?
6. Taking into account that the Western powers control the International
   Monetary Fund and the World Bank, should China seek more or less advice and financial assistance from these organizations?
7. Why has China joined the WTO and agreed to comply fully with all rules
   on the elimination of trade barriers? Is it more advantageous for China to
   negotiate trade agreements on a bilateral basis?
8. Should China take a leadership role or largely be a supporter of third
   world countries on environmental and development issues?
9. In view of China's annual increase in population, should additional steps
   be taken to control population growth? If so, what steps?
10. Keeping in mind China's energy, resource, and developmental needs,
    what additional steps should China take to control population and main-
    tain or improve the quality of its air, water, soil, and forests? In what ways
    should it work with international organizations and other countries in
    dealing with these problems?

Suggested Readings

Boutros-Ghali, Boutros. *An Agenda for Peace*. New York: United Nations, 1992.
Conly, Shanti R., and Sharon L. Camp. *China's Family Planning Program: Challenging the Myths*. Washington, D.C.: Population Crisis Committee, 1992.

Dai Qing, John G. Thibodeau, and Philip Williams, eds. *The River Dragon Has Come! The Three Gorges Dam and the Fate of China's Yangtze River and Its People*. Trans. Ming Yi. Armonk, N.Y.: M. E. Sharpe, 1998.

Edmonds, Richard Louis, ed. *Managing the Chinese Environment*. Oxford: Oxford University Press, 1998.

Fravel, M. Taylor. "China's Attitude Toward U.N. Peacekeeping Operations Since 1989." *Asian Survey* 36, no. 11 (November 1996): 1102–1122.

Gill, Bates. *Chinese Arms Transfers: Purposes, Patterns, and Prospects in the New World Order*. Westport, Conn.: Praeger, 1992.

Gill, Bates, and Kim Taeho. *China's Arms Acquisitions from Abroad: A Quest for "Superb and Secret Weapons."* Sipri Research Report no. 11. Oxford: Oxford University Press, 1996.

Jing, Jun. "Environmental Protests in Rural China." In Elizabeth J. Perry and Mark Selden, eds., *Chinese Society: Change, Conflict, and Resistance*. Asia's Transformations. London: Routledge, 2000, pp. 143–160.

Lee, Yok-shiu, and Alvin Y. So, eds. *Asia's Environmental Movements: Comparative Perspectives*. Armonk, N.Y.: M. E. Sharpe, 1999.

Poston, Dudley L., Chiung-Fang Chang, Sherry L. McKibben, Carol S. Walther, and Che-Fu Lee, eds. *Fertility, Family Planning, and Population Control in China*. London: Routledge, 2004.

Smil, Vaclav. *China's Past, China's Future: Energy, Food, Environment*. New York: Routledge/Curzon Press, 2003.

World Bank. *China: Air, Land, and Water—Environmental Priorities for a New Millennium*. Washington, D.C.: World Bank, 2001.

Notes

1. Embassy of the People's Republic of China, Press Release no. 27, December 27, 1990.

2. Madeleine Albright, *Madam Secretary* (New York: Hyperion, 2003), p. 159.

3. Ministry of Foreign Affairs of the People's Republic of China, *Position Paper of China on the 58th Session of the UN General Assembly*, August 12, 2003, http://www.fmprc.gov.cn/eng/wjb/zzjg/gjs/gjsxw/t24859.htm.

4. Contributors to UN Peacekeeping Operations, *Monthly Summary of Contributors*, http://www.un.org/depts/dpko/dpko/contributors/countriessummarymarch2004.pdf, viewed May 5, 2004.

5. Permanent Mission of the People's Republic of China to the United Nations, *Peacekeeping Operations of the UN*, http://un.fmprc.gov.cn/eng/7283.html, viewed May 12, 2004.

6. Willy Wo-Lap Lam, *South China Morning Post*, November 19, 1992.

7. Peter Grier, "China Arms Policy Puzzles West," *Christian Science Monitor*, July 3, 1992.

8. "China Denounces U.S. Arms Sales to Taiwan," http://wwwchinadaily.com.cn,viewed May 12, 2004.

9. Stockholm International Peace Research Institute (SIPRI), *SIPRI Yearbook 2002*, chap. 8, "International Arms Transfers, 2002," http://editors.sipri.se/pubs/yb02/ch08.html.

10. A. M. Rosenthal, "Missile Mongering," *New York Times*, April 10, 1992, p. A19.

11. For an analysis of U.S. concerns about Chinese missile sales in 1992, see *New York Times,* January 31, 1992, p. A1; April 19, 1992, p. A19; September 11, 1992, p. A3; and December 4, 1992, p. A5.

12. Kerry Dumbaugh, *China-U.S. Relations: Issue Brief for Congress* (Washington, D.C.: Library of Congress Congressional Research Service, May 17, 2002). http://FPC.State.gov/documents/organizations/13412.pdf.

13. "An Introduction of China's Export Control System," statement by Fu Cong, Department of Arms Control and Disarmament, Ministry of Foreign Affairs of China, at Tokyo Workshop on Nonproliferation Export Control Regimes, December 11–12, 1997, quoted in *China/MTCR, Monterey Institute for Nonproliferation Studies,* http://www.nti.org/db/china/excon.htm, viewed May 12, 2004.

14. Ibid.

15. For an analysis of the role played by multilateral economic regimes in the modernization of China, see William R. Feeney, "Chinese Policy Toward Multilateral Economic Institutions," in Samuel S. Kim, ed., *China and the New World: New Directions in Chinese Foreign Relations,* 2nd ed. (Boulder, Colo.: Westview, 1989), pp. 237–263.

16. Feeney, "Chinese Policy," pp. 252–254.

17. "Memorandum of the President of the IBRD and the IFC to the Executive Directors on a Country Assistance Strategy of the World Bank Group for the PRC," January 22, 2003, p. 29, http://www.worldbank.org.cn/english/content/cas03.pdf.

18. International Finance Corporation, http://ifcln1.ifc.org/ifcext/spiwebsite1.nsf/results517200481202pm?openview, viewed May 17, 2004.

19. The data on China's grain production, exports, and imports come from Scott Kilman, "U.S. Steadily Losing Share of World Trade in Grain and Soybeans," *Wall Street Journal,* December 31, 1992, pp. 1, 6. In 1991, the former Soviet Union, prior to its breakup, imported 259 million bushels of wheat, whereas China bought 209 million bushels. Joe Grant, "U.S. 5th in Wheat Production Worldwide," *Charleston Illinois Times Courier,* December 3, 1992, p. A8.

20. Colin A. Carter and Scott Rozelle, "Will China's Agricultural Trade Reflect Its Comparative Advantage?" http://ers.usda.gov/publications/aib775/aib775k.pdf, viewed May 17, 2004.

21. Fred Gale, "China at a Glance: Statistical Overview of China's Food and Agriculture," Economic Research Service/USDA China's Food and Agriculture: Issues for the 21st Century, AIB-775, http://www.ers.usda.gov/publications/aib775/aib775e.pdf, April 2002.

22. Premier Li Peng, Rio Summit Meeting of the UN Conference on Environment and Development, June 2, 1992, Chinese embassy, Washington, D.C., Press Release no. 7, June 15, 1992.

23. Ibid.

24. World Bank, *China: Air, Land, and Water* (Washington, D.C.: World Bank, 2001), p. xvi.

25. Jim Yardley, "Bad Air and Water, and a Bully Pulpit in China," *New York Times,* September 25, 2004.

26. 2004 ESCAP Population Data Sheet, http://www.unescap.org/esid/psis/population/database/data_sheet/2004, viewed September 27, 2004.

27. Nicholas D. Kristof, "China's Crackdown on Births: A Stunning, and Harsh, Success," *New York Times,* April 25, 1993, pp. A1, A12.

28. Quoted in ibid.

29. Quoted in Hannah Beech, "China's Baby Bust," *Time Asia,* July 30, 2001, http://www.time.com/time/asia/news/magazine/0,9754,168514,00.html.

30. Dong Shi, "Water Crisis in North China and Counter-Measures," *Beijing Review* (April 2–8, 1990): 31–33.

31. Bjorn Larsen and Anwar Shah, "Combatting the Greenhouse Effects," *Finance and Development* (December 1992): 20–21.

32. Nicholas D. Kristof, "China Plans Big Layoffs of Coal Mine Workers," *New York Times*, December 12, 1992, p. C1.

Alternative Scenarios

The rise of China, if it continues, may be the most important trend in the world for the next century. . . . China is the fastest growing economy in the world, with what may be the fastest growing military budget. It has nuclear weapons, border disputes with most of its neighbors, and a rapidly improving army that may—within a decade or so—be able to resolve old quarrels in its own favor. The United States has possessed the world's largest economy for more than a century, but at present trajectories China may displace it in the first half of the next century and become the number one economy in the world.

—*Nicholas D. Kristof*[1]

As China's leaders enter the twenty-first century, they see both great challenges and great opportunities. Within China itself, the challenges and opportunities are perhaps greatest because the external environment appears more favorable than at any time in modern history. As Machiavelli, the Italian political realist, pointed out in the sixteenth century, the choices of decisionmakers involve both opportunities and dangers, but may be determined largely by "fortuna" (circumstances beyond the control of decisionmakers). Machiavelli believed the key to effective leadership was how decisionmakers chose their course of action based on the availability of options at the time. The previous chapters have examined the dangers and opportunities facing China's leaders up to the present. This concluding chapter examines China's future role in the emerging global system, a world that looks very different from that of the Cold War era.

China's Role in the Emerging International Security System

China is experiencing a period of vigorous development, with economic construction as the focus. Its foreign policy must help create a long-standing and steady international environment of peace for its economic construction.

> . . . At present, all nations, developed or developing, share the view that a country's national strength, especially in the economic sense, will decide its status in the 21st century. Therefore, they are generally turning their attention to domestic affairs, attaching great importance to economic construction and cooperation. All nations are becoming more interdependent, harmonious, complementary and mutually restricted.[2]

The above statement reveals the essence of China's security approach in the emerging global system. The key seems to be internal stability and economic development in an era in which domestic success is related to good relations and growing economic interdependence with others based on mutual self-interest. Beijing seems more concerned with internal factors that may destabilize the Middle Kingdom than with any military threat from beyond its boundaries. But security, which depends on well-being, also depends on continuing Deng Xiaoping's Open Door policy. Trade and foreign investment are essential to China's development, rising living standards, and ability to develop a modern military capable of protecting the country in the twenty-first century. By maintaining an authoritarian order at home while encouraging economic interdependence and a market economy, Beijing's leaders hope to avoid the Russian syndrome through which the changes introduced by Mikhail Gorbachev appear to have weakened the former Soviet Union's security and well-being.

Although observers mostly agree that there is no emerging global order that ensures security at home and among nations, they also mostly agree that security needs to be defined more broadly than as protection against violence and outside interference in one's internal affairs (all Westphalian values). These concerns remain important in the twenty-first century, but security increasingly will also mean a sustainable environment—the maintenance of spaceship earth. The relationship between humankind and its earthly environment—which provides adequate air, water, soil, and biodiversity to sustain human life and well-being—is the ultimate security envelope.

China's leaders apparently agree with this broader definition of security, which will involve international cooperation to preserve the earth's essential resources. At the same time, although China's leaders include economic, social, and environmental factors in their definition of security, they have not yet chosen to include democracy or freedom of political expression as part of their broader definition of security.

Two Arabic words, *sullah* and *salaam,* may provide a key to China's international security role. In many regions of the world the practice of *sullah* signifies the use of force and coercion, actions designed to solve disputes through domination. On the other hand, *salaam* signifies a willingness to seek security through solutions based on mutual self-interest, trust, and multiple-sum bargaining games in which everyone benefits. In short, one cannot be secure unless one's neighbor is also secure. The fact that China continues to hesitate in supporting the global security role of the United Nations suggests that its leaders may believe that bilateral relations are the best means of promoting Chinese security, especially if China's economy grows more rapidly than that of others, including Japan and the United States, in the twenty-first century.

At the global level, China has been mainly a consumer of security rather than a major contributor to efforts to help provide security for those less fortunate and unable to protect themselves, as in Bosnia, Somalia, and Kuwait. China has been leery of the effort of others, especially the West, to use global institutions to eliminate or at least control security threats, especially if this means international efforts to protect human rights inside the borders of states.

China as a Regional Power

Now China's relations with Northeast, Southeast, South and Central Asia and Russia are all growing and its security environment has improved fundamentally. It is pointed out in a report to the 14th National Congress of the Chinese Communist Party that China's surrounding environment is in the best period since the founding of the People's Republic in 1949.[3]

Based on China's overall regional role in the twenty-first century, China may face a number of difficult choices in Asia. Currently, Chinese policy follows a dual line. Some even call it a Janus-faced policy, one in which China simultaneously pursues military buildup and threats while promising bilateral and multilateral cooperation with its neighbors. For example, increased Chinese naval capabilities could be harbingers of limited conflicts in the region.[4]

Samuel Kim, who has been writing about Chinese foreign policy for many years, observes that "China's regional security policy seems no more than a blurred image of its changing definition of the world situation."[5] In the future, China will find it increasingly difficult to maintain both policies. To maintain good relations with its Asian neighbors, China's leaders must decide whether bilateral cooperation is more important than military buildup.

A Regional Security System in Asia?

In contrast to Eastern Europe and the former Soviet Union, where the disintegration of communist regimes resulted in economic dislocation, political chaos, and even open warfare, Asia outwardly appears to be relatively stable in the post–Cold War era. Yet Western Europe's goals of economic and security integration still elude Asia. In comparing the two regions, a European writer, Peter Sturm, observes that there is little chance that regional economic and security arrangements can be created in Asia similar to those emerging in

Europe. He notes that there is no leader in the region that Asian states would be willing to follow. If Asian countries were forced to defend their interests, he believes that they would be more likely to align with actors outside the region rather than accept the leadership of either Japan or China.[6]

China, too, had been loath to accept a regional security system. Beijing's leaders had rejected all such proposals by regional neighbors, including those put forth by Russia and Japan; however, in the early twenty-first century China seems more willing to engage in multilateral discussions on security in Asia. From the Japanese perspective, an Asian security system is needed to ensure regional stability. But Japan would seek a regional security system only if it included China, because no other arrangement could provide military stability in Asia. Because China seems unwilling to subordinate its security and military interests to a regional organization, the alternative, from the Japanese perspective, will necessarily be continued security arrangements between Asian countries with outside powers such as the United States.[7]

A Regional Economic System in Asia?

Although China has rejected any multilateral approach to security in Asia, it is more likely to agree to multilateral economic cooperation. There are several possibilities, all based on the remarkable economic development in the region, including in China. First, China could join others in seeking a narrow and structured regional market system, which might eventually resemble the North American Free Trade Agreement. Malaysia's former prime minister, Mahathir Mohamad advocated a plan known as the East Asian Economic Grouping, which would "be a narrow regional grouping of East Asia that excluded North America and Oceana." It would seek "to invigorate regional economic transactions by promoting market liberalization and setting up common standards [for the region] . . . in the face of United States–led market liberalization attempts."[8]

A second approach to regional economic cooperation might be a looser arrangement to eliminate trade barriers among all the participating states, which would include North America and Oceana (Australia, New Zealand, and Pacific island states). The Asia Pacific Economic Cooperation (APEC) conference could be the basis for such an approach, because it includes Asian countries as well as Australia, New Zealand, Canada, and the United States. The advantage of this type of arrangement would be that Asia would look outward in its trade relations rather than become a closed trading bloc. APEC is unique in that it is currently the only regional international structure that includes China, Hong Kong, and Taiwan. Should the European Community impose further trade restrictions against both North American and Asian products, then an APEC-type structure could bring these two regions together as a counterforce against European protectionism.

A third approach is reliance on bilateral trade arrangements while at the same time seeking to participate fully in the promotion of a global liberalized market system through membership in the World Trade Organization (WTO). Beijing was so eager to renew its membership in the WTO that it was willing to accept associate status for Taiwan short of membership as an independent state. This gave the advantage of helping China, as a member of the WTO, work out agreements that would in turn enable it to take advantage of the tremendous market potential of greater China. Examples of this might include additional international financial assistance, more overseas investment, and a greater opening of markets for Chinese products.

Japan's policy views will be a major factor in determining which of the three alternatives eventually emerges. Japanese observers recognize that a more open global trading system would be preferable for most Asian countries, including both Japan and China, than a closed Asian trading bloc. The latter alternative would presume Japanese leadership, because Japan is the largest trader and investor throughout Asia as a whole. This is something China and the rest of Asia might object to. Japan, like the rest of Asia, would therefore benefit more from global liberalization of the market than from a limited system in Asia or one including Asia and North America.[9]

China and the Third World

A genuine peace that the people of the world have longed for has not come with the end of the Cold War. . . . New problems [are] added to the old ones and armed conflicts [arise] one after another as a result of disrupted equilibrium. Hegemonism and power politics continue to exist; the attempt of some big powers to control developing countries politically and economically has become more and more obvious; the long-hidden ethnic conflicts have surfaced with a vengeance; and the North-South contradictions have further aggravated. The road to peace and development . . . is covered with thorns.[10]

In 1955, China's prime minister, Zhou Enlai, participated in a conference in Jakarta, Indonesia, that was the forerunner of the nonaligned movement. The purpose of the conference, and later of the nonaligned movement, was to separate participating nations from both superpower blocs as a third force independent of the imperialist West and the "hegemonical" East. The latter term was used by Beijing to categorize Soviet attempts to dominate third world regions.

With the end of the Cold War, the nonaligned movement seems to have lost part of its reason for existing. Nonetheless, third world leaders, including China's leaders, talk about the emergence of neoimperialism—Western economic domination after their soldiers have gone home. China has always seen itself as part of the third world. In varying ways, it has sought to play a leadership role within the third world, largely based on a common desire to change the global economic system so that poorer developing states would receive more help and fairer treatment from the rich Western countries that currently dominate the system.

When non-Western developing states became a majority in the UN General Assembly in the early 1960s, they sought to promote their economic interests by calling for the UN Conference on Trade and Development (UNCTAD), a forum dominated by the third world. China was not an original member of the group, and as the movement continues its efforts, other UNCTAD members seem uncertain about their relationship with China; they are not sure whether it is a rival or a partner. Third world concerns have been further complicated by the collapse of the second world (the Soviet Union and its satellites). The former communist countries, as well as China, vie with third world countries for bilateral and multilateral aid and investment. Like China, Eastern European countries and the former parts of the Soviet Union need help in making the transition to marketplace economies. Increased aid and investment in these regions lessens the amount available to Africa, Latin America, the Middle East, South Asia, and Southeast Asia.[11] Chinese statements about solidarity with the third world are therefore unconvincing to many members of UNCTAD.

China and the Third World: Similarities and Differences

Although China is less developed than some of its neighbors, such as South Korea, Taiwan, Hong Kong, and Singapore, it is much more developed than a majority of third world states, including most of Africa, parts of South Asia, and some areas of Latin America. China, which previously sought to serve as a model to the third world for self-reliant socialist development, now seeks to show the third world how to combine authoritarian political control with spectacular economic growth.

Nationalism and subnationalism. A study of self-determination and nationalistic ideologies in different regions in the wake of the Cold War identifies nationalist ideologies as the great force both uniting and dividing peoples throughout the third world and the former second world.[12] There are severe conflicts between subgroups and self-determination problems in nearly every region of the world.

In comparison with India and many other third world countries, despite serious problems in outlying areas such as Tibet and Xinjiang,[13] China has a high degree of ethnic unity. The danger of disunity based on subnationalist and ethnic sentiments seems much greater in India, as well as in many other parts of the third world, than in China. The large Chinese Han majority controls the heartland, and the odds are heavily against successful revolts by

China's small minorities, which have been oppressed whenever they have resisted Beijing. Conflict inside China is more likely to result from growing unemployment, inequities in economic development, Communist Party corruption, and loss of support for party rule.

Democracy versus authoritarianism. One of the most controversial debates raging in China and the third world involves the advantages and disadvantages of democracy during the transition from traditionalist to modern societies.[14] Many scholars and politicians concur that democracy, based on Western ideas of representative government and individual freedom, is essential to the full development of marketplace competition and economic success. From this perspective, the competitive marketplace of ideas, personal freedom, and competitive popular selection of leaders provide the environment in which the production and distribution of goods is most likely to succeed. However, others believe that democracy must be tempered by respect for authority and willingness to subjugate individual rights to the common interest.

Following the end of World War I, the English political writer Lord Bryce announced the triumph of democracy over other forms of government. In the remaining years of the twentieth century, however, democracy suffered a series of setbacks. The full extent of democratization remains in doubt in the former communist countries and many parts of the third world. The correlation of modernization and development with democracy, touted by theorists in the 1960s, has not become apparent. Indeed, not only has democratization from within been slow to come, but external pressures for change have been muted. For example, during the debate over renewal of China's most-favored-nation status, U.S. business interests strongly lobbied against a link between human rights issues and trade issues. Capitalists who invest in China and many other third world regions are often indifferent to how democratic the political system is. They may actually prefer authoritarian regimes, which promise stability and an absence of democratic labor or other populist movements.[15]

China's leaders believe that the key to human progress lies not in the form of political structures, but in economic growth. Beijing notes that although India calls itself a democracy, as does the Philippines, rural peasants are still exploited by traditional ruling classes, with little effort by government to protect the people's interest and their well-being. A comparison of living standards in rural China, especially with those in countries such as the Philippines and India, shows that conditions in China seem to be more favorable. In many parts of Africa, Latin America, and South Asia, despite efforts to establish democracies, there also seems to be little hope for immediate improvement of life in rural areas.

Should third world countries seriously consider the Chinese model as an alternative means of achieving development and higher living standards, as well as stability and order? How should third world countries view Chinese claims that the most important human rights are those such as order, literacy, education, food, clothing, housing, the right to a job, and health care? Former Chinese foreign minister Qian Qichen, speaking before the forty-seventh session of the UN General Assembly in 1992, said:

> It is obviously irresponsibly one-sided and harmful to make irresponsible comments about the human rights situation in developing countries in disregard of the difference in historical background and cultural tradition as well as the actual conditions in these countries. For the people of developing countries, the right to subsistence and the right to development are undoubtedly the fundamental and the most important human right of all. In those areas hit by severe natural disasters for years, people are starving; in those war-ridden areas, millions are turned into refugees. How can the people living in such conditions enjoy "human rights"?[16]

States like India and the Philippines, with large rural populations, high birthrates, and high levels of unemployment in rural areas, may wish to emulate China's rural development model. For example, they may see the advantages of adopting Deng Xiaoping's policies of encouraging peasants to create their own rural industries, either as collectives, joint ventures, or private businesses. They might also take note that as a result of these reforms since 1978, over half of all income in rural China now comes from nonagricultural work. Furthermore, they may wish to consider both the advantages and the disadvantages of China's dual economic system, in which the public sector is either gradually being privatized or being subjected to the discipline of the market through the elimination of special government loans, subsidies, guaranteed employment, and guaranteed prices. In view of what is happening in former communist states, third world countries may also wish to weigh carefully the contrasting Chinese and Russian approaches. Would China be better off if it had attempted to establish Western-type democracy, as the Russians tried to do, before trying to carry out marketplace reforms?

China as a Third World Leader: Partner or Rival?

At the global level, China has aligned with the third world on development issues. In the 1970s, Beijing's delegates to the United Nations strongly supported third world calls for a new international economic order. Virtually all developing countries felt that the global economic system was unfairly tilted toward the industrialized nations, and they resented the latter's control of the international regimes in trade, finance, and investment. China supported these views and agreed that the industrialized world should provide more aid and better terms of trade and finance. Then, in the 1980s, as the mood in UNCTAD shifted from a policy of confrontation, Beijing did likewise, joining other third world states in seeking to become part of the global economic system as partners rather than challengers.

This is the core of Deng Xiaoping's Open Door policy. Instead of rejecting or seeking to reform the World Bank, the International Monetary Fund (IMF), and the General Agreement on Tariffs and Trade (GATT) and its successor, the World Trade Organization (WTO), Deng sought to join these international regimes in order to get more international aid and investment. In Latin America, Mexico is following a similar policy, as is India in South Asia. China is therefore, in many ways, their rival.

As noted earlier, despite professions of peaceful intent, Beijing sometimes seems to follow a "tragedy of the commons" approach. Especially in arms sales, China is in fact helping to stimulate arms races between third world countries. Iraq and Iran illustrate the problem. Beijing sold arms to both sides in order to get hard currency. China has also been a major arms seller to a number of third world countries that have a reputation of using force to suppress dissent within their borders.

In nonmilitary trade, China has also had a major impact on a number of third world countries because of its comparative economic advantage, especially in light industrial products, which other third world countries also wish to sell to Japan, North America, and Western Europe.[17] As the world paradoxically becomes both more multipolar and more interdependent, the third world (including China) seems to be united only at the rhetorical level. Third world nations seem to be increasingly divided among themselves on political-security as well as economic issues. Capitalism has won out over Marxism nearly everywhere. But this may lead to an economic version of the tragedy of the commons as the third world countries compete against each other for exports, foreign investment, and aid from the first world. Each will be forced to offer more concessions to lure trade, aid, and investment away from its neighbors. In this competition, China frequently seems better situated to offer the West what it wants—larger markets, greater stability, and disciplined but cheap labor. Other third world countries might believe they have to lower their standards to compete with China. Working conditions, including child labor, safety regulations, reasonable working hours, and good wages, are likely to be sacrificed in the process. A new international economic order is largely a mirage because third world nations are unable or unwilling to bargain collectively for better economic terms. In a world of underemployment, unemployment, high third world birthrates, and the overproduction of most commodities, China's comparative advantage in the marketplace may come not only from its disciplined and cheap labor, but also from the stability and order provided by its highly authoritarian regime.

▨ China and the New World Order
Redux: Problems and Solutions

As China's leaders face the future, uncertainties abound over domestic and international challenges that, at best, must seem overwhelming to the leaders in Beijing. In the twenty-first century, the external world looks very different from that of the 1980s and 1990s, but the real challenges appear to be within China's own borders. The leaders in Beijing must feel like they are riding the back of the tiger. They cannot get off for fear that they will be consumed by the forces they have already unleashed. Few ideological guideposts remain from the Maoist era to provide a compass in a sea of storms. Marxism is largely discredited in fact, if not in theory, and Leninism, based on party dictatorship, is also being questioned inside China; this is especially the case with China's youth and intellectuals, even if public protest is forbidden.

Fortunately, as challenges seem to grow from within, the outside world seems less threatening. Except for rigid adherence to Leninist party rule, Beijing's leaders seem willing to proceed pragmatically, adjusting their policies to avoid sudden dangers. Above all else, as China moves into the twenty-first century, its leaders—whether conservatives, moderates, or reformers—keep looking over their shoulders at events in Eastern Europe and the former parts of the Soviet Union. Gorbachev's approach is not a role model for any of China's potential leaders in the post-Deng era. All of China's leaders wish to avoid, at almost any cost, the economic and political difficulties facing those living in these former communist lands.

Future Challenges from Within

In looking to the future, Beijing's leaders can take considerable pride in what has been accomplished inside China since 1978. Although living standards vary by region, many parts of rural China and most of urban China are clearly better off than prior to the communist revolution. Conditions in rural China compare favorably with rural conditions in much of the third world, and this is also true in urban areas. China's people seem to have new energy, especially at the village and township levels, where life is clearly more prosperous now than it was under Mao.

Another important development is the rise of consumerism. Technological innovation, increased production of better-quality goods, and greater availability of a wide range of agricultural and industrial products have helped to create a cultural fad in which the Chinese masses are becoming addicted to material things as well as the pop culture of the West. The consumerism phenomenon is closely related to the rise of global capitalism, in which not only the middle classes but the masses seek satisfaction in mass consumption of goods and services. But with this increased desire for material things comes the danger of future disorders should China's strained infrastructure, accompanied by resource shortages, be unable to satisfy these growing demands for a better life.

Collapse of the economy would no doubt bring new demonstrations and disturbances, something that has always been on the minds of China's leaders since the days of Tiananmen Square. Beijing's leaders will have to make difficult decisions. At one end of the spectrum are past ideologies and practices based on Marxism and Leninism. At the other end of the policy continuum are choices closer to Western values and practices. As China's society modernizes and becomes more complex, China's leaders must feel much like politicians in Western countries. There seem to be no good choices, but only a combination of options in which some are less damaging than others, or choices in which it is hoped the good will outweigh the bad.

How China deals with its internal dilemmas will have a major impact on its global and regional role in the twenty-first century. If these problems can be managed, China will be able to make a major contribution to the international community in promoting stability and economic prosperity. But if there is a breakdown of order, with the possible emergence of regional warlords, it would be difficult to predict China's future. Should power devolve from the center to the different regions, however, China's international role might be changed in a number of ways:

1. Political and economic rivalry inside China might substantially reduce China's influence as an international actor, especially at the regional level.
2. Instability could reverse China's remarkable success in attracting international investment.
3. Instability could also cause discontent and threaten party rule.
4. Some regions, particularly the coastal regions, might seek closer ties with the West in order to protect and promote trade and investment.
5. Domestic instability and decline in party rule are unlikely to bring about Western-type democracy and political freedoms in the foreseeable future. During the past 400 years, China's periods of both stability and instability have been characterized by authoritarian rule. With open political conflict within and between different regions, the personal well-being and rights of the people are likely to suffer severely, just as the post–Cold War era has brought suffering in many regions with the collapse of international communism and the domestic disorder in Africa, the Middle East, Eastern Europe, and Russia.

In spite of China's rapid rise in living standards since 1978, there are unfortunately many signs of discontent that could very well lead to domestic instability. For example, there are over 100 million people, mostly peasants, who have not benefited from the increased agricultural production and industrialization of the past decade. Many of them, without work permits, have migrated to China's rapidly developing coastal regions, where they have been unable to find work. As corruption seems to become more rampant in both the political and the economic systems, those who are less well off show signs of greater impatience. Ominously for the Chinese Communist Party, which historically claims to draw its authority from the peasantry, peasants have recently demonstrated against local corruption and nonpayment for crops. There are also signs of discontent among China's intellectuals, many of whom did not share the benefits of Deng's economic reforms and who regret the failure to achieve greater political freedom and individual rights after Tiananmen Square. Further evidence of current discontent is the willingness of thousands of Chinese in both rural and urban areas to give up their life savings to smugglers who help them migrate illegally to the West in search of a better life. Should there be a major breakdown of order inside China, one result might be a mass international migration of Chinese, dwarfing current levels and creating yet another international refugee crisis.

Future External Challenges

In the post–Cold War era, geopolitics (the conduct of foreign policy based on how resources, geographical location, and changing technology affect the relative capability of states) plays a continuing role in Chinese foreign policy. According to Harold and Margaret Sprout, in their classic study of how environment affects international politics, not only are real capabilities important, but so are decisionmakers' perceptions of each other's capabilities and intentions. Decisionmakers may sometimes decide what to do on the basis of false perceptions.[18] Beijing's current leaders are concerned about the changing perceptions of leaders in countries such as the United States, Russia, and Japan—perceptions that could seriously affect Chinese relations with these countries. To protect itself from policy changes in any particular country, Beijing seems to be trying to balance its relations with key countries such as Japan, the United States, and those in Western Europe in order to avoid relying heavily on any one of them.

Balancing its relations becomes even more important as China becomes increasingly sensitive to the policies of others beyond its shores. Two U.S. international relations theorists, Robert Keohane and Joseph Nye, point out that states are becoming increasingly interdependent as their relations become more complex. Because of this, countries such as China, Japan, and the United States are not only sensitive but sometimes vulnerable as a result of each other's policies. According to Keohane and Nye, a state is sensitive to another's actions if those actions threaten to harm the state's vital interests. A state becomes vulnerable when it is not possible to take corrective actions to avoid these sensitivities, which can result from things such as increased communications, movement of people across international borders, foreign investments, and changes in export and import policies. Sometimes these transnational interactions take place without foreign offices and national authorities even being aware of what is occurring.[19]

Beginning with Deng Xiaoping's Open Door policy, this is what has been happening between China and the outside world. Even with its Leninist authoritarian government, Beijing is losing an increasing amount of control over social and economic transactions taking place across China's borders, especially at the local and regional levels. China's further integration as a result of global trade, finance, investment, communications, and tourism will only speed up the process. Already, millions of overseas Chinese move in and out of China every year, along with hundreds of thousands of other tourists, investors, and professionals.

Conflicting Policies?

China's regional and global policies may in fact be contradictory. On the one hand, China pursues a Westphalian policy to avoid outside cultural pollution and dependence on others for security. On the other hand, with its Open Door policy, a complex approach to economic interdependence that includes joining global economic regimes, China becomes increasingly sensitive and possibly vulnerable to the actions of others.

Even though China makes minimal contributions to global security (through the United Nations), it nevertheless wishes to be consulted, with the right to disapprove global security policies initiated by others. But if China continues at its current rate of economic development and increased economic interdependence with the outside world, China's future leaders may also find it necessary to increase their participation in multilateral political-security fora, at both the regional and the global levels, in order to protect China's economic interests. From the Chinese perspective, complex interdependence may be good or bad, depending on China's ability to play outside forces against each other, including investors, traders, and governments. Beijing's leaders, by accepting interdependence in the economic sphere, seem to be betting that China will grow increasingly powerful in the economic sphere and therefore be better able to use its market leverage to promote its interests, preferably through bilateral transactions but also through global regimes if there is a clear economic advantage. Beijing's leaders are also betting that economic success will ensure the continuation of the Communist Party's political rule over the long term, which was the basic reason from the start for Deng Xiaoping's economic reforms.

▓ Policy Options

Throughout this book a number of conclusions have been drawn about internal and external challenges facing China's decisionmakers. Now we will look at some of China's more general policy options in the twenty-first century:

Option 1: Playing a Minimal Role in Global Security Operations

In the foreseeable future China faces no major external threat, and others have played a more active role in organizing UN security activities. With its currently limited capability to project power beyond its borders, Beijing may therefore wish to minimize its role, except where its own vital interests are at stake:

- At some future date when China has much greater capability, it may wish to assume greater responsibilities. Currently, a low profile seems to best suit China's interests. China is essentially a free rider on global security issues—it lets others do the work.
- China, as a permanent UN Security Council member, nonetheless wishes to be consulted and reserves the right to approve or disapprove initiatives taken by others.

Option 2: Participating More in Global Economic Regimes

Beijing's leaders seem committed to playing an even larger role in global economic structures such as the World Bank Group, the IMF, and the WTO:

- Even if these regimes are market oriented and controlled by the West, China's leaders believe that they have more to gain than lose by supporting them. In fact, Beijing believes that China will benefit from these regimes because as China develops economically, it will be able to exercise greater leverage in international investment, finance, and trade.
- Membership in organizations such as the WTO may also help China reduce bilateral threats to use trade restrictions or avoid regional trade structures (an Asian trade bloc possibly dominated by the Japanese) that might regulate trade in ways detrimental to Chinese interests.

Option 3: Avoiding Entangling Alliances at the Regional Level

With an Asian post–Cold War balance-of-power system in which China faces no major threats, bilateral relations seem preferable to multilateral regional approaches in both political-security and economic relations:

- If China is able to continue its current rate of economic growth, it will be able to exercise more leverage on both security and economic policies through bilateral transactions with its neighbors.
- For the foreseeable future, regional political-security regimes, from the Chinese perspective, are more likely to serve the interests of other Asian states than China (for example, Japan or the ASEAN states in Southeast Asia).

Option 4: Seeking Good Bilateral Relations with All

Historically China has had no permanent friends or enemies and has been suspicious of entangling alliances. Beijing believes that its interests, with few exceptions, are best served by bilateral relations based on pragmatic agreements promoting mutual self-interest. Westphalian values are the cornerstone of such bilateral relations. Beijing seems convinced that political security as well as economic mutual self-interest can be promoted by noninterference in each other's affairs.

Option 5: Domestic Security, Maintenance of the Chinese Communist Party's Mandate of Heaven, and Continued Economic Development

Beijing's foreign policy is clearly dictated by domestic concerns:

- Without continued economic development inside China, party leaders believe they will have no chance to retain power, which traditionally is based on the popular perception that the rulers are meeting the needs of the people.
- A foreign policy designed to achieve minimal Chinese international obligations but considerable economic interdependence best serves China's internal development and its domestic needs.
- China's continued economic development depends on further elimination of domestic contradictions resulting from the dual economy, uneven regional development, and political corruption.
- Beijing's leaders are convinced that Western-style democracy is ill suited to Chinese needs, which can best be met through an authoritarian political system and the absence of organized political opposition or open challenges to continued party rule.

Discussion Questions

1. From the Chinese perspective, what are the favorable characteristics of the emerging global system? What are the unfavorable characteristics?

2. What role does China seek to play in the emerging global security and economic system?
3. How does Beijing view efforts to create regional political-security and economic structures in Asia? Explain the reasons for this point of view.
4. In the case of China, as well as other third world countries, is Western-style democracy essential to the development and practice of marketplace economics?
5. How relevant is the Chinese model of development to the needs of other third world countries in the post–Cold War era?
6. To what extent do other third world countries recognize China as a leader of the third world?
7. How are (a) the Westphalian system of values, (b) geopolitics, and (c) complex interdependence applied in the making of Chinese foreign policy in the emerging global system?
8. Why are domestic challenges likely to pose greater risks to China's leaders than are international challenges?
9. In the promotion of world peace and international security, in what ways is China part of the problem or part of the solution?

Suggested Readings

Boutros-Ghali, Boutros. *Agenda for Peace*. New York: United Nations, 1992.
Faust, John. "The Emerging Security System in East Asia." *Journal of East Asian Affairs* 8, no. 1 (Winter–Spring 1994): 56–89.
Halperin, Morton H., David J. Scheffer, and Patricia L. Small. *Self-Determination in the New World Order*. Washington, D.C.: Carnegie Endowment for International Peace, 1992.
Huntington, Samuel P. *The Clash of Civilizations and the World Order*. New York: Touchstone, 1996.
Kaplan, Morton. *System and Process in International Politics*. New York: Wiley, 1957.
Kim Samuel S., ed. *East Asia and Globalization*. Lanham, Md.: Rowman & Littlefield, 2000.
Klare, Michael T. *Resource Wars: The New Landscape of Global Conflict*. New York: Owl Books, reprint edition 2002.
Krieger, Joel, ed. *The Oxford Companion to the Politics of the World*. 2nd ed. New York and Oxford: Oxford University Press, 2001.
Kristof, Nicholas D. "The Rise of China." *Foreign Affairs* 72, no. 5 (November–December 1993): 59–74.
Mingst, Karen. *Esssentials of International Relations*. 3rd ed. New York: W. W. Norton, 2004.
Nye, Joseph S., and John D. Donahue, eds. *Governance in the Globalizing World: Visions of Governmance for the 21st Century*. Washington: Brookings, 2000.
Robinson, Thomas W., and David Shambaugh, eds. *Chinese Foreign Policy: Theory and Practice*. New York: Oxford University Press, 1994.
Shih, Chih-yu. *China's Just World: The Morality of Chinese Foreign Policy*. Boulder, Colo.: Lynne Rienner, 1992.

Sklair, Leslie. *Globalization: Capitalism and Its Alternatives.* Oxford: Oxford University Press, 2003.
Snow, Donald M. *Distant Thunder: Third World Conflict and the New International Order.* 2nd ed. New York: St. Martin's Press, 1997.

▓ **Notes**

1. Nicholas D. Kristof, "The Rise of China," *Foreign Affairs* 72, no. 5 (November–December 1993): 59–74.
2. Former Chinese foreign minister Qian Qichen, responding to questions by a Xinhua correspondent in an interview on Chinese foreign policy on December 29, 1992. People's Republic of China embassy,Washington, D.C., Press Release no. 11, December 30, 1992, p. 1.
3. Qian Qichen, Press Release no. 11, pp. 1–2.
4. See Nicholas D. Kristof, "China Builds Its Military Muscle, Making Some Neighbors Nervous: Filling a Perceived Power Gap in Southeast Asia," *New York Times,* January 11, 1993, pp. A1, A4. Kristof notes that "the growing strength of the People's Liberation Army would not be so much of a concern if China did not have border disputes with at least seven neighbors." Referring to the possibility of Chinese naval facilities in Myanmar, he notes a growing concern from "mounting intelligence that China may be selling weapons to Myanmar in exchange for the right to set up naval facilities and listening posts in islands off the Burmese coast." Also see David Stenberg, "China Cultivates Its Burmese Connection," *New York Times,* January 19, 1992, p. 14.
5. Samuel S. Kim, "China as a Regional Power," *Current History* (September 1992): 248. Also see Michael T. Klare, "The Next Great Arms Race," *Foreign Affairs* 72, no. 3 (Summer 1993): 135–152. Klare believes that China's military buildup and seizure of islands in the South China Sea is stimulating a regional arms race in which the ASEAN countries in Southeast Asia are now building up their own military forces in response to China's military actions. He also notes a renewed interest among Asian countries in seeking security assurances from countries outside the region. By refusing to support the development of a regional security system based on multilateral consultation, Beijing seems to raise suspicions that it is not really interested in joining its neighbors in preventing regional arms races or creating Asia-wide fora to solve regional disputes.
6. Peter Sturm, "Risks of Conflict Increasing As Asia Becomes Less Stable," *Frankfurter Allegemeine Zeitung für Deutschland,* December 4, 1992.
7. See Takashi Inoguchi (professor of political science, Tokyo University), "Japan's Foreign Policy in East Asia," *Current History* (December 1992): 412. Also see his book *Japan's International Relations* (Boulder, Colo.: Westview Press, 1991).
8. Inoguchi, "Japan's Foreign Policy in East Asia," p. 411.
9. Ibid., pp. 407–412.
10. Chinese foreign minister Qian Qichen, speaking before the forty-seventh session of the UN General Assembly, press release of the People's Republic of China Mission to the United Nations, September 23, 1992.
11. A major problem facing the third world is that most foreign direct investment (86 percent) is between first world countries. However, of the remaining 14 percent, China's importance as a competitor for this investment is revealed by the fact that in 1989 it was the largest recipient of foreign direct investment going to third world countries (16 percent), followed by Mexico (12 percent), Brazil (10 percent), and Egypt (7 percent). Rosmarie Philips and Stuart K. Tucker, *U.S. Foreign Policy and Developing*

Countries: Discourse and Data 1991 (Washington, D.C.: Overseas Development Council, 1991), p. 33.

12. Morton H. Halperin, David J. Scheffer, and Patricia L. Small, *Self-Determination in the New World Order* (Washington, D.C.: Carnegie Endowment for International Peace, 1992).

13. Because of Beijing's encouragement of Han migration to these outlying regions, the native populations are becoming minorities in their own lands. Han Chinese are already a majority in Tibet, and in Inner Mongolia the indigenous Mongol population is only 16 percent of the total. Halperin, Scheffer, and Small, *Self-Determination in the New World Order,* pp. 133–134.

14. See Donald M. Snow, *Distant Thunder: Third World Conflict and the New International Order* (New York: St. Martin's Press, 1993).

15. See D. Decker, J. Frieden, S. Schatz, and R. Sklair, *Post-Imperialism: International Capitalism and Development in the Late Twentieth Century* (Boulder, Colo.: Lynne Rienner, 1987). Also see Leslie Sklair, *Sociology of the Global System* (Baltimore: Johns Hopkins University Press, 1991); and George Sorensen, *Democracy and Democratization: Dilemmas in World Politics* (Boulder, Colo.: Westview, 1993).

16. Foreign Minister Qian Qichen, press release, September 23, 1992, p. 6.

17. See Alexander J. Yeats, *China's Foreign Trade and Comparative Advantage: Prospects, Problems, and Policy Implications,* Report no. 141 (Washington, D.C.: World Bank, 1991).

18. Harold Sprout and Margaret Sprout, *Toward a Politics of the Planet Earth* (New York: Van Nostrand Reinold, 1971), pp. 97–107.

19. Robert O. Keohane and Joseph S. Nye, *Power and Interdependence,* 2nd ed. (Glenview, Ill.: Scott Foresman, 1989), pp. 3–37.

Chronology of
Most-Favored-Nation Status

1934	Most-favored-nation (MFN) status applied to U.S. trading partners.
1951	Trade Agreements Extension Act (P.L. 82-50), Section 5, requires the president to suspend MFN status of the Soviet Union and all countries of the then–Sino-Soviet bloc.
September 1, 1951	United States suspends MFN status for China.
July 14, 1952	United States suspends MFN status for Tibet.
1974	Jackson-Vanik amendment curtails the president's ability to extend MFN status to communist countries; to do so, the president has to negotiate a commercial trade agreement subject to congressional approval and either certify that the country is allowing free emigration or waive this requirement on the grounds that the country is improving its emigration policies.
October 23, 1979	President Carter transmits to Congress a trade agreement with China (signed on July 7, 1979) and the executive order extending to China the Jackson-Vanik waiver.
January 24, 1980	Congress approves the trade agreement with China.

February 1, 1980   Trade agreement enters into force and restores MFN status for China conditionally under the Jackson-Vanik freedom-of-emigration amendment of the Trade Act of 1974.

October 1990   H.R. 4939 passes the House (384–30), requiring the Chinese government to take a number of steps to correct human rights abuses in order to be eligible for MFN renewal. The Senate does not take up this bill or adopt a measure of its own.

February 1, 1992   Trade agreement with China renewed (through January 31, 1995).

March 2, 1992   President George H. W. Bush vetoes H.R. 2212, which set conditions for China's MFN status. The veto is overridden in House (357–61) but sustained (60–38) in the Senate.

September 28, 1992   President Bush vetoes H.R. 5318, which withdrew MFN status for products of Chinese state-owned enterprises only; products of private Chinese companies and foreign joint ventures could still be imported under MFN status whether or not conditions were met. The veto is sustained by the Senate (59–40) on October 1, 1992.

April 28, 1993   H.R. 1890 is introduced, prohibiting the president from extending MFN status in 1994 to state-owned industries unless human rights and international security conditions are met. The bill is referred to committees on ways and means and rules.

May 5, 1993   H.R. 1991 is introduced, prohibiting the president from extending MFN status in 1994 to state-owned industries unless human rights and international security conditions are met; the bill also specifies cessation of coercive abortion or involuntary sterilization. The bill is referred to committees on ways and means, foreign affairs, and rules.

May 26, 1993   S. 1034 is introduced, prohibiting the president from renewing China's MFN status in mid-1994 unless he can determine that China is not manipulating its currency to gain an unfair competitive advantage. The bill is referred to the finance committee.

May 28, 1993   President Bill Clinton issues a determination extending for one year China's Jackson-Vanik waiver and thereby its MFN status. Clinton also issues Executive Order 12850, extending MFN conditionally.

July 21, 1993   H.J. Resolution 208 is introduced to disapprove the extension of China's Jackson-Vanik waiver, but it fails to pass the House (105–318).

May 18, 1994   In a news conference, House Speaker Thomas S. Foley says withdrawal of trade benefits will cause "a trade disruption" and will make the United States "less influential, not more influential" with the Chinese on human rights. On May 16, 106 other House members—including Representative Lee Hamilton (D–Indiana), chairman of the House foreign affairs committee; Robert Michel (R–Illinois), the minority leader; and Newt Gingrich (R–Georgia), the minority whip—had signed a letter urging unconditional renewal of China's MFN trade status and the creation of a bilateral commission to deal with human rights issues.

May 23, 1994   Secretary of State Warren Christopher reports to President Clinton that China has met the two mandatory requirements of Executive Order 12850: cooperation on ending the export of prison-made goods to the United States, and allowing close family members of certain dissidents to leave the country.

May 26, 1994   President Clinton announces he will extend MFN status and end the policy of setting human rights conditions as part of trade policy.

June 2, 1995   President Clinton extends China's Jackson-Vanik waiver and MFN status for one year.

October 10, 2000   P.L. 106-286 signed by President Clinton, granting China permanent MFN status.

Acronyms

ADB	Asian Development Bank
APEC	Asia Pacific Economic Cooperation
ASEAN	Association of Southeast Asian Nations
CCP	Chinese Communist Party
CSCE	Conference on Security and Cooperation in Europe
FAO	Food and Agricultural Organization
FDI	foreign direct investment
FDSP	Federal Directorate for Supply and Procurement
GATT	General Agreement on Tariffs and Trade
GDP	gross domestic product
GNP	gross national product
IBRD	International Bank for Reconstruction and Development
IDA	International Development Association
IFC	International Finance Corporation
IMF	International Monetary Fund
KMT	Kuomintang
MFN	most-favored nation
NAFTA	North American Free Trade Agreement
NATO	North Atlantic Treaty Organization
NEPA	National Environmental Protection Agency
OECD	Organization for Economic Cooperation and Development
PLA	People's Liberation Army
PRC	People's Republic of China
SARS	severe acute respiratory syndrome
SCO	Shanghai Cooperative Organization
SEZ	special economic zone
SOE	state-owned enterprise

TVEs	township and village enterprises
UN	United Nations
UNCTAD	United Nations Conference on Trade and Development
UNDP	United Nations Development Programme
UNESCO	United Nations Educational, Scientific, and Cultural Organization
UNHCR	United Nations High Commissioner for Refugees
WHO	World Health Organization
WTO	World Trade Organization

Selected
Websites

Asia Pacific Economic Cooperation. http://www.apecsec.org.sg
Asian Development Bank. http://www.adb.org
Association of Southeast Asian Nations. http://www.aseansec.gov
China Daily. http://www.chinadaily.com.cn
ChinaOnline: The Information Network for China. http://www.chinaonline.com
ChinaSite.com: The Complete Reference to China/Chinese-Related Web Sites.
    http://www.chinasite.com
Embassy of the People's Republic of China in the United States. http://www.china
    -embassy.org/eng
Far Eastern Economic Review. http://www.feer.com
Ministry of Foreign Affairs of the People's Republic of China.http://www.fmprc.gov
    .cn/eng/default.htm
National Committee on U.S.-China Relations. http://www.ncuscr.org
People's Daily Online. http://english.peopledaily.com.cn
Permanent Mission of the People's Republic of China to the United Nations. http://
    un.fmprc.gov.cn/eng/index.html
United Nations Conference on Trade and Development. http://www.unctad.org
U.S.-China Business Council. http://www.uschina.org
U.S. Department of State. http://www.state.gov
World Bank. http://www.worldbank.org
World Trade Organization. http://www.wto.org

Index

About the Book

This fully revised and updated text introduces students to China's foreign policy—past and present—and the factors that may influence the country's future policy agenda. Exploring the new dynamics of China's regional and international roles, the authors outline the political, security, economic, and social issues the country faces in the emerging twenty-first century.

Each chapter of the book familiarizes students with the Chinese framework for analyzing the issues in question. Alternate policy choices are suggested, along with supporting data for each course of action. Discussion and essay questions, as well as suggested readings and a bibliography of Internet resources, are also included.

Judith Kornberg is dean of the School of Continuing and Professional Studies at the Fashion Institute of Technology. **John Faust** is professor emeritus of political science at Eastern Illinois University and research associate at the Eastern Illinois University Public Policy Institute.